$8\frac{95}{3}$ AD

THE
POLITICS
OF MASSIVE
RESISTANCE

THE
POLITICS
OF MASSIVE
RESISTANCE

by Francis M. Wilhoit

GEORGE BRAZILLER

NEW YORK

To the memory of my mother

"Man makes his own history, but he does not make it out of whole cloth; he does not make it out of conditions chosen by himself, but out of such as he finds close at hand. The tradition of all past generations weighs like a nightmare upon the brain of the living."—KARL MARX,
The Eighteenth Brumaire of Louis Bonaparte

PREFACE

THIS BOOK PROVIDES a descriptive analysis and critical discussion of the origins, politics, and ideology of Massive Resistance, the right-wing movement that surfaced in the mid-1950's as the white South's response to the United States Supreme Court's desegregation decision. The main emphasis is on describing the development stages through which Massive Resistance evolved and analyzing the interrelationships of mythic ideas and political action in each of the stages. A secondary purpose, dealt with in the last chapter, is to propose an interpretive explanation of the factors that led thousands of decent, God-fearing white southerners to support the movement. While the book was written for the general reader, it is hoped that its analysis and conceptualization will be of benefit to professional students of southern politics.

The materials on which this study is based were derived from a variety of primary and secondary sources. These included legislative records of the southern and border states, state and federal court opinions, gubernatorial and presidential pronouncements, congressional and other government documents, political propaganda, general historical records, autobiographies and memoirs, scholarly and journalistic books about southern politics, and a selective survey of southern newspapers and periodicals for the period of the 1950's and 1960's.

The most useful source of primary data was *Southern School News* of Nashville, Tennessee, the official publication of the Southern Education Reporting Service. This unique experiment in journalism, funded by the Ford Foundation, provided continuing information about the rocky course of school desegregation from September 1954, through June 1965. Unless otherwise noted, the general expository materials of the text, as well as the numerous quotations from public figures, were taken from this source. It did not seem appropriate to footnote every such reference.

It may well be that data based on interviews with selected Massive Resistance figures would have strengthened the conclusions of this study and added color to them. However, since the book is more concerned with politics, process, programs, and policy than with attitudes or personal impressions, conducting formal interviews did not appear essential to the achievement of the book's purposes. It is nevertheless a fact that because of long-standing contacts in the South, I was able in many cases to "flesh out" my personal judgments of particular events with corroborating impressions from acquaintances on the spot.

I have endeavored to center my analysis on the ideological, symbolic, tactical, and strategic aspects of Massive Resistance politics while using the traditional form of historical narrative as the skeleton on which to build.

As far as the subject of the present book is concerned, political scientists, by and large, have abdicated their responsibilities to sociologists, psychologists, journalists, and historians. Indeed, beyond scrutinizing the public law aspects of Massive Resistance, political scientists have scarcely touched the subject. The recognition of this fact was one of the major reasons for my initiating the inquiry which gave rise to the present volume.

This book has had a long intellectual history since 1958, when, in quite a different form, it was presented as a thesis to Harvard University in partial fulfillment of the requirements for the degree of Doctor of Philosophy in Political Science. There is also a large accumulation of personal debts to go with it, only the more important of which can be acknowledged here.

My biggest debt of all is to those hundreds of southerners of both races who, over a period of almost thirty years, helped shape my own "southern experience." A native of North Carolina, I was never outside the South until I joined the U. S. Army Air Corps in 1942. After World War II, following study at Harvard, I taught for about a decade in Florida and Georgia, where I happened to be living when Massive Resistance peaked. Although I have not lived in the South since the early 1960's, I continue to be influenced in a thousand ways by such "southern" things as a tragic sense of history, an awareness of the centrality of race consciousness in American life, and an appreciation of the awesome complexity of black-white relations. I had friends and relatives on both sides of the Massive Resistance battle. And almost every page of the present work reflects, in one way or another, the tensions, ambiguities, and resonances of the southern experience that I knew.

I am also greatly indebted to four of my Harvard professors. They are Professor Samuel H. Beer, who first suggested I do such a study as this; Professor Arthur Maass, who initiated me into the mysteries of political science; Professor Louis Hartz, whose stimulating lectures and writings on southern political thought were a spur to my own imaginings; and the late Professor Robert Mc-Closkey, whose incisive analyses of court opinions in the field of race relations are still unequalled.

In 1957 the Southern Fellowships Fund provided a grant-in-aid for terminal thesis research, which helped me through a difficult period. Eleven years later the Drake University Research Council made available funds for clerical help in preparing the final manuscript. With those funds I was able to avail myself of the secretarial services of two of the most competent ladies of the Drake staff—Mrs. Pauline Holt and Mrs. Phyllis Lawless.

I would be disingenuous if I pretended that I had excluded evaluation from the scholarly analysis of this study. On the contrary, I have sought throughout the book not merely to understand and describe the political phenomenon of Massive Resistance, but also to evaluate its strengths and weaknesses from the perspective of American democratic values. It is my feeling that the proper course for the South—and the nation—to follow is that charted by the ideals of the egalitarian revolution which go back to the founding of the Republic. This is simply to say that I am a constitutional democrat, not a counterrevolutionary. It is not necessary here to give a detailed exposition of the reasons for this preference, but I thought it ought to be noted.

Finally, for all interpretations, value judgments, and factual errors, the author (left no honorable alternative) assumes full responsibility.

F. M. W.
February 1973

CONTENTS

11. AN INTERPRETIVE EXPLANATION (continued)

INTRODUCTION

I. AMERICAN POLITICS AND RACE RELATIONS

THE RACE PROBLEM in American society and politics is as old as the Republic and, indeed, a lot older. One might, in fact, trace the roots of the problems posed by Massive Resistance all the way back to 1619.[1] For it was in that year that a Dutch man-of-war brought twenty African "Negars" with Spanish names to Jamestown, Virginia, and sold them to local white planters as indentured servants. This was one year before the arrival of the Mayflower Pilgrims and almost a century after the Spanish explorers had introduced blacks to the New World. At the start, neither institutionalized racism nor slavery existed in what came to be known as Virginia. Yet, by the end of the seventeenth century, all the English colonies in the New World had legalized black slavery. Ironically, it was also in 1619 that our English forebears established at Jamestown the first representative legislative assembly in this hemisphere.

It would be hard to exaggerate the cruelty of the African slave trade, which, paradoxically, began to supply slaves to the New World as serfdom was disappearing in Europe. It began in West Africa with the systematic hunting of young, able-bodied blacks, and was facilitated by the local wars that divided the African peoples and by the success of the slave-traders in "buying off" some of the local rulers. After the kidnappings came the horrors of confinement, shipment, "seasoning," and the auction block. Today it is generally believed that only a minority of the kidnapped Africans lived long enough to become slaves of the white man—and to enrich and trouble his new land.

The parallel growth of slavery and white racism met little opposition at first, but with the passage of time opposition increased. The slaves themselves sometimes revolted and courageously fought for their freedom. Quaker leaders frequently denounced the enslavement of blacks. And quite a few intellectuals, moved by the humanitarianism of the Enlightenment, openly attacked the slavery system. But until the middle of the nineteenth century, the protesters represented only a small minority of whites.

The existence of black slavery created both moral and practical problems for American political leaders during the Revolutionary War. In his first draft of the Declaration of Independence, Jefferson strongly condemned slavery and the slave trade. However, the pro-slavery delegates in the Continental Congress protested and forced the deletion of the critical passages.[2]

The politicians also at first excluded blacks from the Revolutionary Army, even though blacks had fought in the colonial wars against the French and Indians. After the British promised freedom to all blacks who enlisted in His Majesty's forces, and after thousands of slaves accepted the offer, Washington and the Continental Congress reversed their policy against black enlistments. All told, probably more than 5,000 blacks fought for the independence of the United States—and, if slaves, won their freedom thereby.

In 1787 the short-lived Confederation Congress adopted the Northwest Ordinance, which helped to curtail the spread of slavery. Article 6 of the law provided that "There shall be neither slavery nor involuntary servitude in the said [Northwest] territory, otherwise than in the punishment of crimes whereof the party shall have been duly convicted." In practical terms this meant that slavery was excluded from those territories that later became the states of Ohio, Indiana, Illinois, Michigan, Wisconsin, and Minnesota.

Also in 1787 our Founding Fathers wrote at Philadelphia a new federal Constitution to replace the Articles of Confederation. Slavery was not much debated at the Convention, and the words slave and slavery nowhere appeared in the final document they produced. There were, however, several provisions included in the Constitution that directly affected the slavery system. Article I, for example, provided that in census enumerations three-fifths of "other Persons" (slaves) were to be counted both for taxation and congressional apportionment purposes. This meant that the Fathers viewed slaves as three-fifths human and two-fifths non-human and considered five slaves to be the equal of three white men. As chattel, slaves were excluded from the "privileges and immunities" of U. S. citizenship by a provision in Article IV requiring state officials to return all escaping persons "held to Service or Labour in one State, under the Laws thereof." Congress was also forbidden to end for at least twenty years the "Migration or Importation of such Persons as any of the States now existing shall think proper to admit" (African slave trade). Even more callous was the provision that Congress not impose "on such Importation" a tax of more than ten dollars per head. These provisions make it clear that the politicians of 1787 based the new Constitution on the premises of white racism, with its central concept of black inequality. American politics have been bedeviled ever since by that decision—one of the most fateful in the nation's history.

As the nineteenth century wore on and the slaves became the great prop of the South's economy, a kind of Abolitionists' revolution arose which was countered by a slaveocracy counterrevolution. The political and social issues raised by this "irrepressible" conflict eventually brought about the Civil War. Though at first the War was basically a fight to preserve the integrity of the Union, it was transformed, after Lincoln's Emancipation Proclamation of January 1, 1863, into a moral crusade for the total abolition of slavery.

Certainly the Civil War was the single most important event in the history of the black man in this country. Practically speaking, the chief result of the War was the "federalization" of black rights and liberties through a series of new laws and constitutional changes. These included the thirteenth amendment freeing some four million slaves (1865), the fourteenth amendment making native-born blacks full citizens (1868), the fifteenth amendment forbidding state deprivation of the freedmen's right to vote (1870), and the Reconstruction Civil Rights Act guaranteeing the freedmen access to all public places. While later Supreme Court interpretations of these measures weakened their values as a tool of black emancipation, they collectively legitimated, both morally and legally, the black man's fight for first-class citizenship.

With the dawn of the twentieth century, the black man had moved from bondage to legal freedom, yet he remained a kind of quasi-slave. The forces largely responsible for aborting the Reconstruction revolution included the postwar decline of American idealism, the 1877 withdrawal of federal troops from the South, the recapture of southern governments by white supremacists, the onrushing industrial revolution that muted concern with the race problem, the emergence of the sharecropping system in southern agriculture, the Supreme Court's invalidation of key parts of the Reconstruction "settlement," the white terror waged against blacks by the Ku Klux Klan, southern disfranchisement of black voters, and—most crucial—the appearance in the 1890's of a structural surrogate for slavery—the Jim Crow or segregation system.

Early in this century a kind of neo-Abolition movement developed, the aim of which was to crush the newly institutionalized system of segregation. Scholars usually trace this development to the founding by W. E. B. Du Bois and other militant black intellectuals from 14 states of the Niagara Movement at Niagara Falls (Canada) in the summer of 1905. This Movement was partly a response to the "accommodationist" policies of Booker T. Washington, expressed in his famous 1895 Atlanta speech.

The Niagara Movement was in effect succeeded by the National Association for the Advancement of Colored People (NAACP), which was founded in 1909 in Lincoln's home town of Springfield, Illinois. The NAACP's founding was to a great extent a response to the Springfield race riots of August 14 and 15, 1908. By the 1920's, there were at least two other important black organizations working with the NAACP to promote the black cause. These were the National Urban League (founded in 1910–1911) and Marcus Garvey's ill-fated (but prophetic) Universal Negro Improvement Association, which first popularized the "black is beautiful" slogan.

The New Deal marked a turning point in American race relations. In political terms the 1932 election was the final chapter in the black man's long flirtation with Lincoln's party and his defection to the party of Jackson and FDR. Under the New Deal blacks gained many advantages and got more prominent political positions than at any time since the Taft Administration. More important, President Roosevelt, after being threatened with a march on Washington by A. Philip Randolph, issued on June 25, 1941, Executive Order 8802 barring "discrimination in the employment of workers in defense industries or government." Soon after that, a Fair Employment Practices Committee (F.E.P.C.) was set up.

The politics of the Fair Deal were even more pro-black than those of the New Deal. Whatever one's view of Harry Truman as a chief executive may be, there can be little doubt that his commitment to civil rights was as genuine as that of any of our Presidents. His greatest monuments in this area were the report *To Secure These Rights,* produced by his Committee on Civil Rights, and his revolutionary Executive Order 9981 decreeing an end to racial discrimination in the military.

For the first time in our history the issue of race was now being viewed as a *national* political problem. Even the Supreme Court, as evidenced by a number of "pro-black" decisions, was beginning to see the light. By the early 1950's the black protest movement had clearly reached the take-off point from which it would shortly grow into a full-scale political revolution. That take-off point became dimly visible in the late fall of 1952 when the Supreme Court agreed to hear five consolidated segregation cases that flatly posed the question of segregation's constitutionality. The impossible, at last, had become possible.

II. THE BROWN DECISION

O N MAY 17, 1954, the United States Supreme Court, in the most important twentieth-century case on race, outlawed governmentally imposed segregation of blacks in the public schools.[3] In a series of cases decided over the next few years, the Court's holding was amplified and extended to every kind of tax-supported public service.

In the Brown opinion the Supreme Court flatly rejected the plea of the southern states that it reaffirm the separate but equal doctrine. As Chief Justice Warren put it for a unanimous Court, "we cannot turn the clock back to 1868 . . . or even to 1896 when Plessy v. Ferguson was written." Then, after noting that education is "the most important function of state and local governments," the Court faced up to the central question posed by the case: "Does segregation of children in public schools solely on the basis of race, even though the physical facilities and other 'tangible' factors may be equal, deprive the children of the minority group of equal educational opportunities?" The Court's answer was unequivocal: "We believe that it does."

The basic holding of Brown was stated in a single paragraph:

> We conclude that in the field of public education the doctrine of "Separate but equal" has no place. Separate educational facilities are inherently unequal. Therefore, we hold that the plaintiffs and others similarly situated for whom the actions have been brought are, by reason of the segregation complained of, deprived of the equal protection of the laws guaranteed by the Fourteenth Amendment.

At the same time Brown was announced, the justices, in a companion case, invalidated public school segregation in the District of Columbia.[4] Here the legal issue was different, since there is no equal protection clause in the Bill of Rights limiting federal authority. This case, therefore, was decided on the basis of the due process clause of the fifth amendment. The Court held that

> Segregation in public education is not reasonably related to any proper governmental objective, and thus it imposes on Negro children of the District of Columbia a burden that constitutes an arbitrary deprivation of their liberty in violation of the Due Process Clause.

The Court still had to face one further question: should the black litigants be granted admission to white schools at once or should enforcement of the desegregation holding be postponed? Understandably, the NAACP lawyers argued for immediate admission, while the South's attorneys argued for a delay. To the surprise of many observers and to the dismay of most blacks, the Court decided not to order the immediate end of school segregation. It followed this course "Because these are class actions, because of the wide applicability of this decision, and because of the great variety of local conditions." The consolidated cases were restored to the Court's docket, and the interested parties were asked to present additional argument concerning the formulation of decrees to provide appropriate relief.

Approximately one year later, on May 31, 1955, the Supreme Court announced its enforcement decree in what has come to be known as Brown II.[5] The Brown Court did not hold that the black plaintiffs had a personal and immediate right to an integrated education, nor did it order the admission of any particular black students to white schools. Rather the justices, sitting as a court of equity, fashioned a novel and controversial method of relief. They accepted, in effect, the South's request for a gradual phasing out of school segregation and remanded the cases to the lower courts, which were ordered to supervise and enforce desegregation within a reasonable time. Specifically, the justices directed the lower courts "to take such proceedings and enter such orders and decrees consistent with this opinion as are necessary and proper to admit to public schools on a racially nondiscriminatory basis *with all deliberate speed* the parties to these cases." [Emphasis added by author.]

Equitable decrees traditionally have allowed delayed relief under a variety of situations not involving constitutionally guaranteed rights—most typically in nuisance and antitrust cases. It seems, however, that the second Brown opinion was the first to hold that vindication of *constitutional* rights may also be deferred if this is deemed essential for the protection of other legitimate interests.

In any case, the Supreme Court in Brown II threw out the remains of the "separate but equal" doctrine as it applied to public education and started the erratic career of the "all deliberate speed" formula. Though ambiguous, this new judicially constructed phrase would remain the law of the land until 1969 when the Court lost its last shred of patience with the South's foot-dragging and ordered all school districts to "operate now and hereafter only unitary schools."[6]

In terms of its overall impact, perhaps the most important thing to say about Brown is that it constituted a fundamental value revolution in American jurisprudence. Up until May 17, 1954, the moral authority of the "supreme law of the land" lay with the segregationists rather than with their opponents in the sense that school segregation had a legal basis and had not been invalidated by the United States Supreme Court. After "Black Monday," however, attempts to prop up the Jim Crow system would be devoid of a legal or moral sanction and, if state action were involved, they would also be unconstitutional.

There were, of course, other kinds of revolutionary "fall-out" from Brown. The decision, for example, generated a contagious excitement among blacks that for a time reached utopian proportions. It was responsible for a new mood of hope and activism among black leadership elites and their white supporters. It led in succeeding years to a spiraling series of lawsuits by black organizations seeking the end of dual school systems, which Justice Jackson predicted with his phrase "a generation of litigation." It sparked the rise of new militant black groups whose goal was the revitalization of the American Dream. And, not least in importance, it directly contributed to an increase in black unity and cohesion, the full consequences of which would not be realized until the emergence of black political power in the 1960's. As for the decision's effect on the white community, it provided the stimulus for the rise (and fall) of Massive Resistance.

In conclusion it should be stated that the Warren Court in the Brown decision was not only giving new meaning to the equality concept of the Declaration of Independence and the fourteenth amendment, but was also showing an almost poetic sensitivity to the unique problems and nuances of a biracial society in mid-century America. In so doing, it demonstrated a high gift for judicial imagination and made, in effect, a prophetic judgment about the future of American democracy. By unanimously revising a public policy decision arrived at in the late nineteenth century by the South's political leaders, the Court (to quote the words of Justice Frankfurter from another context) was piercing the curtain of the future and giving "shape and visage to mysteries still in the womb of time." Equally important, it was performing that fundamental duty of democratic decision makers: drawing the line between the majority and the minority, between liberty and authority.

Because of Brown, 1954 was the year when—briefly—the forces pushing for a truly integrated America seemed about to impose true democracy on the South. White supremacy and the Jim Crow institutions it inspired had been morally and legally discredited, and the spirit of egalitarianism was on the rise. The South's politicians, however, opted for Massive Resistance instead of peaceful change, and the dreams of 1954 became the nightmares of the terrible decade that followed. This book is the story of their failures—of their demagoguery that drove a confused South to seek a reversal of Brown and a petrification of the status quo, and of the Deep South's collapse into white terror and brutal violence.

It may be, as many charge, that the Supreme Court in the two Brown decisions committed the country to a guarantee of equality that popular convictions were not prepared to sustain, and that constitutional commitments overreached moral persuasion. But if that is so, the fault lies not with the Warren Court but with the Reconstruction Congress that drafted the fourteenth amendment.

In any event, the Supreme Court had boldly forged a new direction in a crucial area of civil rights, though the egalitarian revolution's ultimate destination was uncertain, indeed unknowable. Still, for all the imponderables that lay ahead, it was generally agreed that the makers of the revolution were traveling the central (if bumpy) highway of American democracy.

I.

First Reactions of the Segregationists

I. OVERVIEW

THE FIRST RECORDED REACTIONS of white southerners to Brown I were varied and, more often than not, cautiously phrased. The extreme white supremacists, who would later be the shock troops of Massive Resistance, viewed Brown as an unmitigated tragedy. Moderate whites, especially those in journalism, were less pessimistic and saw the opinion as more or less inevitable. Public officials, by and large, tended to be more outspokenly critical than private citizens, and lower-class whites seemed to be more embittered than those from the middle and upper classes. Viewed in retrospect, there appears to have been initially more calm resignation than rebellion among whites, more fatalism than rabid defiance.

To be sure, white southerners, when speaking for public consumption, rarely went so far as positively to praise Brown. Still it is a fact that at least a small number of white southerners, not known as integrationists, did speak up in the summer of 1954 in support of the opinion. An American political scientist, for example, has reported that when the news of Brown was revealed to a Rotary meeting in Savannah, Georgia, it evoked a hearty burst of applause.[1] Atypical perhaps, but probably not as much as is commonly assumed.

Southern senators and congressmen in Washington were all but unanimous in their condemnation of Brown. This was notably true of the leaders of the so-called "southern bloc," whose word had long been law for millions of their faithful constituents. And far from ebbing as it became clear that Jim Crow was legally dead, this negative attitude among the South's national solons persisted well into the 1960's.

Senator James O. Eastland, the arch-segregationist from Mississippi, quickly came forward with the charge that the Supreme Court had been "indoctrinated and brainwashed by Left-wing pressure groups."[2] Equally negative were the reactions of the veteran senators from Virginia and Georgia, Harry F. Byrd and Richard B. Russell, both of whom blasted the Court for its Brown opinion in an idiom reminiscent of the pre-industrial conservatism of Burke and Calhoun.

It needs to be noted at this point that in the summer and fall of 1954 the white South was reacting not only to the words and phrases of the Supreme Court's desegregation decision, but also to the reactions of the rest of the nation and the world. Those reactions were in nearly every instance highly favorable, and for several days they were given a prominent place in media reports about the decision. The *Hartford Courant* hailed Brown as a "milestone in our history." The *New York Times* described it as a reaffirmation of the American faith "in the equality of all men and all children before the law." To the *Amsterdam News* (a black paper) it was "the greatest victory for the Negro people since the Emancipation Proclamation." And in Britain, the *London News Chronicle* headlined its story of the decision: "A Black Stain Wiped Out." To make sure that the entire world would be informed of the significance of Brown for American democracy, the Voice of America started broadcasting the news within an hour of the announcement of the decision. These editorial reactions to

Brown from outside the South were dinned into the ears of white southerners day after day for several weeks. Given the tendency to xenophobia on the part of many southerners, it is quite likely that this continuous "outside" praise of Brown was one of the many factors that, some months later, coalesced to form a vigorous southern backlash.

While no southerner—or any other American for that matter —was wise enough in 1954 to predict with any degree of certainty the ultimate outcome of the desegregation struggle, it seems clear in retrospect that a large number of the white South's leaders were sufficiently perceptive to realize that a genuine social and political revolution was in the making. How else account for the gloomy pessimism of so many of them? They disliked both the substance and rationale of Brown, and they foresaw only trouble, and perhaps tragedy ahead. Not the least of the ironies of the 1950's was the fact that the white South's reaction to Brown amazingly resembled the white North's reaction, a century earlier, to the famous Dred Scott case.[3] In both instances, a revolution and counterrevolutionary backlash followed a controversial Supreme Court decision.

II. EXECUTIVE REACTIONS

AFTER THE SUPREME COURT had had its say, journalists and students of southern politics turned their attention to the region's governors. They were interested in gubernatorial reactions for several reasons. Southern governors are the acknowledged heads of their state governments. They serve as a link between their own state and other states. They wield substantial internal political power. They have the responsibility for law enforcement and public safety, "the pivot on whose action the public order turns."[4] It was generally assumed that unless a majority of the governors gave at least tacit assent to the desegregation decision, it would stand scant chance of being quickly or peacefully implemented.

From the data now available, it appears that the extent of a governor's approval or disapproval of Brown was largely a function of geography. With some exceptions, governors from the Deep South (Louisiana, Mississippi, Alabama, Georgia, and South Carolina) were strongly critical of Brown. Those from the upper South (Arkansas, Tennessee, North Carolina, and Virginia) tended to be more restrained in their comments. Only the governors from the border states (Delaware, Maryland, Kentucky, Missouri, Oklahoma, and West Virginia), where segregation had also been required by law, felt secure enough to respond more positively to the opinion.

Of the 1954 incumbent governors in the border states, one of the first to make a statement about Brown was Governor J. Caleb Boggs of Delaware, whose state was a party to the Brown litigation. In a matter of days, he informed his State Board of Education that it would be the policy of his administration "to work toward adjustment to the United States constitutional requirements." At the same time he requested the Board to "proceed toward this objective."

The governor of neighboring Maryland, Theodore R. McKeldin, a Republican, stated that "Maryland prides itself on being a law-abiding state, and I am sure our citizens and our officials will accept readily the United States Supreme Court's interpretation of our fundamental law." West Virginia's Governor William C. Marland made it clear that his state would abide by the Court's decision. In Kentucky, the most "southern" of the border states, Governor Lawrence Wetherby promised that Kentucky would "do whatever is necessary to comply with the law." Missouri's official reaction was suggested on July 1 by Attorney General John M. Dalton, who confirmed that Brown had invalidated all state constitutional and statutory requirements for segregation. Because of this, he told local school districts they were free to integrate their facilities whenever they chose. He stressed, however, that until the Supreme Court handed down its implementation decree, school integration was not obligatory.

Governor Johnston Murray of Oklahoma, whose state had seen little open racial controversy, was a little more negative in his reaction than one might have expected. He said, "I don't believe in forcing people to do something they don't want to do." Later he suggested a "liberal transfer policy" for the benefit of both races.

Among governors from the upper South, Governor Frank G. Clement of Tennessee seems to have been the most moderate in his attitude toward Brown. He reminded his people that "it is a decision handed down by a judicial body, which we, the American people under our Constitution and law recognize as supreme in matters of interpreting the law of the land." But he also conceded that "no change is anticipated in our school system in the near future."

Governor William B. Umstead of North Carolina, who died soon after Brown was announced, confessed that he was "terribly disappointed," but was generally conciliatory toward the Court. "The Supreme Court of the United States has spoken," he told his fellow Tar Heels. "It has reversed itself and has declared segregation in the public schools unconstitutional. . . . This reversal of its former decisions is in my judgment a clear and serious invasion of the rights of the sovereign [sic] states. Nevertheless, this is now the latest interpretation of the Fourteenth Amendment."

In Virginia, the state that would play a pivotal role in the creation of Massive Resistance, Governor Thomas B. Stanley issued an official statement within two hours after Brown's announcement. Though he would later turn to defiance of the Court, Governor Stanley's initial reaction was a call for "cool heads, calm, steady and sound judgment." He also made it known that he would "call together as quickly as practicable representatives of both state and local governments to consider the matter and work toward a plan which will be acceptable to our citizens and in keeping with the edict of the court."

Governor Francis Cherry of Arkansas, a racial moderate, stated on May 18 that "Arkansas will obey the law. It always has." Taking a somewhat different line, the state's Education Commissioner, on July 2, made the following prophetic remarks before the Little Rock Rotary Club:

> *We will continue to have segregation unless and until the people at the local level are willing to accept integration. In my opinion, integration will come in some communities*

within a relatively short period of time. In others it will perhaps be many years. It is apparent that there can be no general statewide pattern of integration in our public schools.

Governor Cherry, a sick and colorless individual, lost in the August run-off primary to Orval Faubus in the race for the Democratic gubernatorial nomination. While Faubus went on to become a leading Massive Resister, Cherry ended his aborted career as chairman of the Subversive Activities Control Board in Washington.

Few observers were surprised when the governors of the Deep South attacked Brown more vehemently than did their counterparts from neighboring states. Governor Hugh L. White of Mississippi castigated Brown as "the most unfortunate thing that ever happened." White, who is remembered today for luring new industry into the state with long tax moratoriums, insisted that it is "impossible to mix the races together in the public schools of Mississippi." Furthermore he predicted, inaccurately as it turned out, that his state was "never going to have integration in its schools."

James F. Byrnes, who himself had once sat on the United States Supreme Court, was governor of South Carolina in 1954. Though he said he was "shocked" by the decision, he urged all of his state's citizens, "white and colored, to exercise restraint and preserve order." He also stated the opinion that the South would somehow devise "ways to lawfully maintain segregation." Although Byrnes had earlier been a chief spokesman for the New Deal in the South, he had become more conservative by the 1950's and would shortly take the leap into Massive Resistance.

Louisiana's Governor Robert Kennon, a former state judge, reminded his people that "It is not a violation of the Supreme Court ruling to continue a dual school system. The Supreme Court does not have jurisdiction over the state school systems." Anticipating the Massive Resisters' "freedom of choice" ploy, Kennon suggested that "building equal facilities for both races largely will solve problems brought about by the Supreme Court decision."

Somewhat surprisingly, the most moderate gubernatorial voice from the Deep South was that of Alabama's Gordon Persons, whose brother was one of President Eisenhower's close advisers. Governor Persons was a conservative, but he refused to attack the integrity of the nation's highest tribunal. A few months after Brown, in the fall of 1954, he showed considerable courage when he refused to call a special legislative session to consider a legislative committee's proposals for new segregation laws.

Alabama's Governor-Nominate, James E. ("Big Jim") Folsom, was likewise a racial moderate. His first reaction to Brown was to say, "I don't know what we are going to do about it." A little later he said publicly, "When the Supreme Court speaks, that's the law." Many students of southern politics believe that if genial Jim had not had such a weakness for booze, Alabama might have been spared the more gothic extremes of Massive Resistance politics, as exemplified by the career of George Wallace. In any case, Alabama would rather quickly do an about-face and go from moderation to something like racial fanaticism.

More typical of Deep South reactions to Brown was the defiance of Georgia's Governor Herman Talmadge (later to be a United States Senator), who bluntly stated that Georgia would not accept racially mixed schools whatever the Supreme Court said. Talmadge received strong support from Attorney General Eugene Cook, an arch-white supremacist, who said that Georgia would have nothing to do with the arguments before the Supreme Court regarding Brown's implementation. Though Talmadge later moderated his racial rhetoric, Cook never did.

Florida and Texas are geographically part of the Deep South, but they are usually viewed as separate entities since, politically and ideologically, they tend to follow an independent course. Charley E. Johns was Acting Governor of Florida when he heard about Brown, and he seems not to have been overly upset by the news. He said he saw no reason to call a special session of the legislature to deal with issues raised by the decision, as many of the state's segregationists were demanding. The semi-public Continuing Education Council, whose views were generally close to those of the state school superintendent, announced that it would do everything legally possible to postpone school integration. A heated gubernatorial primary was in progress in Florida when Brown was handed down, but none of the candidates made much of segregation as a major campaign issue.

Down in Texas, Governor Allan Shivers won an unprecedented third term nomination in the August Democratic primary and promised to strive for continued segregation. But he also stressed law and order, as these comments show:

> *We don't need the help of any night-riders or moon-lighters or cross-burners roving about with bedsheets over their heads, attempting to hide their faces from God and man while they take the law into their own hands. Texas saw an era of that at one time, and as long as Allan Shivers is Governor we are not going to have another.*

It is a fact that during much of this country's political history, the governorship has been little more than a ceremonial post, and incumbents have as often been figureheads as real leaders. In the South, however, the governor has almost always been a man of considerable power and high status, and in the Massive Resistance era this was even more the case than usual. That is why every public statement of a southern governor was closely scrutinized in the wake of Brown for clues about future state policy toward integration. It is also why even restrained criticism of Brown, such as that by Shivers, was taken by many observers to be an omen of serious trouble ahead.

III. LEGISLATIVE REACTIONS

SOUTHERN LEGISLATURES traditionally have confined their business to biennial rather than annual sessions, and only Louisiana's was at work in May 1954, when Brown was announced. This largely accounts for the fact that in most of the South legislative reactions to Brown took a little longer to crystalize than gubernatorial reactions. However, as the legislatures convened in regular or special sessions in the ensuing months, the spotlight shifted from governors to legislators.

Within three days after Brown was announced, a resolution was introduced into the Louisiana legislature censuring the Supreme Court for "usurpation of power." Only four legislators voted against the resolution—three in the house, one in the senate. Less than a month later, three bills designed to preserve segregation were introduced and enacted into law. In a very real sense, this trio of bills marked the first fateful step on the road to legislative Massive Resistance.

One of the measures adopted by the 1954 Louisiana legislature was a so-called "police power" constitutional amendment, which was submitted to the voters in November. Predictably, the voters approved the amendment by a five to one majority. The purpose of the amendment was to establish the principle that segregation was a matter of "health and morals," and therefore subject only to regulation by the state's inherent police power. The courts would later invalidate the amendment. Yet its rationale and summary manner of adoption accurately reflected the hostile reception of Brown by most of the Deep South's legislators.

Alabama's legislators rather quickly showed that they intended to take a back seat to nobody in defense of Jim Crow. And almost from the beginning, they made "NEVER!" their rallying cry. Within weeks after the announcement of Brown, a special state legislative committee, set up by the 1953 legislature, recommended to Governor Persons that a constitutional amendment be offered to the voters that would permit the legislature, in extreme circumstances, to abolish the state's public school system. A few years later, when Massive Resistance was at flood-tide, it seemed that several southern states might take that extreme step, but, in the end, only a few schools were actually closed. It should be stressed, however, that Alabama's legislators were slower than their counterparts in other parts of the Deep South to convert their anti-Brown rhetoric into actual legislation. But once they forsook the road of legislative restraint, they legislated aginst Brown with a vengeance.

Mississippi's legislators convened in special session on September 7 and promptly approved a constitutional amendment. Like the one proposed in Alabama, it permitted the total abolition of public schools if other ways of preventing school integration failed. It also authorized local school authorities to abolish specific schools under integration orders, and provided for the payment of tuition grants to children attending private schools. The "tuition grants" provision was a preview of one of the most controversial (and expensive) tactics devised by the Massive Resisters to counter Brown.

In Virginia, Governor Stanley appointed State Senator Garland Gray of Waverly to head a 32-member Virginia Commission on Public Education, whose task was to analyze school problems raised by Brown. Gray was a leading figure in the Byrd organization that dominated the legislature, and as a white supremacist he passionately opposed desegregation. Before assuming the chairmanship of the new Commission, Gray had served as spokesman for a group of segregationist legislators who met in mid-June to announce their "unalterable opposition to the principle of integration of the races in the schools." In addition, they served notice that they would use all available resources "to evolve some legal method whereby political subdivisions of the state may continue to maintain separate facilities for white and Negro students in schools." It appeared that most Virginia legislators, while opposed to Brown, were biding their time until Senator Byrd would supply them with specific guidelines for future action. Once that word came, and it did come soon, equivocation on the part of the state's lawmakers virtually ceased.

It needs to be stressed at this point that neither legislators nor governors, in the summer of 1954, discussed extra-legal or violent resistance to Brown's implementation. When they spoke of defiance and resistance, as they increasingly did, they virtually always prefaced their remarks with the adjective "legal." Whatever else they might do, the South's public officials had no intention of mounting a full-scale counterrevolution against Brown until the Court had announced its implementation decree and until legal avenues of resistance had been tried.

IV. PRIVATE REACTIONS

ANY APPRAISAL of the reactions to Brown by private individuals and groups must obviously be quite selective in view of the thousands of such reactions that were recorded. Likewise, it is difficult today to say which reactions, if any, were typical. Yet despite these difficulties, a summary survey of private reactions is needed here lest too much emphasis be put on the attitudes and actions of public officials.

As could easily have been foreseen, segregationists in private, as in public, life attacked Brown, while moderate whites not involved in politics or government often praised the opinion, or at least refrained from criticizing it. Southern editorial reaction, which was available in a matter of hours, was generally cautious and temperate. True, in the Deep South and in scattered areas elsewhere, a few editors responded with unabashed hostility, such as would become commonplace in a few years. But far more editors muted whatever objections they may have had and concentrated on pointing out the obvious difficulties in carrying out a desegregation policy. Typical of this pessimism was a statement in the *New Orleans Times-Picayune* that "the ensuing strife will probably react unfavorably on public-school support and multiply the problems with which the schools are already faced." The *Birmingham Post-Herald* hinted at resistance, but only through legal means: "Acceptance of the decision does not mean that we are stopped from taking such honorable and legal steps as may be indicated to avoid the difficulties it presents to both races."

Almost all of the nationally-known papers of the South reacted editorially in a calm and often quite constructive way. The highly regarded *Atlanta Constitution* said: "Our best minds must be put to work, not to destroy, but to arrive at constructive conclusions." Equally moderate was the Chattanooga *Times*, which editorialized: "The *Times* believes that most of the Southern states will meet the situation calmly." The *Richmond News Leader*, soon to become the authoritative voice of Virginia's Massive Resisters, speculated that "If the court were to fix, say, a ten-year period, and permit the states to integrate 10 per cent of their schools a year . . . a solution might be found."

In August, 1954, a scientific analysis of white and black reactions to Brown in the state of Florida became available, when the results of a Florida State-University of Miami questionnaire survey were made public. Among the more interesting findings of the survey were these:

1. Roughly one-fourth of white leaders polled agreed, in principle, with Brown.

2. A minority of whites vigorously rejected Brown to the point of promising active opposition to its implementation.

3. The great majority of black leaders hailed Brown as a triumph for social justice.

4. White leaders ("influentials") for the most part preferred gradual to immediate adoption of a school desegregation policy.

5. The majority of both white and black leaders doubted that serious violence would accompany desegregation, though many were skeptical of the state's ability to handle violence if it should come.

6. Elective white officials tended to be more strongly opposed to Brown than the average white Floridian.

7. Finally, the survey analysts concluded that a peaceful transition to school desegregation in Florida would require five preconditions: (1) strong public support for desegregation by white influentials; (2) vigorous enforcement of Brown by school as well as other public authorities; (3) prompt prosecution of any segregationist who might try to disrupt the desegregation process; (4) a firm resolve on the part of courts and other involved public agencies not to tolerate direct or indirect defiance of desegregation orders; and (5) a continuing effort by community leaders to rally popular support for desegregating schools by appeals to moral, religious, and democratic principles. Quite aside from the substantive findings of the Florida survey, the very fact that a scholarly group of white moderates could initiate and publicize such a survey in the summer of 1954 would seem to be proof that southerners had the freedom to agree or disagree with Brown, with little fear of reprisal, at that time. Later, of course, that freedom would be severely restricted or nonexistent.

Among private groups that generally reacted positively to Brown were most of the area's churches. In fact, it is now well established that initially nearly all general denominational convocations acclaimed it. The Southern Presbyterian General Assembly of 1954, for example, urged "all our people to lend their assistance to those charged with the duty of implementing the decision, and to remember that appeals to racial prejudice will not help but hinder the accomplishment of this aim." The Assembly also pronounced enforced segregation to be "out of harmony with Christian theology and ethics" and requested local congregations and church-related colleges to open their doors to people of all races.[5] The very conservative Southern Baptist Convention of 1954 agreed that Brown was "in harmony with the constitutional guarantee of equal freedom to all citizens, and with the Christian principles of equal justice and love for all men." The Convention likewise implored Southern Baptists "to conduct themselves in this period of adjustment in the spirit of Christ," and to give "a good testimony to the meaning of Christian faith and discipleship."[6]

It is also well documented that several state and district convocations of Protestant denominations reacted favorably to Brown. The Southern Presbyterian Synods of Virginia and Arkansas followed the lead of the General Assembly in praising the Supreme Court and in criticizing segregation as "out of harmony with Christian theology and ethics." There were similar endorsements of Brown from the North Carolina, Little Rock, North Arkansas, and North Texas Methodist Annual Conferences. Ironically, one of the strongest endorsements of Brown came from the Baptist General Association of Virginia, which acknowledged "the fact that, regardless of our own personal views, the decision of the . . . Supreme Court . . . is the supreme law of the land which does not violate any cardinal principle of our religion, and . . . as Christian citizens we should abide by this law."[7]

It would be misleading, however, to suggest that in 1954 local congregations and individual church members were as sympathetic to Brown as religious editors and denominational spokesmen were. That was simply not the case. Moreover, as the months went by, the cleavage between leaders and rank-and-file members widened sharply. This became so marked that by 1956 pastors and denominational officials virtually ended their former frank comments on the race issue, apparently unwilling to incur further risks to their security. This was especially true in the Deep

South where loyalty to regional traditions soon overrode loyalty to abstract Christian ideals. As for the Catholic and Jewish minorities, their leaders also spoke favorably of Brown, but it is not clear that their statements made any deeper inroads on their followers' prejudices than did the statements of Protestant leaders on theirs.

It is generally agreed, then, that the white South's first reactions to Brown were a mixed bag. There was the expected criticism, but an unexpected amount of praise. One might say, in light of subsequent events, that the southerners' first impressions were a sort of cameo in which strategies and tactics of the future could be dimly seen. Certainly the Brown decision did not win immediate acceptance from many segregationists nor did it instantly alter the South's racial status quo. Yet a growing awareness of the failures of basic American principles such as freedom and equality, as well as controversy over them, attested to the existence of the democratic ideal as a living factor in our legal order. Whatever sentiments white southerners may have voiced in reacting to Brown, none of them denied that an ideal of constitutionalism is and must remain central in the traditions by which we relate law and life in the United States.

This positive conclusion, however, must be balanced by the fact that the adverse reactions to Brown, especially those by public policy-makers, confirmed once more that freedom and equality are the most paradoxical and protean of political terms, and the most difficult to realize in practice.

2.

Rise of Southern Resistance

═══════════

I. GOVERNMENTAL RESISTANCE

THE FIRST CLEAR SIGNS of organized attempts to circumvent Brown appeared in the fall of 1954 with the reopening of the South's public schools. The Supreme Court had not yet handed down its implementation decree, and there was thus only minimal pressure to integrate southern schools. Such integration as did take place in the first post-Brown school year was largely confined to peripheral areas: Arkansas (Charleston and Fayetteville), Delaware (Wilmington), Kansas, Maryland (Baltimore to a small extent), Missouri (nine school districts), New Mexico, Oklahoma (only at the college and parochial school levels), West Virginia (in 25 of the state's 55 counties), and the District of Columbia. In terms of pupils involved, it was not a great deal. Yet it was sufficient to generate the first stages of a segregationist backlash.

What appears to have been the first case of serious resistance to desegregation occurred in mid-September in the rural community of Milford, Delaware, about 65 miles from Wilmington. After the school board agreed to desegregate the local schools, a white protest movement, accompanied by threats of violence, emerged, and frightened school officials temporarily closed the schools. Although it was private individuals who took the initiative at Milford, local officials precipitated the trouble by giving almost no advance notice of desegregation plans, and by doing little to prepare either the school personnel or the community for the transition from separate to unitary schools.

About the time that Milford was experiencing its troubles, Newark, Delaware, located a few miles to the north, was also having desegregation problems. In Newark, however, disturbances were minimized because of the prompt actions taken by school and law enforcement officials. The Newark pacification did not entirely end the threat of racial violence in the border state of Delaware, but it provided a useful example of how future violence might be anticipated and averted. It is also worth noting that the desegregation troubles in Delaware in September 1954 were the first of scores of dramatic crises in the Massive Resistance era that would be brought home to every American through the saturation coverage of the national media. Experts in the field of communications are still debating the pros and cons of this kind of coverage.

In the state of Georgia, after an ugly racist campaign involving nine candidates, Marvin Griffin of Bainbridge won the Democratic gubernatorial primary on September 8, and thus was assured of succeeding Governor Talmadge in January 1955. If there had been any doubts as to the state's position on school desegregation under Talmadge, there would obviously be none under Griffin. Governor-Nominate Griffin pledged that "Come hell or high water, races will not be mixed in Georgia schools." He also stated that "The meddlers, demagogues, race baiters and Communists are determined to destroy every vestige of states' rights." As for integrationists, they should be chased out of town "with a brushy top saplin'." Surely few governors who embraced Massive Resistance worked harder to redeem their racist pledges then Marvin Griffin did. In the process he gave his state an incredibly corrupt administration.

In Louisiana in the fall of 1954 talk of resistance to Brown centered around discussions of the "police power" amendment, which the voters approved on November 2. It was during the campaign for the ratification of this amendment that the name of State Senator W. M. Rainach, destined to become a Massive Resistance stalwart, first came into prominence. As head of a joint legislative committee supporting the amendment, Senator Rainach served as master of ceremonies for a 15-minute television film expounding its virtues. He did a masterful job as he traced segregation back to God and cleverly manipulated those forensic techniques and symbols that in a few years would become so familiar to the nation's television viewers and newspaper readers. During the New Orleans school crisis, Rainach would go so far as to advocate civil disobedience and a scorched-earth policy to forestall integration.

On November 23, 1954, President Eisenhower made one of his rare public statements about Brown, which may well have stiffened governmental resistance in the South. Without approving or disapproving the Supreme Court's holding, President Eisenhower said he expected the Court to decentralize the carrying out of Brown in view of the difficult problems involved. The next day, U. S. Attorney General Herbert Brownell released to the press the contents of the brief his office had filed with the Supreme Court respecting Brown's implementation. The brief suggested a policy of localized gradualism, and on two key points it coincided with the briefs filed by eight southern states and a South Carolina county. These points were the request that the Court grant southern school boards sufficient time to comply with Brown and the proposal that the lower federal courts be given the job of supervising the desegregation process. The NAACP, on the other hand, argued for a clear-cut decree that would set a definite time limit for desegregating the South's schools. When Brown II was finally announced, it turned out to be a good deal closer to the southern position and to that of the Attorney General's *amicus curiae* brief than it was to the NAACP suggestions.

Although Mr. Eisenhower would later push through the military integration begun by Mr. Truman, oversee the integration of the District of Columbia schools, stand firm at Little Rock, and defend the correctness of Brown in his memoirs, it is a matter of record that he never publicly expressed his approval of the decision during his eight years in the White House.[1] This is of more than passing importance, for it was precisely those years that constituted the heyday of the Massive Resistance backlash. Stung by criticism of his public neutrality toward Brown, President Eisenhower, at one point in the late 1950's, stated that it was not his prerogative as chief executive in a separation-of-powers government to approve or disapprove Supreme Court decisions. Whatever the merits of such a hands-off policy, there can be little doubt that some of the South's political leaders took the President's continued neutrality to mean that he was secretly on their side. This misunderstanding, as Little Rock apparently proved it to have been, led to an enormous amount of mischief, at least some of which might have been averted by a different kind of moral and political leadership in the White House.

Shortly before President Eisenhower made his cautious comments on Brown, the Southern Governors Conference met at Boca Raton, Florida. Naturally the question of desegregation loomed large in the Conference's deliberations. The most publicized action taken by the governors was the issuance of a defiant statement protesting the forced integration of public schools. The signatories pledged every legal effort "to preserve the right of the states to administer their public school system to the best interest of all the people." An interesting footnote to the meeting was the fact that Governor-Elect Folsom of Alabama, though present, did not sign the statement.

During the early months of 1955 several southern legislatures were in session, and all of them were preoccupied with the problems and challenges posed by Brown. By mid-April most had adjourned, and pro-segregation legislation in one form or another was adopted by the legislatures of Mississippi, North Carolina, and South Carolina. "Resistance legislation," however, failed to pass in Arkansas and Tennessee, which would suggest that in the upper South at least the dominant public attitude was one of "wait and see" rather than open defiance.

In the wake of Brown II's announcement on May 31, 1955, the South's public officials for the most part discarded their "wait and see" posture and began evolving a state policy of in-depth resistance and legal challenge. In this regard, Louisiana was again in the forefront as its Board of Liquidation of the State Debt granted the sum of $100,000 to the State Attorney General's office for hiring lawyers to fight integration suits in the courts. State Senator Rainach, as chairman of the legislature's Joint Segregation Committee, had requested the funds. Though there was a good deal of public opposition to this unusual diversion of state funds, it apparently was not taken very seriously by the officials involved.

Other southern states copied Louisiana's tactic of hiring high-priced legal talent to fight every NAACP suit, with the result that southern taxpayers soon realized the bitter truth that fighting the Supreme Court was going to be a long and financially costly battle. And worse from the South's point of view was the fact that there was no assurance of final victory even if millions of dollars of tax funds were paid out in legal fees. The other side, after all, had the full resources of the federal government behind it as well as some of the best legal brains in the nation.

Though southern resistance perceptively hardened after Brown II, the resistance had not yet taken on the form of overt violence that would be so much a part of the South's backlash in later years. For most of 1954 and 1955 defiance of federal authority expressed itself through political maneuvering, legal challenges, and propaganda campaigns. At the center of the controversy was the "battle of the courthouse" between the NAACP's lawyers and lawyers representing southern school districts. An indication of the scope of this battle was the fact that in the fall of 1955 there were almost 30 lawsuits in the courts directly concerned with the issue of school segregation. Most of these were actions that black parents, aided by the NAACP, had brought in federal district courts with the object of getting black students admitted to all-white schools, and, in a few cases, to all-white colleges. In almost every instance, southern officials went to court to oppose the black students' requests.

With the advent of 1956, the upper South and border states reported slight progress toward desegregation, but the Deep South was still promising continued defiance. By this time, the segregationists had developed an arsenal of slogans, symbols, and legal-constitutional concepts, such as states' rights and interposition, with which to discredit Brown, but they still lacked strong leadership and a southwide organization. True, a few local and state leaders, notably Senator Rainach and Leander Perez in Louisiana, were coming into national prominence, but no segregationist had yet emerged with sufficient charisma and leadership ability to unite the South's still fluid resistance forces.

More and more of the South's spokesmen were demanding some kind of southwide coordination of resistance efforts, as evidenced by this South Carolina newspaper editorial:

> *If the Southern states will stand together on the Doctrine of Interposition, they will find strength in unity. Successful defense of states rights, though presently forming around the explosive issue of race, would go far beyond segregation below the Mason-Dixon Line. . . .*
>
> *Now is the time, we believe, for the strong voices of the South to be raised. There are many names in the South that command respect throughout the country. . . .*
>
> *Let our spokesmen be heard from Virginia to Texas. Each will give support to the others.*[2]

In January of 1956 Alabama apparently became the first southern state to pass a legislative resolution declaring the Supreme Court's desegregation opinions to be "null, void and of no effect." Actually the measure was a resolution of interposition, a legal ploy that was fast becoming the key feature of the Massive Resisters' strategy. It passed almost without debate—in the house by a vote of 86 to 4 and in the senate unanimously.

In February Alabama was again in the spotlight, when the court-ordered admission of Miss Autherine Lucy to the University of Alabama incited a three-day demonstration which became so riotous that university officials, fearing for her safety, indefinitely suspended Miss Lucy. The demonstrators appear to have been led by a pre-law student, who was later expelled. Miss Lucy, the first black student to be admitted to an all-white Alabama school, allegedly accused university officials of conspiring with the rioters, and after that her suspension was made permanent.[3] As a result of the Lucy affair, school segregation in Alabama was strengthened, and white supremacists all over the South were jubi-

lant. Why not? A precedent had been set of governmental deference to mob hysteria, which meant that desegregation orders
could be nullified if enough white people would stand up and defy
them.

Governor Allan Shivers, in the fall of 1956, demonstrated his
determination to take full advantage of the Lucy precedent. He
did this by defying not one but *two* federal courts. This came
about after the Governor intervened in the two Texas communities
that were under federal court orders to desegregate their schools.
The institutions involved were Mansfield High School and Texarkana Junior College. Both had agreed to accept black applicants
when ordered by federal district courts to do so, but Governor
Shivers spared them the ordeal of desegregation. In putting interposition to its first practical test, he sent Texas Rangers to both
Texarkana and Mansfield, allegedly to prevent violence and assure
order, but chiefly to defend segregation. As in Alabama, judicial
authority had proved to be a frail reed for blacks to lean on when
government and community leaders were not on their side.

One may well ask what the federal government did when
faced with a clear-cut case of state defiance. The answer is nothing
—or almost nothing. About a week after Shivers "interposed" his
rangers to save Jim Crow, reporters asked President Eisenhower
at a press conference what he thought of the actions of the Texas
Governor. The President, refusing a chance to commit himself to
Brown, pointed out that in this country the maintenance of public
order is chiefly a responsibility of the states. Then, in rather
murky prose, he added: "Now, in the Texas case there was—the
attorney for the students did report this violence and asked help,
which apparently was the result of unreadiness to obey a federal
court order. But before anyone could move, the Texas authorities
had moved in and order was restored, so the question became
unimportant."[4]

The question may have seemed unimportant to the President,
isolated in Washington, but it was not unimportant to the whites
and blacks of the communities concerned or to the South's attentive
politicians seeking a way to combat the egalitarian revolution. By
asserting that desegregation was a responsibility of the states and
the federal courts, the President was in effect washing his hands of

the controversy—as, to some extent, the Supreme Court was then doing. In any event, the Texas showdowns proved that the white South was no longer willing—if it ever had been—to take court-imposed integration lying down. And throughout the region, public officials, buoyed by the coup of Governor Shivers, increasingly moved from moderation to verbal defiance.

II. PRIVATE RESISTANCE

THIS STUDY is not premised on the "hearts and minds" theory of Massive Resistance, which holds that the South's backlash had its chief basis of support in the affections of the white populace. It stresses state action more than private action and assumes that the people of the South followed more often than led. Still, thousands of whites did follow, more or less freely, their political leaders, and to such an extent that the growth of governmental resistance in 1954 and 1955 was closely paralleled by a rise in private resistance—some carefully contrived, some spontaneous.

Rather surprisingly, one of the first groups in the private sector to propose organized resistance to Brown was Louisiana's Association of Catholic Laymen. The Laymen opposed even token integration, and restricted their membership to "persons of the Caucasian race who profess the faith of the Holy Roman Catholic Church." Their resistance ran counter to the official position of the Catholic Church as well as to the stated policy of Archbishop Joseph Francis Rummel of New Orleans who, back in 1953, had ordered an end to *church* segregation in his diocese.

It will also be recalled that in 1954 Archbishop Rummel made it known that he was about to order the complete desegregation of his parochial schools, which constituted a large segment of southern Louisiana's educational system. Such an order, however, was not actually issued until eight years later, well after Massive Resistance had passed its peak. Indeed, it was not until 1956, two years after Brown I, that the Archbishop, in a pastoral letter, unequivocally branded school segregation as "morally wrong and sinful." As for the actual desegregation of Louisiana's Catholic schools, that did not take place till two years after the start of public school desegregation in the state, and it ultimately led to the excommunication of three Catholic white supremacists, the most important of whom was Leander Perez.

Another sign of rising resistance in the private sector was the formation in Durham, North Carolina, of the North Carolina Association for the Preservation of the White Race, Inc. There was an irony in this, for Durham had long been one of the southern strongholds of the black bourgeoisie and of black economic power. In South Carolina at about the same time a States Rights League was being formed in Sumter County, the precursor of many such resisters' groups in the Deep South.

The desegregation troubles that had flared up in southern Delaware in the fall of 1954 were made worse by the sudden intrusion into the state of Bryant W. Bowles of Washington, D. C. Bowles was the self-styled president and founder of the National Association for the Advancement of White People as well as the prototype of the professional racist agitators who played such a key role in Massive Resistance in the late 1950's. After inflaming the Delaware situation, Bowles moved on to Baltimore and Washington, where he urged whites to stand firm for segregation. Bowles ultimately fared less well than most of the demagogues who came after him. He dabbled in local Delaware politics for a time and then moved to California. Some time after that, he was convicted of murder in Texas and sentenced to life imprisonment.

A milestone in the rise of Massive Resistance occurred in July 1954, when the Indianola Citizens' Council was formed at Indianola, Mississippi, by a cadre of the town's civic and business leaders that included the mayor, city attorney, and a Harvard-educated attorney. The key figures in the founding of the group were Mississippi Circuit Judge Thomas Pickens Brady (the chief ideologue), Robert B. Patterson (former Mississippi State football star and World War II paratrooper), and Arthur B. Clark, Jr. (the Harvard-trained attorney). Indianola was an altogether fitting place for the foundation of the Council movement. Located in the heart of the Deep South on the banks of cypress-studded Indian Bayou, it was the seat of Sunflower County, where Senator Eastland's huge plantation is situated, and had long been regarded as the center of the cotton-rich, ideologically conservative Delta area of the state. It is also interesting that while blacks constituted almost 70 per cent of the county's population in the early fifties, they comprised but .03 per cent of the registered voters. The acorn that was planted in sleepy Indianola shortly after Brown was announced would grow in an amazingly brief time into the tallest and most admired oak in the tangled forest of Massive Resistance.

But other private groups were springing up at this time to compete with the Councils for the hearts of segregationists. They included the White Brotherhood and White Men, Inc., the Defenders of State Sovereignty and Individual Liberties in Virginia, the Patriots of North Carolina, the States' Rights Council of Georgia, and the Tennessee and Florida Federations for Constitutional Government. In most cases, the influence of these groups was limited to a single state or section of a state.

If the Councils were the power to be reckoned with in the Deep South, it was the Defenders of State Sovereignty and Individual Liberties who, as allies of the Byrd machine, led the resistance troops in Virginia. The Defenders were founded early in the post-Brown era—on October 8, 1954—and throughout their career they seem to have felt somewhat above the more blatantly racist Councils of the Deep South. The permanent president of the Defenders was Robert B. Crawford of Prince Edward County (one of the original parties to the Brown litigation), who, like so many Massive Resistance leaders, was unknown before being thrust onto center stage by the desegregation crisis. A dry-cleaner and ex-member of the Prince Edward County school board, Crawford turned out to be a talented leader and, as a confidant of Virginia governors, a potent influence in state politics. His organization had around 2,000 members at the end of 1954, around 8,000 a year later, and some 12,000 by the end of 1956. Eminently respectable and thus in tune with the genteel tradition of Virginia politics, the Defenders were resolute opponents of all egalitarian revolutionaries. They were in fact so respectable that state officials and politicians-on-the-make rarely passed up a chance to speak at their numerous rallies.

In 1955 Louisiana segregationists set up a new resistance group called the Knights of the White Christians. The avowed purpose of the group was to save "Christianity, States' Rights, Segregation and the Traditions of the South as well as the Purity of the White Race." The Knights never achieved anything like the influence of the Councils, but their name and objectives were a good example of how the new resistance groups were mixing regional, Christian, Calhounian, and white supremacist values in their backlash rhetoric.

A more ominous development was a marked increase in Ku Klux Klan agitation going back to mid-1955. One of the first post-Brown Klan rallies to be widely reported was held in Sumter County, South Carolina, early in June of 1955. After that, there were frequent reports of Klan activity in virtually every part of the South, save Virginia and the border states. Even in the border states there was some activity, notably in southern Delaware.

What seems to have been one of the first serious acts to impede integration by physical violence took place in Florida in late 1955. This invoved an unidentified group of men who tried to set fire to the home of Allen Platt, whose five children, alleged to be black, had been ousted from a Lake County white school they had integrated only to be returned by another court order. Plagued by continued harassment and constant threats against his home and family, Platt changed his residence four times in a few months to evade his harassers. The police never made any arrests in the case.

The momentum of both public and private resistance to Brown steadily mounted in 1954 and 1955. In 1956 it would become truly massive.

III. THE SOUTHERN MANIFESTO

IF ONE CAN SET A DATE on which the South's resistance to Brown turned into something close to a political counterrevolution, that date would have to be March 12, 1956. For it was then that

Georgia's Senator Walter George, speaking for the southern bloc, introduced their "Declaration of Constitutional Principles" or Southern Manifesto. As an evolving counterrevolution, Massive Resistance had, of course, grown organically out of the South's violent past. And the shape that it acquired with the proclamation of the March 12 Manifesto stemmed largely from the unresolved tensions of that past, which Brown had brusquely brought to the surface of southern politics.

The Manifesto initially bore the signatures of 19 senators and 77 representatives from 11 southern states. Five more representatives signed later. The document itself had no legal standing and required no congressional action, yet it was a dramatic challenge of the South's ruling oligarchs to the supremacy of federal law and authority in the states of the old Confederacy.

It began by charging that the Supreme Court had handed down an "unwarranted decision" in the Brown case and had thereby substituted "naked power for established law." It then alleged that since the constitution can be changed only by formal amendment, "the decision . . . in the school cases . . . [was] a clear abuse of judicial power." Rejecting the Warren Court's construction of the equal protection clause, the Manifesto noted that the framers of the fourteenth amendment "subsequently provided for segregated schools in the District of Columbia." Moreover, since the separate but equal doctrine announced in Plessy was the proper interpretation of the fourteenth amendment's equal protection clause, all judicial decisions rejecting that precedent are invalid. In the Brown case, the justices of the Supreme Court in effect "substituted their personal, political, and social ideas for the established law of the land." And what is worse, they opened the flood-gates to "outside agitators" and "revolutionary changes" in the South. The Manifesto closed with the following statements:

> *We decry the Supreme Court's encroachments on rights reserved to the States and to the people, contrary to established law and to the Constitution.*
>
> *We commend the motives of those States which have declared the intention to resist forced integration by any lawful means.*
>
> *We appeal to the States and people who are not directly*

affected by these decisions to consider the constitutional principles involved against the time when they, too, on issues vital to them, may be the victims of judicial encroachment. . . .

We pledge ourselves to use all lawful means to bring about a reversal of this decision which is contrary to the Constitution and to prevent the use of force in its implementation. . . .[5]

The framers of the Manifesto at first meant it to be a flat endorsement of interposition, but they could not get a consensus for that idea. Senator Strom Thurmond of South Carolina seems to have first conceived the idea of such a document, and he prepared at least three early drafts. Senator Harry Byrd endorsed Thurmond's idea, which makes Thurmond and Byrd the real fathers of the Manifesto.[6]

The original draft bristled with defiance, but it soon became clear that a broad consensus could be achieved only if the language were more moderate. Five rough drafts of the Manifesto were made and circulated; none got the desired amount of support from southern congressmen. Senators Thurmond, Russell, Stennis, Fulbright, and Daniel worked together on a sixth and final draft. This proved acceptable to most of the southern bloc, and it was then introduced into the House and Senate.

Doubtless the Manifesto's framers had several purposes in mind when they drafted and circulated their statement. A retrospective analysis would suggest that at least ten were uppermost in their minds. They were: (1) to reassert an antebellum conception of federalism; (2) to stress the illegitimacy of the Brown decision; (3) to rehabilitate Plessy's view of the equal protection clause of the fourteenth amendment; (4) to convince southern opinion that the Brown opinion was an act of naked usurpation by the Supreme Court; (5) to urge states'-rightists throughout the nation to make the South's cause their own; (6) to give hope to local officials who were seeking ways to avoid desegregation; (7) to put the prestige of a part of the United States Congress behind southern resistance; (8) to scare white southerners with threats of invasions by outside agitators; (9) to polarize white opinion in the South by forcing moderates to come out for or against Brown; and

(10) to nip in the bud the undercurrent of "inevitability" about desegregation that had been rising in the South since the spring of 1954. The fact that most of these purposes were not explicitly discussed does not, of course, refute their existence.

In view of the pressure that was put on southern congressmen to sign, the wonder is that the Manifesto was not signed by every southerner in Congress. Yet two senators flatly refused to sign—Gore and Kefauver of Tennessee—along with 24 southern House members. Several of these later became *defeated* "Profiles in Courage." Senate Majority Leader Lyndon B. Johnson and House Speaker Sam Rayburn, both of Texas, were not asked to sign the Manifesto. In the end, seven state delegations had 100 per cent participation in the signing. These were the delegations from Alabama, Arkansas, Georgia, Louisiana, Mississippi, South Carolina, and Virginia. There were no signers at all from the border states of Kentucky and Oklahoma, and 16 members of the big Texas delegation in the House refused to sign.

How well did the Manifesto realize the framers' goals? An honest answer would have to be not very well. Certainly it provided a boost to the morale of the South's segregationists, and on the surface it seemed to endow southern resistance with a new legitimacy and aura of respectability. Yet these gains were ephemeral, for in the long run the Manifesto simply did not achieve the decisive or dramatic impact its creators envisioned. Most important, it did not succeed in either repealing or discrediting Brown, nor did it seriously retard the slow march of tokenism.

Perhaps one of the greatest victories achieved by the Manifesto's framers was one that has been little noticed. That was their success in widely disseminating their extraordinary document while provoking only minimal criticism from their non-southern colleagues. Critics of the Manifesto in the House scarcely protested at all, and in the Senate the non-southerners' reaction was muted to say the least. After Senators George and Thurmond extolled the Manifesto, four opponents briefly—almost apologetically—stated their views. Senator Lehman said he would "have more to say on this subject at an early date." Senator Morse praised the Brown decision and equated the Manifesto's principles with the Calhounian doctrines of interposition and nullification.

Senator Humphrey seconded the views of the Senator from Oregon and said that "The Supreme Court decision should be a stimulant for further orderly progress." Senator Neuberger thought the Manifesto would be a boon to the Soviet Union's propaganda campaign, since it confronted the United States government "with a choice between anarchy and the rule of law." He also suggested that the "President should call a White House conference" of southern officials and use his "great influence and authority" to reestablish domestic unity and solidarity.

As for Eisenhower, who would soon be wooing the South in his second presidential campaign, he stressed that the Manifesto mentioned only legal defiance, and let it go at that. Adlai Stevenson, who was expected to be the President's Democratic opponent for a second time, pretty much ignored the Manifesto.

Shortly after the Manifesto's proclamation, the first public utterance of the phrase "Massive Resistance" was heard. Senator Harry Byrd of Virginia seems to have been the first member of Congress to use the phrase.[7] While seeking to justify the Manifesto to his colleagues, Byrd observed that its drafting was "part of the plan of massive resistance we've been working on and I hope and believe it will be an effective action." So it came about that the South's emergent counterrevolution, though not very cohesive, had at last acquired a label and a powerful Senate sponsor. Both would stay with the movement till the end.

Since the demise of Massive Resistance, students of southern politics as well as ordinary Americans have asked themselves whether its rise in the mid-1950's was inevitable. It may well be, as the old saw holds, that nothing is really inevitable save death and taxes. But if Massive Resistance was not wholly inevitable, it was not too great a surprise to those intimately familiar with southern history and politics.

3.

The Ideology of
Massive Resistance

I. THE NATURE OF IDEOLOGY

THE MAKERS of counterrevolutions have traditionally rationalized their movements with a conservative or reactionary
ideology, and the leaders of the South's backlash to Brown were
no exception. The ideology of Massive Resistance in the final
analysis came down to a kind of regional nationalism which, for
all its surface bravado, revealed a deep uncertainty and *Angst*
about key aspects of the southern way of life. True, this *Angst* was
never publicly admitted, but it was always there.

Ideology in the broadest sense is the value system and mythology held by a party, class, or group. A counterrevolutionary
ideology, like that of Massive Resistance, serves three basic functions. It legitimates a given social system; it promotes group cohesion; and it provides its adherents with propaganda ammuniton
for psychological and political warfare against revolutionary opponents. One may also say that an ideology both describes a
special view of reality and prescribes what ought to be.[1]

Scholars have defined myth, a chief component of ideology, in a wide variety of ways. They have equated it with sacred tale or cosmogony (theologians), a primitive tribe's fantasy story (Lévi-Strauss), a charter for social action (Malinowski), a functional ritual (Frazer), a historical rationalization (historians), a personalized legend (literary critics), a traditional folk tale (social anthropologists), an ancient people's fairy tale (classicists), a temporization of essence (Kenneth Burke), and a vision that individuals have of the human situation (Northrop Frye). One of the first social scientists to use the concept defined it as the non-scientific, non-technological, value-impregnated aspects of a society whose function it is to sustain a given society and its culture.[2] The man whose name is most closely associated with the term today used myth to mean a value-laden, apocalyptic symbol to be consciously manipulated by leaders as a way of inspiring oppressed minorities to seek political power.[3]

All of these definitions of myth have their points, and none is perhaps a great deal better than the others. As used in the present analysis, myth is defined as an aspect of ideology which is manifested through symbols, emblems, stereotypes, totems, taboos, rites, and verbalized propositions. The ideology of Massive Resistance contained two basic myths and dozens of sub-myths. The basic ones were the psycho-social philosophy of white supremacy racism and the politico-legal doctrine of states'-rights federalism.

It is trite but true to say that every person and every culture is a creature of myth. And since that is so, it is obvious that one of the best ways to understand a society is to explore its mythology. The analyst must not be put off by the fact that myths may be, and often are, veiled explanations of the truth or gross distortions of reality. For despite (perhaps because of) these characteristics, they have the power to grip men's minds and hearts as they provide an understandable image of the surrounding world.

Since myths are largely non-rational and emotive, they can tell us much about the fears, sorrows, joys, illusions, and dreams of individuals and groups. Indeed, the noted expert on mythology, Joseph Campbell, recently wrote that "myths are public dreams" in his *Myths to Live By* (New York, 1972). And in a very real sense they are. As a medium of communication between man's conscious and unconscious, myths have a dream-like quality, and like dreams may turn into nightmares.

In the post-Brown politics of conflict, the South's revolutionaries and counterrevolutionaries were fighting over mythic abstractions as much as over material things. And it has been clear since World War I that the more ideologized a conflict becomes, the more difficult its final resolution will be. It is never easy to say how crucial myth and ideology are in a given conflict, yet one can be certain of their presence in this Age of Ideology. In regards to its mythology, the South after 1954 was experiencing the agonies of reorientation. Its old myths, though still tenaciously clung to by the militants, had lost much of their life-supporting potential since Brown threw them into moral disequilibration. But no consensus was yet in sight for the counter-myths of integration and social equality. So, as the dialectic of conflict intensified, a new synthesis was waiting to be born.

II. THE MYTH OF WHITE SUPREMACY

THE BASIC SOCIAL PHILOSOPHY of Massive Resistance was the myth of white supremacy, a doctrine that almost all social scientists view as a type of racism.[4] This seems reasonable if one accepts the common definition of racism as the theory which holds that there is a genetic link between skin color and psychocultural traits, that some races are innately superior to others, and that race purity should be the highest social goal. Of course, it must be conceded that few if any of the Massive Resisters ever referred to themselves as racists. And, in fact, most seemed to resent being so described.

Like all myths, the myth of white supremacy includes quite a panoply of symbols, emblems, totems, and taboos. These are important. But far more important are the verbalized propositions that rationalize the trappings and give meaning to them. Ten of these will be summarized below, having been generalized for analytical purposes from a broad range of books, pamphlets, speeches, journal articles, and public documents.[5] A few quotations from typical segregationists—some living, some dead—are included in order to suggest the tone and flavor of southern racist rhetoric. It did not seem unfair to include old quotations along with new ones, since it is generally assumed that the myth of white supremacy goes back at least to the seventeenth century.

1. Blacks and whites are fundamentally different—psycho-culturally as well as physically—and the observable differences between them are greater than the inherited likenesses they share as human beings. This view seemed to be implicit in Chief Justice Taney's reasoning in the Dred Scott case, when he wrote: Negroes are considered "a subordinate and inferior class of beings, . . . subjugated by the dominant race," and they have had "no rights or privileges but such as those who held the power and the Government might choose to grant them."

2. Since blacks are inferior beings, the normal courtesy titles of "Mr.," "Mrs.," and "Miss" should not be applied to them, whatever their station in life.

3. The crucial difference between whites and blacks is the general superiority of the former over the latter. This is proved by the fact that it has been the white race that has been responsible for the achievements of civilization. It is also proved by the black man's demonstrated addiction to laziness, thriftlessness, immaturity, immorality, criminality, ignorance, unreliability, and hyper-sexuality. Wrote an early twentieth-century racist: "Since the dawn of history the Negro has owned the Continent of Africa—rich beyond the dream of poet's fancy, crunching acres of diamonds under his bare black feet. Yet he never picked one up from the dust until a white man showed him its glittering light. . . . He lived as his fathers lived—stole his food, worked his wife, sold his children, ate his brother, content to drink, sing, dance and sport as the ape!"[6]

4. The self-evident inferiority of the black race is something God predestined. As such, it is an inherent part of the natural order and eternally fixed. It also means that there is a biological ceiling above which education cannot improve the

black man's intellect, and no amount of environmental change can remove this inherited debility. In the words of Senator W.M. Rainach of Louisiana: "Segregation is a natural order—created by God, in His wisdom, who made black men black and white men white."[7]

5. Since in the beginning God created separate races, it is important for society and government to be imbued with a thorough-going social sense of racial classification. Racial identities must not be confused, which means that every descendant of African slaves, however light-colored, shall be considered, for legal and social purposes, a black person. As a character in southern racist fiction put it, "One drop of Negro blood makes a Negro. It kinks the hair, flattens the nose, thickens the lips, puts out the light of intellect and lights the fires of brutal passion."[8]

6. The blacks' inferiority being a natural thing, their segregation from whites by law is an example of honest race consciousness, not bigotry or race prejudice. In the Brown case, the South's lawyers argued that segregation is neither race hatred nor intolerance, but rather "a deeply ingrained awareness of a birthright held in trust for posterity. . . . This doctrine of separate and equal schools was not the result of official or governmental prejudice or a desire to discriminate against either race nor caused by any hatred or feeling of superiority."[9]

7. A public policy of racial segregation is not only natural and compassionate, but also Christian, democratic, and traditional. The evidence for this is that the early Christians practiced it, our Founding Fathers sanctioned it, and until 1954 the Supreme Court approved it. Early in this century, Bishop William Montgomery Brown of the Protestant Episcopal Church wrote, "From every point of view, the conclusion is unavoidable that it is not only right for Anglo-Americans to recognize the Color-Line in the social, political and religious realms, but more than that it would be a great sin not to do so."[10]

8. Knowing their weaknesses, most blacks neither wish nor seek the end of segregation. They realize it is a protective

device that shields them from the competition of superior whites. Those who espouse integration sentiments are simply the victims of outside agitators. Only the native white southerner truly understands the black man's child-like psyche and has his real interests at heart.

9. Largely because of segregation, southern white Anglo-Saxons are the purest representatives of the white race. And of all the races of man, none has done more for America and western civilization than those whites with Anglo-Saxon blood in their veins. As Henry W. Grady, the prophet of the New South, once put it: "The Anglo-Saxon blood has dominated always and everywhere. . . . Never one foot of . . . [land] can be surrendered while that blood lives in American veins, and feeds American hearts, to the domination of an alien and inferior race."[11]

10. The end of segregation and the triumph of egalitarianism would inexorably lead to miscegenation in light of the hyper-sexuality of blacks. This in turn would bring about the decline of the white race and the triumph of a decadent race of half-breeds. This would follow, for there is a kind of Gresham's Law at work in race relations, whereby bad black blood corrupts and drives out good white blood and, in the process, mongrelizes the white race. Georgia's Senator Herman Talmadge has noted that "history shows that nations composed of a mongrel race lose their strength and become weak, lazy and indifferent. They become easy prey to outside nations."[12] Even blunter was Sutton E. Griggs, when he observed in an earlier time that "the problem of keeping Negro blood out of the veins of the white race is the paramount problem with the Southern white man, and to it all other questions, whether economic, political or social are made to yield."[13]

Since very few social scientists regard the myth of white supremacy as having scientific support, there would be little point in again rebutting the propositions here. Suffice it to say that most (though not quite all) scholars today view this myth as a blend of negrophobia, spurious biology, romantic eugenics, culturebound ethics, faulty psychology, perverted Christianity, and hysterical hyperbole about sex. [14] It need hardly be added that the Supreme Court's holding in Brown was far closer to the American Creed than the Massive Resisters' myth of white supremacy—at least closer since the adoption of the fourteenth amendment's equal protection clause.

One, of course, does not kill a myth just by demonstrating its empirical invalidity. "Myths are created to fill psychological needs,"[15] and that being so, the myth of white supremacy will live in southern hearts as long as it satisfies felt needs of whites—such as the need to feel superior to blacks. No amount of statistical data or hard scientific evidence suggesting a sociological rather than a genetic origin of black-white differences will change a "true believer's" mythic ways. Just as the Nazi counterrevolutionaries of the 1930's were unmoved by evidence disproving their racist myths, so the South's Massive Resisters were—and are—unimpressed by the piles of social science data revealing the fallacies of white supremacy. Faced with this imperviousness to reason, one is tempted to say: once a racist, always a racist. But that, too, would be unscientific—and uncharitable.

III. THE MYTH OF STATES'-RIGHTS FEDERALISM

THE MYTH of states'-rights federalism, like that of white supremacy, was a mixture of slogans, symbols, and verbalized propositions, most of which were born in antebellum political theory. To illustrate the core of the myth, ten propositions will be generalized below from such diverse sources as the Southern Manifesto, legal briefs filed in the Brown case, the theoretical works of Calhoun, and the mass of polemical writings by southern apologists for slavery and segregation that have flourished in the past two centuries.

After 1954, white supremacy and the states'-rightist view of federalism were so interwoven in the ideology of Massive Resistance that it is impossible to say that one was more important than the other to the South's counterrevolution. Neither was temporally prior to the other in all respects—though racism might seem more ancient—and neither was a necessary and sufficient cause of the other. A given individual might hold to one and reject the other. But in practice the myths were perfectly complementary, since both were created by white people with the interest of the white race in mind.

The myth of states'-rights federalism is a good deal more respectable than white supremacy, and intellectually more sophisticated. Because of this, a brief critique has been appended to the description of each proposition.

1. The federal Constitution is fundamentally a *compact* of independent states. The state governments existed before the national government was born, and it was the states which created the latter as their agent.

The only accurate thing about this proposition, which goes back to English Calvinist thought, is the claim of the temporal priority of the states. As for the origins of our federal system, the Preamble to the 1787 Constitution makes it clear that the creators of the new government were not the states, which did indeed establish the Confederation government of the 1780's, but "We the people." As Hamilton wrote in *Federalist* No. 22, it is the people of the whole nation who are sovereign—i.e., "the original fountain of all legitimate authority." Furthermore it was the popularly elected delegates in state ratification conventions, not the state legislatures, who ratified the 1787 Constitution. Also relevant are the oft-quoted words of Chief Justice John Marshall in the case of *McCulloch* v. *Maryland* (1819): "The government of the Union . . . is emphatically and truly a government of the people. In form and in substance it emanates from them, its powers are granted by them, and are to be exercised directly on them, and for their benefit."

2. The Supreme Court has no authority to amend the Constitution, which is what it tried to do in the Brown case. That document may be amended only if two-thirds of both

houses of Congress and three-fourths of state legislatures or conventions approve a formal resolution of amendment, introduced by a member of Congress or drafted by a convention called by Congress at the request of the legislatures of two-thirds of the states.

The second sentence of this proposition is an accurate summary of the two methods for the *formal* amendment of the Constitution as set forth in Article V. But it is no secret that the Constitution may be, and often is, changed by legislative elaboration, executive interpretation, judicial construction, as well as by evolving usage and custom. The Founding Fathers deliberately stressed brevity and "creative ambiguity" in drafting the 1787 Constitution. And while that laid a heavy burden on the courts, which must interpret the document's generalities, it facilitates adjustment to changed conditions and makes frequent resort to the formal amendment procedure unnecessary.

3. The tenth amendment is the heart and capstone of our system of federalism. It limits the federal government to those national powers *explicitly* enumerated in the Constitution, reserving all other powers "to the States respectively, or to the people."

There was a time when the post-Civil War Supreme Court interpreted the tenth amendment as a significant check on federal power. But most Supreme Court justices, beginning with John Marshall, have construed this so-called "states' rights" amendment as no more than a "truism," to use a phrase popularized by Chief Justice Stone. Under this construction, state and local governments are empowered to do those things which the national government may not do either in the exercise of its enumerated *or implied powers*—such as, for example, the collecting of local garbage and the establishment of public schools. But it must be stressed that the tenth amendment nowhere mentions the restrictive adverb "explicitly." In fact, some members of the first Congress that met under the new Constitution proposed including that word in the amendment, but the proposal was defeated by a large majority. As for the view that this amendment is the "heart" of our Constitution and federal system, this would seem to be denied by the fact that it took more than four years after the writing of the Constitution before what is claimed to be its most vital organ was finally inserted—at the *end* of the Bill of Rights. The important point here is that the reservation of certain powers to the states via the tenth amendment does not exclude the national government from regulating the subjects of that power under one of its express, implied, or inherent powers.

4. As a general principle of government, decentralization is to be preferred to centralization. This is so, for the state governments are closer to the people and thus they more accurately reflect the people's wishes than does the national government. No matter how democratic it may be, any national government will be viewed as a distant and essentially external authority by the average citizen. Mississippi's Senator Eastland was giving expression to this view when he said some time ago that what we need is a "return to the genius of the American system of government, which is local government, by the people of the communities."[16]

The alleged universal superiority of decentralization over centralization is a value judgment that lacks empirical confirmation. It is well to recall that it was not until we had centralized the collection of taxes and the formulation of basic national socio-economic policies that we began to make any real headway in solving the nation's urgent problems. Furthermore, it is no longer true—though it once may have been—that the national government is a distant, foreign entity. And even more to the point, state governments speak only for some of the people, while the national government alone speaks for all the people. Few today would deny that in beating the drums for decentralization, the South's Massive Resisters were simply rationalizing their selfish desire to shake off federal interference with the "southern way of life."

5. Federal judicial review of the acts of executive and legislative bodies at the state-local level is invalid, for it is a "usurped" power. If there has to be supervision of local pol-

icy making, a better procedure would be to set up a "Court of the Union" comprised of state chief justices.

It is, of course, true that the Constitution does not explicitly give the federal judiciary the power of judicial review. Yet a joint reading of Article III ("The judicial power of the United States . . . shall extend to all Cases . . . arising under this Constitution") and Article VI ("This Constitution . . . shall be the supreme Law of the Land") would seem to imply that this contingent veto power lies with the courts. Moreover, Alexander Hamilton, a member of the 1787 convention, argued in *Federalist* No. 78 that the federal courts would quite obviously have the power of judicial review. In any event, the judiciary has exercised this power since the early 1800's. And usurped or not, its right to do so has rarely been seriously contested. Even the Plessy Court, which Massive Resisters revere as the pinnacle of judicial wisdom, was exercising this power when it reviewed Louisiana's Jim Crow transportation law to see if its provisions conformed to the supreme law of the land. The fact that the Plessy Court found a consonance in this case does not alter the fact that the members of the Court were assuming that they had the right to invalidate the Louisiana law if a conflict with the federal Constitution were found.

In regard to a "Court of the Union," such an agency was actually proposed in one of three states' rights amendments which conservatives, in the South and elsewhere, sought to push through state legislatures in the 1960's. That fifty state-oriented magistrates would be more fit than the Supreme Court to construe our federal Constitution is not an idea that commends itself to reasonable men. Clearly if we wish to preserve minimal uniformity in the political systems of the states, while making sure that every citizen gets his constitutionally guaranteed rights, we cannot do without a national umpire, which is what the Supreme Court really is.

6. The President of the United States has no constitutional or other right to intervene in the affairs of any state or local government unless specifically asked to do so by state or local authorities.

As every schoolboy knows, several of our Presidents have violated this canon of states'-rights federalism. Washington did it during the Whiskey Rebellion. Cleveland did it during a rail strike. Eisenhower did it at Little Rock. And Kennedy did it in Mississippi and Alabama. Actually there is no constitutional requirement that a President first get permission from state or local authorities before dispatching marshals, troops, or other agents to enforce the law of the land. Indeed, the pertinent constitutional clauses provide for unilateral executive action. For example, Art. II, Sect. 3 states that the President "shall take care that the laws be faithfully executed," and the "laws" include court constructions of statutes and the Constitution itself. In addition, Art. IV, Sect. 4 provides that "the United States shall guarantee to every State in this Union a republican form of government." And while no President has actually implemented this provision, it is clearly a grant of unilateral federal authority. There are also numerous federal statutes, many going back to Reconstruction, which specifically authorize presidential intervention in certain circumstances. In sum, when executing the law of the land, the President, on his own initiative, may intervene anywhere and in any way he deems fit, provided only that he not violate federal law or the Constitution.

7. The framers of the fourteenth amendment, which has been the rationale for most federal "usurpations" of state powers, did not "contemplate and did not understand that it would abolish segregation in public schools."[17] Therefore, if the people's legislative representatives in a given state decide, by majority vote, to make segregation a state policy, the federal government can do nothing about it, since this right is clearly one of those which the tenth amendment has "reserved to the States." But even if this be denied, one must still face the fact that the fourteenth amendment with its equal protection clause may itself be unconstitutional, as the Reconstruction Congress forced a prostrate South to ratify it.

In the Brown case, the Supreme Court concluded that it is impossible to say with any degree of assurance exactly what were the intentions of the fourteenth amendment's framers vis-à-vis school segregation. Most constitutional experts concur in that conclusion. As for segregation being an inviolate state's right, it is well to remember that nowhere does the Constitution legitimate the concept of segregation or mention the phrase "state's right." Regarding the fourteenth amendment, Congress certainly did apply pressure on the defeated South to secure its ratification. But questioning the legitimacy of the amendment at this date is a constitutional red herring that reveals more about the rewriting of history by Massive Resistance leaders than about the true principles of our federal system.

8. The Bill of Rights, which the federal courts are increasingly using to restrict state-local autonomy, should be construed as a limitation on the federal government only, for the Founding Fathers never intended it to curtail state powers.

This may well have been the intent of the Founding Fathers, since the first amendment begins with the words, "Congress shall make no law" abridging our basic freedoms. Moreover, when this issue was first adjudicated in the Jacksonian Era, the United States Supreme Court held that the Bill of Rights was "intended solely as a limitation on the exercise of power by the government of the United States, and is not applicable to the legislation of the states."[18] While the Court consistently stuck to this view throughout the nineteenth century, it changed its mind in the 1920's and began incorporating parts of the Bill of Rights into the word "liberty" of the due process clause of the fourteenth amendment. As of the present time, it has not adopted the doctrine of "total incorporation" nor has it made the fourteenth amendment's due process clause a "mirror image" of the Bill of Rights. But it has come very close to that position. This "near-nationalization" of the Bill of Rights by the Supreme Court annoys states' rightists, but it has protected individual liberties from a variety of governmental abridgements.

9. Since ours is a dual system of government, it is extremely important that the boundaries of national and state authority be sharply defined and strictly adhered to.

This is a hair-splitting conception of federalism that was quite popular before the Civil War. It is not, however, a necessary deduction from the Constitution, nor is it warranted by actual experience in meeting national challenges. The Founding Fathers almost certainly intended state and federal authorities to carry out the functions of government not in an abrasive adversary relationship but in a spirit of harmonious cooperation. That spirit we today call "creative functional federalism." Such a conception of federalism, which has the Supreme Court's seal of approval, is solidly in the American pragmatic tradition, since it subordinates jurisdictional and ideological conflict to a concern with meeting national crises in the most expeditious way possible. Unless one assumes—as many Massive Resisters did—that the states have a right to use their reserved power to frustrate national policies, one can scarcely say that functional federalism is a denigration of valid states' rights.

10. The alpha and omega of American federalism is, in the final analysis, the sovereignty of state governments. Therefore, if federal authorities attempt to coerce the states into acting against the expressed will of their people, the states have the right, and indeed the duty, to resort to interposition or nullification to prevent the unconstitutional exercise of federal power.[19]

This proposition obviously is a logical extension of the compact theory of federalism discussed above. It was the major unarticulated premise of the Southern Manifesto and the explicit rationale of many of the laws which Massive Resistance legislators enacted after 1954. One might well say that it is the fundamental error from which flow all the other mythic aberrations of states'-rights federalism. It is, of course, a fact that the states were sovereign in the 1780's according to Art. II of our first national constitution, the Articles of Confederation. In 1787, however, the drafters of our present Constitution dropped the concept of state sovereignty and replaced it with federal sovereignty. This was done in Art. VI, which reads in part: "This Constitution, and the Laws of the United States which shall be made in pursuance thereof; and all Treaties made, or which shall be made, under the authority of the United States, shall be the supreme Law of the Land . . . *any Thing in the Constitution or Laws of any State to the Contrary notwithstanding"* (Italics added). As for the merits of interposition, the courts have long held that there is nothing in American constitutional law that justifies, directly or indirectly, that doctrine as a state device for invalidating the supreme law of the land as declared by the federal judiciary. Of course, if one construes a state's interposition resolution as nothing more than an official state protest against some federal action, it may be regarded as a relatively harmless, though still eccentric gesture, but not the absurdity it becomes when it is presumed to be a constitutional check on federal authority.

When one has carefully scrutinized the myth of states'-rights federalism, one wonders why so many intelligent southerners were taken in by it. An amorphous *collage* of theory, fancy, fact, half-truth, aspiration, and plain old rationalization, this myth really came down in the end to a kind of "political expressionism," characterized as it was by distortion of constitutional reality, and by the profligate use of symbols and slogans to give eccentric expression to subjective regional values.

Yet, in spite of their intellectual and moral sterility, the myths of white supremacy and states'-rights federalism formed the hard core of the legitimizing ideology of the South's counterrevolution. Designed as much as anything to palliate southern guilt over discrimination against blacks, these myths were conceived in the Old South and were revived and refurbished in the wake of Brown. Their persistence into the New South was one of the fundamental causes of the "culture lag" and tension that characterized southern society after 1954.

4.

Leadership Elites

I. SAINTS AND MARTYRS

NO ANALYSIS of the Massive Resisters' politics of conflict would be realistic if it failed to appraise the movement's "Leaders." One can, of course, go too far in this direction, as happened in the nineteenth century when scholars went overboard in favoring the "Great Man in History" thesis, while neglecting the long-range, impersonal forces stressed by most post-Marxian theorists. But since both leaders and impersonal forces were clearly involved in the history of Massive Resistance, both are legitimate concerns of the analysis of this book.

At the outset, several obvious questions come to mind that relate to political leadership as a generic phenomenon. Who, for example, are the key leaders? How do they lead? How important are they to their movements? What produced them? How did events and experiences shape them? Are they "charismatic" or "organizational" men? How do they relate to ideology? Do they shape ideology unilaterally or are they themselves shaped by ideology? This random sample by no means exhausts the list of possible leadership questions, but it includes enough to suggest the complexity and importance of the subject. Most of the analysis of this chapter will focus on these and related questions as they pertain to Massive Resistance leaders.[1]

The South's counterrevolutionary leaders were both top-level decision makers and lower echelon spokesmen whose job was not so much to make decisions as to spread propaganda and manipulate symbols. Still, whether decision makers or mere spokesmen, the leaders were all agreed on the necessity to throw back the egalitarian revolution and thereby deny socio-political equality to blacks. It is also well to bear in mind that the leadership elites were on the cutting edge of the South's politics of conflict, where concern with ideological purity is most acute, and deviation therefrom most dangerous.

A number of social scientists, including Karl Marx, have maintained that both revolutionary and counterrevolutionary leaders constitute elitist conspiracies. In a loosely defined sense that may well be the case, since it is obvious that revolutions and counterrevolutions invariably involve a good deal of plotting for or against the status quo. On the other hand, it would clearly be wrong to suggest that the leadership elites of most mass political movements, whether of the right or left, are monolithically united on strategy, tactics, and ideology. The truth of the matter is that there is often but minimal cohesion among such leadership groups. And in the case of Massive Resistance, that was unquestionably the situation.

While recognizing that leadership typologies can easily become procrustean beds, the analytically inclined will find it hard to dispense with them entirely in a study of such a complex thing as Massive Resistance. It will, therefore, perhaps be useful to distinguish five categories of leaders and spokesmen who led the Massive Resistance counterrevolution. These are saints and martyrs, tutelary geniuses, charismatic demagogues, pragmatic self-aggrandizers, and intellectual ideologues.

It is doubtful that there has ever been a mass movement in history that did not get around, sooner or later, to setting up a pantheon of hallowed saints and martyrs. In one sense, such figures are not leaders at all, for they are usually dead when the mass movement that venerates them is formed. Nevertheless they would seem to merit a place among leadership elites for two reasons.

Their "sacred writings" are often the core of mass movement ideologies, and their exemplary lives are constantly held up to the masses as models they should emulate. Thus, they are in a sense posthumous "leaders."

Among the saints canonized by Massive Resistance, none stood higher in the South's pantheon than John C. Calhoun, a states' rightist first, last, and always.

The salient facts of Calhoun's long and fruitful career are well known. Born into a prosperous South Carolina family in 1782, he was graduated from Yale, studied law, and in the early 1800's entered the South Carolina legislature. In 1811 he went to Congress, and came to national prominence as a hawk and strong supporter of the war with Great Britain. He served for seven and a half years as Monroe's Secretary of War, and was elected Vice President in 1824. Elected for a second term in 1828, with Andrew Jackson heading the ticket, he served three additional years as Vice President, and then resigned to return to Congress as Senator from South Carolina. In the Senate, he quickly became the leader of the southern bloc, a role that Georgia's Senator Russell would play in the 1950's. In that position, he became the chief source of arguments, policies, and political theory for the slaveocracy's counterattack against the Abolitionists. It was during these years in the Senate that he formalized the mythic doctrine of nullification. Later, in the 1840's, he served as Secretary of State under President Tyler, after which he returned to the Senate in 1845 and died in Washington in 1850.[2]

While Calhoun's writings were not often directly quoted in Massive Resistance politics, the principles of his political thought colored and shaped virtually every aspect of the movement's mythology and ideology. Moreover, at least one oracle of the defiant South, the *Richmond News Leader*, confirmed the hagiographic status of Calhoun by printing a three-column portrait of him in several of its issues during the height of the interposition controversy.

As the chief saint of the white South, Calhoun may be said to have made at least five contributions to the segregationists' counterrevolution. He provided a handy theoretical rationale for the doctrines of state sovereignty and states' rights. His writings legitimated, for segregationists if not for others, the myths of interposition and nullification. He made a strenuous effort to invest white racism with an aura of high morality. He offered a constant source of inspiration to those southerners who distrusted the federal government and sought a way back to the "Golden Age." And in his famous *Disquisition on Government*, he laid the groundwork for the South's best tool of legislative obstruction, the Senate filibuster. This he did by arguing, quite cogently, that in a pluralistic society, justice cannot be achieved by majority rule, but only by obtaining for every public policy the concurrent agreement of all concerned interest and sectional groups.

Calhoun's public career, like that of so many southern statesmen, had elements of Greek tragedy about it. Endowed with enormous talents and an upper-class background, he deliberately chose to exhaust his great powers in a futile defense of slavery and states'-rights federalism. He did not live to see the carnage his political theory helped to cause, though it is unlikely he would have shrunk from the logical or practical conclusions of his principles. In any case, the Civil War exposed the moral and legal bankruptcy of his thought, without preventing his canonization by the unrepentant South.

Within a few years after his death, Calhoun had become a kind of Arthurian figure among southern saints, ever ready to return to the political wars if a new generation of abolitionists should threaten white supremacy and states' rights. Yet it is ironic that while the Massive Resisters constantly bandied his name about in the 1950's, it was left to liberal academicians, mostly in the North, to read and rehabilitate his theoretical works.

The segregationists, especially those of Virginia, also venerated Jefferson and Madison. It must, however, be stressed that in this case their veneration was of a highly selective kind. A cursory survey of Massive Resistance propaganda would seem to suggest that Jefferson and Madison were praised for three things chiefly: their devotion to states' rights, their alleged belief in "strict construction" of the Constitution, and their suggestion in the 1790's of interposition resolutions as a possible way of checking the growth of federal power. Beyond these things, their seminal contributions to American government were little noted by the segregationists. One must conclude, therefore, that the white South venerated Jefferson and Madison for their eccentric deviations rather than for the main thrust of their political philosophy.

In discussing heroic saints of the South, one must not forget the name of Edmund Burke. To be sure, the white South's ethnocentric leaders rarely if ever mentioned Burke by name—he was after all a foreigner. Nonetheless it can be argued that a large part of the rhetoric propagated by those leaders amounted to a neo-Burkean philosophy. This was evident in their stress on tradition, their preference for conservative values, their espousal of the Aristotelian notion of "natural slavery," their belief in a preordained social hierarchy, their implicit support of social organicism, their fear of innovation and rapid change, and their gut pessimism about human nature. If Burkeanism remained an unarticulated premise of the Massive Resisters' rhetoric, it was perhaps because Burke's agrarian conservatism had already been absorbed into the legacy of Calhoun's political thought.

Of the South's honored martyrs, two towered above the others. These were General Robert E. Lee and Jefferson Davis, who was the one and only President of the Confederate States of America. While neither of these men paid the ultimate price of martyrdom—death in line of duty—both suffered a series of traumatic shocks and persecutory wounds (not all Union-inflicted) that might well have driven lesser men to a mental collapse or suicide. It was these shocks and wounds, unmerited in the eyes of segregationists, that led white southerners to venerate Lee and Davis as heroic martyrs while the North was vilifying them.

First and foremost, the segregationists honored Lee and Davis as heroes and martyrs because after the War they had stoically endured the twilight ordeals of the selfless martyr: defeat of their ideals, a loss of stature, vilification by their foes, ingratitude from many of their friends, and the total eclipse of their careers. The ordeal of Davis was intensified by a frantic and futile flight from his conquerors and, later, a two years' imprisonment at Fort Monroe, Virginia, shackled at the ankles in a casement cell with one barred window facing the moat.

Lesser martyrs of the white South included all civil and military officers of the Confederacy, especially those who were generals; politicians and others who were disfranchised by the Reconstruction settlement; widows of Confederate soldiers; and the impoverished plantation owners who, at one stroke, were deprived of their entire labor force. It is true that none of these martyrs were ever venerated in the way that Lee and Davis were, yet they did become the subjects of hundreds of postbellum popular songs and literary romances that kept alive the bittersweet memories of The War Between the States.

In light of the fact that religion stands at the core of the southern way of life, it is a remarkable fact that the saints and martyrs revered by the Massive Resisters were to a man secular rebels rather than religious saints. Over the years the South has produced a vast number of famous preachers and "prophets," but not a single one has approached the saintly status of those tough secularists—Jefferson, Calhoun, Lee, and Davis. Maybe one day the Reverend Billy Graham, who came to prominence in the Massive Resistance era, will achieve such a status. But on second thought, he probably will not, for he opposed both segregation and white supremacy.

II. TUTELARY GENIUSES

THE TUTELARY GENIUSES of Massive Resistance were those men who exercised a kind of guardian authority over the movement by determining basic strategy while avoiding involvement with everyday tactical problems. Four southern leaders appear to merit the tutelary genius label, and all of them were members of the United States Senate in the post-Brown era. Heading the list was Senator Harry Flood Byrd of Virginia, who was the chief inspirer of Massive Resistance and who, more than any other single individual, determined the shape and style of the movement as it evolved in the decade after 1954. To understand Byrd—no easy task—is in a real sense to understand Massive Resistance.

A man of few words and fewer public appearances, Senator Byrd may be longest remembered as the man who presided over the christening of Massive Resistance. But that was the least of his contributions to the counterrevolution. He was also mainly responsible for turning Virginia from reluctant compliance with Brown to bitter-end defiance. He was the originator and leading sponsor of the Southern Manifesto. He was still resisting tokenism when a majority of Virginians seemed resigned to that compromise. He gave aid and comfort to the bizarre revival of the myth of interposition. And, though he said very little in public about the subject of race, what he did say was invariably on the side of reaction.

After the Supreme Court's announcement of Brown, Byrd was among the first of the South's leaders in Washington to denounce it as an attack on states' rights.[3] True, he did not at first call for all-out resistance, yet implicit in his criticism was the assumption that defiance would be in order "after sober and exhaustive consideration." In the summer of 1954, Byrd spoke through his docile disciple Governor Stanley to let Virginians know that his political organization had decided to use every legal means available to prevent the desegregation of the state's public schools. As a result of that decision, there was an escalation of attacks on the Supreme Court all over Virginia as racist rhetoric replaced reasoned dialogue.

Just before Christmas of 1955, Senator Byrd broke a long silence to say that he personally favored the calling of a constitutional convention to draft certain constitutional amendments, proposed in the so-called Gray Report, whose purpose was to prevent integration of the state's schools. Byrd also let it be known that the local option feature of the Gray Plan, favored by moderates, would have to be scuttled on the apparent assumption that though states' rights were vitally important, local rights were not. This was at the peak of the fight over interposition in Virginia. And while there was substantial opposition to the tuition-grant plan in the Gray Report, the voters approved it in a referendum election, largely because of the unprecedented pressure exerted by the Byrd organization.

Early in 1956 when editor James Jackson Kilpatrick, Jr.,

was urging Virginia's legislature to "interpose its sovereignty" against court-ordered desegregation, Byrd observed on the floor of the U. S. Senate that "Mr. Kilpatrick has presented a fine service to the State of Virginia." After that go-ahead signal from Washington, the legislators responded in Pavlovian fashion by passing, almost unanimously, an interposition resolution. It was also about this time that Senator Byrd publicly stated that "In interposition, the South has a perfectly legal means of appeal from the Supreme Court's order."

One of the most extraordinary events in Byrd's career was set in motion by his sudden announcement on February 12, 1958, that he would not run for reelection. Virginia's Massive Resisters, taken wholly by surprise, were aghast at the news. One of them, State Senator Mills E. Godwin, speaking in funereal tones, said sadly, "We shall never look upon his like again." The legislature promptly passed a resolution of appreciation for the Senator's forty-two years of public service, after which they passed another urging him to reconsider his plan to resign. Two weeks after he had made his startling announcement, Byrd did change his mind and promised his followers he would run for reelection after all. The jubilation in the Massive Resistance camp was unbounded.

Today one cannot say with certainty what made the Senator act as he did in February 1958. Massive Resistance was still riding high, and, indeed, it looked as though the egalitarian revolution might yet be thrown back. But appearances were deceptive, and within a matter of months the segregationists would suffer a series of critical defeats. It may just be that Byrd, with his keen political sense, had a premonition of those defeats and wished to remove himself from the battlefield before the "deluge." In any event, his equivocation in this matter was one of the few times he was guilty of political indecisiveness.

Despite Byrd's strategic direction of the opposition, the egalitarian revolution rolled on, and by the 1960's the Senator had lost control of events. After his death, his son Harry Byrd, Jr., took over his Senate seat, but the son lacked both the prestige and the political savvy of his father. Senator Byrd had given his all to the South's counterrevolution, but at most he helped to postpone tokenism by maybe a year or two. Unfortunately, he also helped to inflame tensions and prejudices that several times brought violent clashes between blacks and whites.

As students of Massive Resistance make a final audit of Byrd's tutelary guardianship, they are likely to judge him less harshly for his political authoritarianism—though that could be ruthless—than for his encouragement of southerners to hope for the impossible: the immortalization of Jim Crow. When that possibility turned out to be a chimera, there was massive disillusionment among segregationists, which no amount of soothing talk could dissipate. It is ironic that though Byrd and his ilk bitterly decried egalitarian utopianism, he himself was a classic example of the romantic utopian.

Ranking just a notch below Byrd as a leading tutelary genius of Massive Resistance was Senator Richard Brevard Russell. As chief spokesman for the Senate's southern bloc in the 1950's, Russell must share with Byrd a large part of the blame for unleashing the southern backlash to Brown. For Russell, like Byrd, was both a creator of Massive Resistance strategy and an architect of the illusions and fantasies that went along with that strategy.

One might sharply dispute Russell's views on race and federalism, and still concede his bona fides as a dedicated, selfless public servant. After serving with distinction as the governor of Georgia, Russell went on to the United States Senate, where he remained until his death. A close-lipped bachelor and guardian angel of the Senate's "Inner Club," Russell shunned Washington society and spent his time mastering the intricacies of parliamentary maneuvering in the world's proudest gerontocracy. By the 1950's he was recognized as the grand master of senatorial maneuver, and among his fellow southerners his word had the force of law. Patrician in appearance and usually courtly in manner, he could be ruthless to opponents in the give and take of Senate combat.

Russell's services to the cause of Massive Resistance were many and varied. Like Byrd, he was among the earliest southern critics of the Brown decision. It was, he said, a "flagrant abuse of judicial power," and of course he considered the decision a blow to states' rights. With apparent relish, he assisted Byrd and others in concocting the Southern Manifesto. Year in and year out he organized southern senators to filibuster against civil rights bills until they were changed or withdrawn. He even once introduced a Senate bill to "reduce and eliminate racial tensions and improve the economic status of the American people by equitably distributing throughout the several states those citizens belonging to the two largest racial groups included in the population of the United States who of their own volition desire to change their place of residence."[4] On numerous occasions he urged southern legislators to enact "private school" bills as a way of evading school integration. And, like his friend Senator Byrd, he callously deceived his followers into thinking, and hoping, that there really was a way to prevent *all* desegregation in the public schools. Indeed, Russell was so opposed to even the slightest concession to the enemy that he once observed, "There can be no such thing as token integration. This is merely a device of the race mixers to obtain total and complete integration."[5] It is interesting that though Russell often called the U. S. Constitution "the ark of the covenant," he acted as if that document were a white southern Bible whose only categorical imperative was: Thou shalt preserve white supremacy and states'-rights federalism forever and ever.

Standing next in influence among the South's tutelary geniuses was Senator Strom Thurmond of South Carolina. More flamboyant and extroverted than either Byrd or Russell, Thurmond embraced the myths of Massive Resistance with a passion that few of his colleagues could equal. He had also had an amazingly varied public career, which included membership in three political parties and successive roles as teacher, athletic coach, county superintendent of education, city attorney, county attorney, state senator, circuit judge, decorated World War II hero, governor, presidential candidate, and, finally, United States Senator. Throughout his long career, Thurmond has exhibited a positive genius for manipulating words that block reasoned argument by arousing racial emotions and prejudice. And whether initiating "bold maneuvers" or "impudent plots," Strom Thurmond was rarely silent or inactive in the decade after Brown.

Thurmond's concern with the egalitarian revolution went back at least to 1948, when he was the States' Rights party candidate for the presidency, carrying four states and getting 39 electoral votes. In November of 1954 he achieved quite a coup by winning election to the United States Senate as a write-in candidate. It is perhaps no coincidence that his victory occurred at a time when opposition to Brown was significantly increasing in the South.

While Byrd and Russell were reluctant to address large public rallies of segregationists, Thurmond rarely passed up a chance to appear at one. He pulled out all the oratorical stops when he lit into the Supreme Court and the "race mixers," and the Massive Resisters loved him. It is to be doubted that any of his colleagues in Congress's southern bloc ever approached his record for persistent, unrestrained criticism of Brown.

Thurmond's role in the birth of the Southern Manifesto has been noted, but that was only one of his many contributions to Massive Resistance. Perhaps his most spectacular input to the southern cause was his solitary Senate filibuster against the 1957 Civil Rights bill. After Senate Majority Leader Lyndon Johnson agreed to delete most of the enforcement provisions from the bill, the southerners agreed not to filibuster. Thurmond, however, had other ideas. On the night of August 28, he took the Senate floor and filibustered against the bill for the next twenty-four hours and nineteen minutes—a record for an individual filibusterer. Ironically, in 1971 when Senate liberals were threatening to filibuster against extension of the draft law, Thurmond, for the first time in his life, voted for a successful cloture motion which nipped the liberals' plans in the bud.

Thurmond reserved his sharpest invective for white moderates and the NAACP's "outside agitators." They, even more than the Communists, were the real threat to America, for they operated openly and with the approval of northern opinion. He was convinced they would stop at nothing to subvert the southern way of life. And by the end of the 1950's, most white southerners seemed to agree with him. But, like most statesmen, Thurmond had a fatal flaw. His racist rhetoric was so extravagant that only those who were already true believers took him or his message seriously. The rest dismissed him as a fanatic on race—clever but still fanatic.

The fourth of the South's tutelary geniuses, Senator James

Oliver Eastland of Mississippi, spoke for the Deep South as Byrd spoke for the upper South. An expert at the rhetorical art of *argumentum ad populum*, which attempts to win people's support by appealing to tradition and group loyalties rather than to facts and reasons, Eastland had a sixth sense for divining what southerners in the mass wanted to hear. And, without exception, that is what he told them. Of course, what he told them came down to a highly simplistic vision of "reality," but better to be simplistic and loved than honest and rejected.

As was the case with Thurmond, Eastland's record of counterrevolutionary action went back to 1948, when he defected from the Democratic party and supported the Dixiecrat ticket. The only penalty he suffered for this defection was the loss of certain patronage he would normally have received from the Truman Administration. The penalty was, in fact, so slight that it amounted to a green light for future counterrevolutionary defections.

Eastland made it clear that he detested the Brown decision when he first heard of it, and there is no evidence that his detestation has lessened with the passing years. As militant segregationist groups began springing up all over the South, Eastland, along with Thurmond, quickly emerged as a star performer at the rallies on the "Jim Crow Circuit." He particularly favored the rallies of the White Citizens' Councils. As early as February 1956, before the creation of the Southern Manifesto, the Councils were hailing him as the "Voice of the South." At about the same time, he appeared at a rally in the State Coliseum in Montgomery, Alabama, which turned out to be one of the largest rallies of segregationists ever held there. More than twelve thousand people rabidly applauded the Senator, whose give-'em-hell oratory was accompanied by the strains of "Dixie" and the waving of masses of Confederate flags.

Though he never quite put it that way, Eastland clearly believed that what was good for the white South was good for all America. Thus, as chairman of the powerful Senate Internal Security Subcommittee, he chased not only racial "agitators" but also political "subversives," since, in his mind, the two were one and the same. The fact that most Americans seemed able to distinguish between American nationalism and southern racial nationalism did not bother him in the least. The southern way of life, with all its manifestations, was the highest form of Americanism.

Eastland was so sure that a threat to the southern way of life was also a threat to national security that in May of 1955 he introduced a resolution demanding an inquiry into the extent of subversion behind Brown. He alleged in a widely publicized Senate speech that the authorities on whose writings the Supreme Court relied in drafting Brown were "to a shocking degree" interlocked with "the worldwide Communist conspiracy," and that many of them had "citations in the files of the Committee on Un-American Activities." He, therefore, felt it was proved "that the decision of the Supreme Court in the school segregation cases was based upon the writings and teachings of pro-communist agitators and other enemies of the American form of government."[6]

Not content merely to make rhetorical waves, Eastland dreamed of building a nationwide, grass-roots organization that would be "a great crusade to restore Americanism and return the control of our government to the people." The agency that he envisioned would "carry on its banner the slogan of free enterprise" along with states' rights, and if successful would prevent "the death of Southern culture and our aspirations as an Anglo-Saxon people." If such a crusade could get started, Eastland predicted that "Generations of Southerners yet unborn will cherish our memory because they will realize that the fight we now wage will have preserved for them their untainted racial heritage, their culture and the institutions of the Anglo-Saxon race."[7]

It seemed that Eastland's dream was about to be realized when segregationists formed the Federation for Constitutional Government in December 1955. But for a number of reasons, the Federation never became the central clearing house for all Massive Resisters that Eastland hoped it would be. Even so, its formation under the sponsorship of a powerful United States Senator was yet another sign that the South's leaders were deadly serious about their counterrevolution.

Another of Eastland's important contributions to Massive Resistance was his clever use of the Senate Judiciary Committee to obstruct the passage of civil rights bills in Congress. According to the *New York Times*, he boasted in the 1966 campaign that his Judiciary Committee and its Civil Rights Subcommittee had successfully bottled up no less than 127 civil rights bills. It was a record that he was proud of, and one that he made sure the segregationists knew about.

Eastland also used the Judiciary Committee to hold up liberal judicial appointments in the North until they could be "balanced" by conservative appointments in the South. He was doing pretty much what southern congressmen did in the early nineteenth century when they refused to vote for the admission of a new free state unless a new slave state were admitted at the same time. His most famous "balancing act" in this regard was his successful effort to force President Kennedy to appoint his old college roommate, Harold Cox, to a federal judgeship in the South in exchange for the Judiciary Committee's approval of Thurgood Marshall's elevation to the Second Circuit Court of Appeals. Eastland's bargaining with Attorney General Robert Kennedy lasted almost a year, and in the end President Kennedy capitulated. In light of Cox's subsequent record as a notorious segregationist judge, it is hard to view the "balancing act" as a bargain for either blacks or the nation.

Two more facts about Eastland are relevant to this analysis of his role in Massive Resistance strategy. The first is that as a protégé of the late Senator Theodore Bilbo, Eastland, like his mentor, sometimes did or said things that smelled of anti-Semitism. Thus, in 1965 in a dispute with Mississippi's Freedom Democratic Party, Eastland denounced a New Jersey lawyer who was aiding the blacks for having changed his name in 1939 from Moses Isaac Stavisky to Morton Stavis. It turned out that Stavis had indeed changed his name as Eastland charged, but it had all been done quite legally. The change should therefore have been of no concern to Eastland—unless he wished to emphasize the "Jewishness" of Stavis's original name.

Finally, despite his reputation as a man who never deviated from his principles, Eastland was not in fact a consistent "anti-federalist." Thus, for example, he has long been known in Washington as the Senate's staunchest foe of "federal socialism" and "hand-out welfarism." Yet despite his anti-federalist polemics, he received from the federal government in the post-Brown era hundreds of thousands of dollars in farm subsidies by virtue of owning vast tracts of land in the rich Mississippi delta country. Perhaps if Congress had had the guts to label such subsidies "A.D.F." (Aid to Dependent Farmers), Eastland's reputation for "anti-federalism" would not have been so high, and he might even have felt a little more sympathy for the poor blacks on welfare in Mississippi whose federal subsidies were minuscule compared to his.

The fact that all the tutelary geniuses of Massive Resistance were "up there" in the United States Senate reconfirmed the old adage that absence makes the heart grow fonder—even in politics. Observers were quick to note that whereas the segregationists would often criticize their state and local leaders for ineptitude or lack of zeal in fighting integration, they rarely had anything but kind words for their solons in the Senate. They obviously looked upon their guardian senators as statesmen in the grand manner of Calhoun, who had scaled the peaks of true civility and who could do no wrong. They, of course, failed to perceive that democracy requires a rather different kind of civility—a non-paternalistic civility that understands and accepts the imperatives of equality. That kind of civility the South's tutelary geniuses neither practiced nor understood.

III. CHARISMATIC DEMAGOGUES

LIKE OTHER POLITICAL counterrevolutions, Massive Resistance had its share of charismatic demagogues. This was perfectly natural, for demagogues have always flourished in the politics of conflict. These men are charismatic in the sense that their leadership is dynamic, inspirational, emotionally moving, and persuasive—at least to the faithful. They are demagogic because of their appeals to unreason, their reliance on emotion-swaying oratory, their practice of the "cult of personality," and their conscious manipulation of myths and symbols to hide the complexities of divisive social issues. They differ from tutelary geniuses in at least three ways. They are closer to the people, they are more involved in day-to-day tactics, and they are more willing to adopt the most extreme means to achieve their ends.

After 1954 the South was blessed (or cursed) with a host of charismatic demagogues, all deeply committed to the myths of Massive Resistance. Most of them were leaders in state government, and they included Leander Perez, "Bull" Connor, Ross Barnett, Herman Talmadge (before he went to the Senate), Orval Faubus, George Wallace, Marvin Griffin, and Lester Maddox. These were the men who led the South's shock troops into action, manned the barricades, and spoke the thoughts that were in the hearts of the segregationists, while the Byrds and the Russells remained secluded in Washington away from the post-Brown battlefields.[8]

The charismatic demagogues who played the key roles in Massive Resistance politics validated Shakespeare's belief that "There is a tide in the affairs of men which, taken at the flood, leads on to fortune." They were among the first to see that Brown had unleashed just such a tide, and if that tide did not bring all of them fortune, it brought most of them fame and mass adulation. The careers of all of the demagogues merit more study than they have so far had, for they help to explain a lot about the South and about counterrevolutionary politics. Two of these will be discussed here—George Wallace and Ross Barnett, who were typical of the group in many ways, if atypical in some.

People have said many things about Alabama's George C. Wallace, but few have denied his charisma. Like most charismatic demagogues, Wallace was as quixotic as the visionary, as full of *hybris* as a Greek hero. One almost feels that he was born politicized and Puckish, with a physiognomy to match. One feels too that it was not so much the policies of Massive Resistance that excited him but the drama of peddling to anxious constituents mythic dreams—honest and wish-fulfilling dreams in the eyes of white southerners. Wallace differed from his fellow demagogues in two key ways. He proved to be more durable. And after catching the presidential bug, he went on to become a national leader before he was shot and crippled in the 1972 Maryland Democratic presidential primary.

Wallace was a state judge in the 1950's and not yet in the

front ranks of the South's counterrevolution. But in 1963 he succeeded the hard-core segregationist John Patterson as Alabama's chief executive, and he served in that capacity until 1967, when his wife Lurleen succeeded him. Before her term expired, she succumbed to cancer. Some months after that, Wallace reentered state politics and in 1970 won a hotly contested gubernatorial election.

Wallace's crusades through his adoring Dixie for the cause of Massive Resistance resembled both southern revival meetings and those "countryfied" medicine shows that played the backwater areas of the South in the depression years. Just as the medicine shows brought the simple people of the South country music and health panaceas, Wallace brought the same people country music and political panaceas. Where the old "hell-fire" evangelists had inveighed against sin and the devil, Wallace inveighed against modern demons—the NAACP, outside agitators, integrators, bureaucrats, subverts, perverts, and pseudo-intellectuals, who "couldn't park a bicycle." As a born politician (and revivalist *manqué*), he naturally loved to wow crowds. If in the process he lit piney-wood fires of hate and prejudice all over the South, that was the integraters' fault, not his.

George Wallace was a many-sided demagogue. At one and the same time he was a fiery orator, preacher, politician, popular entertainer, soured Populist, patent-medicine purveyor, devoted father and husband, rabid segregationist, and fearless slayer of federal dragons. Indeed, these varied roles were so mixed up in his career that it is hard to say where one stopped and the others began. It seems probable that in his own mind he conceived of himself as primarily a Dixiecrat St. George, single-handedly slaying the dragons of race-mixing that were threatening to destroy the southern way of life.

Wallace was probably the closest thing to a full-time political pro among the South's charismatic demagogues, and some of his Alabama friends have said he will be running for office as long as there are elections. A compulsive campaigner, he ran in six races from 1958 to 1970, a track record unequaled by anyone save congressmen who must run biennially. It may not be fair to say that he is totally consumed by political ambition and racism, for he is after all a staunch Methodist, but in the Indian Summer of Massive Resistance he was an ever-present, multi-media campaigner for states' rights and "freedom of choice." Though at times his campaigns were touched with a singular imagination, even artistry, he borrowed shamelessly from such earlier Dixie demagogues as Huey Long, Tom Watson (Populist presidential candidate), Bibb Graves (Alabama governor in the twenties and thirties), and Ben Tillman.

Despite his undoubted talents, Wallace was unable to roll back or seriously impede the forward thrust of the egalitarian revolution. But no Massive Resister worked harder or longer at trying to do that. Almost everybody agrees that he reached the peak of his personal popularity when he delivered his demagogic 1963 inaugural address:

> Today I have stood where Jefferson Davis stood, and took an oath to my people. It is very appropriate then that from this Cradle of the Confederacy, this very heart of the great Anglo-Saxon Southland, that today we sound the drum of freedom. . . . In the name of the greatest people that ever trod this earth, I draw the line in the dust and toss the gauntlet before the feet of tyranny. And I say, Segregation now! Segregation tomorrow! Segregation forever!

More demagogic but less charismatic than Wallace, Mississippi's Ross Barnett likewise played a seminal role in the South's counterrevolution. He lacked the intelligence as well as the artistry that characterized Wallace's leadership, but in many ways he was closer to the men in the Massive Resistance ranks. His ascent to the top was far from easy. In fact, it took him three tries to win the governorship in the nation's poorest state. However, after he finally won the post in 1959, he quickly emerged as a living symbol of bitter-end resistance to all forms of desegregation.

More canny than cerebral, "Ole Ross" raised himself by his bootstraps, as it were, and thus he was able to articulate the rednecks' anxieties with consummate skill. His folksy, homespun style made him a hero to his state's segregationists, and his disarming penchant for verbal gaffes helped rather than hurt his political career. Segregation, of course, was always the chief plank in his platform. But until he reached the pinnacle of state power, he had generally had a lackluster career.

Barnett reached the pinnacle when he assumed the governorship of Mississippi on January 19, 1960. From that moment on, he drawled defiance of federal authority at every opportunity. In his inaugural address, which preceded Wallace's by three years, he told Mississippians that their schools would remain segregated "at all costs." That was vital in his view, because "a dual system of education" is always best "for both races." While governor he had a favorite saying that was indicative of his faith in white supremacy. "The good Lord," he liked to say, "was the original segregationist. He put the Negro in Africa—separated him from all other races." Unlike his relatively moderate predecessor, Barnett assiduously courted the Citizens' Councils and gave them a kind of quasi-governmental status. He spoke often at rallies of the Councils and was for a time a Council recruiter.

Barnett's chief weapon in the fight against desegregation was the State Sovereignty Commission, which Governor James P. Coleman had got the legislature to set up in 1956. Though Coleman eschewed police-state methods, Barnett converted the Commission into the spearhead of his state's counterrevolutionary strategy. The Commission, at his direction, financed speakers to spread "The Message from Mississippi" around the nation, kept tabs on "racial agitators" through a network of black informers, and, until the contributions stopped in 1964, gave almost $200,-000 of public funds to the Citizens' Council private "Forum." Approximately $169,000 of that sum is estimated to have been given during the Barnett Administration. It would appear that the Mississippi State Sovereignty Commission, with Barnett's backing, was seeking to realize the grand vision of southern unity that Senator Eastland had earlier described.

Few subjects got Barnett's dander up quicker than tokenism. When somebody once asked him what he thought about tokenism, he answered that southerners who favored a little desegregation were like the common burglar who "comes into your house and tells you that if you give him just a FEW of your valuables, he'll go away. Just sort of a 'token burglary,' you might call it."[9] He also told his supporters many times that "Ross Barnett will rot in jail before he will let one Negro ever darken the sacred threshold of our white schools." In the end, he reneged on that promise, to the dismay of the zealots. And when he tried to recapture the governorship in 1967, he ended up fourth in a seven-man primary, with only 9 per cent of the vote. But as late as 1972 he was still decrying desegregation and racial intermarriage, proving that he remained a Massive Resister.

In evaluating the importance of the charismatic demagogues, one must keep in mind that they themselves viewed their role as primarily that of defenders of an ancient tradition, whose chief components were republican virtue, constitutional rectitude, and class harmony. Imbued with this conception of their role, they elaborated ingenious, sometimes bizarre rationalizations for the Jim Crow system, and branded the Supreme Court and the egalitarians as the main threats to the peace and prosperity of the South. By the end of the 1950's the charismatic leadership of the demagogues had hung over the South a "magnolia curtain" whose job was to protect southern orthodoxy by stopping the flow of liberal ideas from the North. But, like other curtains in other places, the South's magnolia curtain was unable to halt for long the flow of those humane ideas that were slowly but steadily eroding the foundations of the southern way of life.

The fatal flaw in the politics of the charismatic demagogues was the extremity to which they carried the myth of states'-rights federalism. Not content to espouse—as did all Massive Resisters —the idea of state sovereignty and the compact theory of the Union, they went far afield to portray state and local governments as mere appendages of an all-powerful central government increasingly dominating every phase of American life. It was a popular view in the South, but it amounted to a static view of federalism, in which increased national power was assumed automatically to mean reduced state and local power. This non-symbiotic conception of federalism is fallacious, for government activity has been expanding at *all* levels. And were it to be legitimated by the Supreme Court—most unlikely—it would strap the national government, perhaps permanently, in a constitutional straitjacket.

IV. PRAGMATIC SELF-AGGRANDIZERS

THOSE SPOKESMEN for Massive Resistance who were below the top ranks and who were motivated more by political opportunism than by ideological conviction may be denoted pragmatic self-aggrandizers. Although they paid the proper lip-service to the ideology of the movement and never publicly questioned its values, they were not the passionate zealots or the true-believing ideologues that the tutelary geniuses and charismatic demagogues were. It is doubtless true that all leaders of mass movements are to some extent ideologized and rigid, but some are more so than others. It is also true that a pragmatic leader, in the long run, will put expediency above ideological principles whereas a true demagogic bigot will not.

The pragmatists in the Massive Resistance movement were found in a wide variety of fields. They served (and are still serving) as governors, legislators, mayors, city councilmen, school board members, school superintendents, as well as spokesmen for business and professional groups. In the 1950's they were probably more numerous in business and the professions than in state and local government. There is a good deal of evidence to suggest that the businessmen who were most flexible in matters of race were those involved in enterprises that were capital-intensive, technologically advanced, and nationally oriented. Until the 1960's these men had only limited influence on the legislators and executive officials who controlled southern governments. Even after the heyday of Massive Resistance, their influence was largely confined to such "New South" bastions as Atlanta, Miami, and Houston.

Since the pragmatic self-aggrandizers were of secondary importance in determining the course of the South's counterrevolution, the mere listing of a few of their names will adequately serve the purpose of this analysis. At the national level, one thinks of such men as Senator Sparkman of Alabama and Senator Fulbright of Arkansas. Among governors, typical pragmatists were James E.

Folsom, Ernest Vandiver, J. P. Coleman, Luther Hodges, Lindsay J. Almond, Jr., Farris Bryant, Haydon Burns, and Frank Clement. Alabama's Albert Boutwell, who briefly occupied center stage in the post-Brown era, exemplified this category in three different roles: as state legislator, lieutenant governor, and mayor (of Birmingham). After the mid-1960's, the number of southern politicians in this category dramatically increased.

One of the tragedies of counterrevolutionary leadership is the fact that the pragmatists, who are relatively rational spokesmen for conservatism, are at first so cowed by the demagogues that they dare not speak up for reason. They come into their own only when a new synthesis, melding both old and new values, is being created. They are thus the architects of a new status quo, but their job is rendered more difficult than need be as a result of the legacy of hate and bigotry that their prudential silence earlier helped to breed.

V. INTELLECTUAL IDEOLOGUES

THE INTELLECTUAL IDEOLOGUES of the South's counterrevolution—its "men of words"—were theorists rather than political activists. Their job was to provide a rationale for the movement's resistance strategy, and thereby expand its popular appeal. In carrying out that task, the ideologues revived, updated, embellished, and popularized the mythic doctrines and slogans which the saints and martyrs had earlier constructed in "the Golden Age."

The intellectual ideologues were all social scientists or journalists, and most, but not all, were native southerners. While committed to the whole range of myths and sub-myths of the segregationists' ideology, they seemed most preoccupied after 1954 with the myths of white supremacy and states'-rights federalism. Scholars through the years have pinned many labels—mostly pejorative—on these cheerleaders for the southern way of life, virtually all of which they have disdained.[10] But, then, all labels are lies in the strict sense of the word.

One of the most important services rendered by the ideologues was that of combating the egalitarians on their own ground by developing "scientific" evidence to contradict the social science data cited by the Supreme Court in Brown. This involved, among other things, a conscious effort to revive old ideas about the black man's "differences" and "inequality" which, though once fashionable, had been rejected by a majority of social scientists since at least the 1930's.[11]

In addition to writing extensively about race and education, the ideologues sometimes appeared as expert witnesses in segregation court cases. The first of their number to testify in such a case seems to have been Dr. Lindley Stiles, Dean of Education of the University of Virginia. A New Mexico native with a doctorate in education from the University of Colorado, Dean Stiles testified as an expert on a broad range of subjects and, by so doing, appeared to give a scientific warranty to many of the segregationists' arguments.

Dean Stiles was quite convinced that school segregation was positively beneficial to black people. As he saw it, the system provided assured jobs for educated blacks, gave blacks control of their own schools, protected black children from the prejudices of white students and teachers, and, in the long run, retarded the growth of racial prejudice.

Dean Stiles was testifying in the Prince Edward County case about the merits of high school desegregation, and he gave as his view that desegregation at that level was unworkable. On the other hand, he conceded that desegregation at the graduate, professional, and elementary levels might be feasible. Stiles went on to explain that he justified southern segregation laws on the grounds of practical necessity, although he himself was a theoretical integrationist—something few Massive Resisters ever owned up to.

More influential as an apologist for the counterrevolution was Professor Henry E. Garrett, who was a past president of the American Psychological Association. He was a Virginian by birth, had a Ph.D. degree from Columbia, and was a member of Columbia's psychology department until his retirement in 1956. Ironically, three of the "liberal" psychologists used by the NAACP as expert witnesses in school cases had been students of his: Kenneth Clark, Mamie Clark, and Isidor Chein.

Like Stiles, Garrett testified in the Prince Edward County

case, and vigorously upheld the southern position. He flatly endorsed the segregation system, denying in the process that schools segregated by race are any more discriminatory than schools segregated by religion. It was also his view that black students should normally get a better education in segregated than in integrated schools.

Garrett was on firmer ground when he stressed, quite rightly, that psychology and the social sciences are still infant disciplines, inexact and easily manipulated. In later years, Massive Resistance leaders would hammer away at that point in hopes of undermining the Brown rationale. Garrett, however, eventually changed his mind, and began arguing that social science evidence clearly demonstrates the inferiority of blacks and the rationality of segregated education.

Professor Frank C. J. McGurk was another Massive Resistance ideologue with impressive credentials as a social scientist. Originally from Philadelphia (and presumably more "objective"), McGurk earned a Ph.D. from Catholic University and in the late 1950's was a psychology professor at Villanova.

A specialist in the comparative testing of white and black intelligence, McGurk had written a doctoral dissertation in 1951 with the title, "Comparison of the Performance of Negro and White High School Seniors on Cultural and Non-Cultural Test Questions." In 1956, he published a highly controversial article in *U. S. News and World Report*, which is generally considered to have been the first systematic attempt by a social scientist to "debunk" the scientific data cited by the Supreme Court in deciding Brown.

In his 1956 article and in other writings, McGurk manifested a concern with deflating the so-called "Culture Hypothesis," which holds that psychological test score differences between blacks and whites are the result of cultural differences. It was (and apparently still is) his opinion that this hypothesis is invalid, for scientific evidence, he thinks, refutes the claim of radical equality in psychological test performance. As regards the article, it reached two quite controversial conclusions: one, that blacks are substantially behind whites in educational capacity; and two, that their incapacity is not changed by a switch in their socio-economic environment.

The spokesmen for the counterrevolutionary South, especially the charismatic demagogues, hailed McGurk's conclusions as a real step forward in their anti-Brown crusade. To the segregationists, they were proof positive that school integration was not only "anti-southern," it also violated both the laws of nature and empirical science. Nobody was therefore surprised when McGurk's writings were given mass circulation as the Massive Resisters stepped up the pace of their backlash after 1956. Of course, in their own way, the White Citizens' Councils and the Ku Klux Klan had long been saying that white people have a greater innate capacity to respond to a favorable environment than do blacks. But it was obviously far more significant when a professional social scientist said essentially the same thing.

From the Massive Resisters' point of view, an even more important work on black intelligence than McGurk's studies was a long treatise, *The Testing of Negro Intelligence*, which was published in 1958 (and later revised) by Professor Audrey M. Shuey, chairman of the psychology department at Randolph-Macon Woman's College of Lynchburg, Virginia. The author was born in Illinois, studied under Professor Garrett, received a Ph.D. from Columbia in psychology, and held teaching positions at Barnard and Washington Square College of New York before going to Randolph-Macon in 1943.

Professor Shuey's *Testing* was an exhaustive cataloging of the statistical results of 240 studies of black students' performances on psychological and intelligence tests conducted in the 1913–1958 period. Her most important conclusions were these: one, the average IQ for blacks of pre-school age was the best relative performance made by blacks; two, black college students, though more highly selected than whites, performed poorest of all in comparison with whites; three, blacks did consistently better on "concrete" tests than on tests involving abstract concepts; four, black soldiers of World War II performed on tests as poorly as did blacks of World War I; and five, the average IQ differences between northern-born and southern-born black children were relatively small.

A majority of social scientists seriously questioned both the conclusions and methodology of Professor Shuey's book. But the Massive Resisters, naturally, were elated with it and began to tout the Shuey findings as final confirmation of the black man's innate inferiority. They were also pleased that Professsor Garrett wrote the *Foreword* for his former student's book, since this, they felt, considerably enhanced its scholarly standing.

Of the criticisms leveled at the Shuey book by social scientists, these appear to have been most damaging: that Dr. Shuey interepreted all her materials in the manner most favorable to white supremacy; that she accepted without question all studies suggesting black inferiority; that she dealt only with the statistical results of the cited studies; that she treated as equally valid studies made in 1913 and 1957; that she failed to distinguish adequately between studies that tried to control environmental variables and those that did not; that she was largely uncritical of the tests themselves; and that Dr. Shuey herself, for all her disclaimers, was not entirely free of preconceived racial bias. Of course, none of these criticisms bothered the Massive Resisters. They saw them simply as the sour grapes of liberal academicians who had finally been exposed as frauds.

In addition to the social scientists who supported the South's case, there were popular journalists who played the role of intellectual ideologues. Of these, the most influential were Carleton Putnam and James Jackson Kilpatrick, Jr.

A Yankee by ancestry but a southerner by inclination, Putnam was a native New Yorker who claimed descent from Israel Putnam, the famous Revolutionary War general. He studied at Princeton, where he took honors in the department of history and politics, and at Columbia, which awarded him an LL.B. degree in 1932. After that he spent considerable time in the South and Washington, D. C., serving as an airlines executive and working on a multi-volume biography of Theodore Roosevelt.

Putnam's book, *Race and Reason, A Yankee View* (1961), was one of the most widely circulated defenses of segregation in the post-Brown era. In fact, it eventually became something of a Bible to the counterrevolutionary South. Its distribution in the South was aided by right-wing, patriotic bookstores as well as by white supremacy groups, which seem to have given away large numbers of copies to people who would not or could not buy the book.

In *Race and Reason* the segregationists found a lot of things that were pleasing and useful to them. The book summarized, for example, most of the arguments against desegregation. It linked the post-Brown egalitarian revolution with the New Deal and left-wing liberalism. It vehemently attacked the federal establishment. It included a passionate plea for the protection of states' rights. And it proposed, as our only salvation, a return to the Protestant Ethic of Middle America. The segregationists were also pleased with the basic assumption of the book, which was that the preponderance of scientific evidence points to the existence of important genetic differences in intelligence and temperament between whites and blacks.

Ross Barnett was so impressed by the Putnam book that he designated October 26, 1961, as "Race and Reason Day" in Mississippi. Putnam, said Barnett, had written "a significant and valuable new book" that "meets a long-recognized need in improving communications between patriotic Americans" and in showing "responsible Northern citizens . . . the viewpoint on race relations held by loyal Southerners." Barnett also told Mississippians that "Race and Reason Day" might best be observed by bringing Putnam's book "to the attention of friends and relatives in the North, and by participating in appropriate public functions, thereby demonstrating the appreciation of the people . . . for Mr. Carleton Putnam and for his splendid book."

At about the same time, the Louisiana State Board of Education was recommending the book to all Louisiana school administrators and public school teachers. The irony of canonizing a thoroughbred Yankee as one of the top ideologues of Massive Resistance does not appear to have bothered the South's segregationists. It is, of course, possible that many of them were not aware of Putnam's background.

James Jackson Kilpatrick, Jr., was a native of Oklahoma who achieved the status of Massive Resistance ideologue by serving as editor of the *Richmond News Leader* during the heyday of the South's counterrevolution. He had succeeded Douglas Southall Freeman as the paper's editor in 1951, and within a short time he had become more "Virginian" than most of the natives.

Kilpatrick's best known contribution to Massive Resistance

was the considerable part he had in the rehabilitation of the myth of interposition. But he was also a major (and quite effective) propagandist for the myths of white supremacy and states'-rights federalism, with the latter seeming to have his greatest sympathy. Indeed, he tirelessly argued the point that the segregation crisis was really a constitutional crisis, in which the issue was states' rights versus federal "usurpation." Integrationist propaganda, he believed, had obscured this central issue, the outcome of which would ultimately determine the future of the South.

Kilpatrick had been one of the first to denounce Brown. And on June 1, 1955, the day after Brown II was announced, the *News Leader* came out with a long editorial on Brown that bristled with defiance. In light of the subsequent influence of Kilpatrick and his paper, it seems well to quote at length from the June 1 editorial:

> *In May of 1954, that inept fraternity of politicians and professors known as the United States Supreme Court chose to throw away the established law. These nine men repudiated the Constitution, spit upon the Tenth Amendment, and rewrote the fundamental law of this land to suit their own gauzy concepts of sociology. If it be said now that the South is flouting the law, let it be said to the high court,* You taught us how.
>
> *From the moment that abominable decision was handed down, two broad courses only were available to the South. One was to defy the Court openly and notoriously; the other was to accept the Court's decision and combat it by legal means. To defy the Court openly would be to enter upon anarchy; the logical end would be a second attempt at secession from the Union. And though the idea is not without merit, it is impossible of execution. We tried that once before.*
>
> *To acknowledge the Court's authority does not mean that the South is helpless. It is not to abandon hope. Rather, it is to enter upon a long course of lawful resistance; it is to seek at the polls and in the halls of legislative bodies every possible lawful means to overcome or circumvent the Court's requirements. Litigate? Let us pledge ourselves to litigate this thing for fifty years. If one remedial law is ruled invalid, then let us try another; and if the second is ruled invalid, then let us enact a third. . . .*

When the Court proposes that its social revolution be imposed upon the South "as soon as practicable," there are those of us who would respond that "as soon as practicable" means never at all.[12]

The resistance tactic recommended in the *News Leader* editorial—endless litigation—was quickly adopted by the South's leaders, and after 1955 it became one of the key weapons in their counterrevolutionary arsenal. Kilpatrick eventually left the *News Leader* to become a syndicated columnist and TV personality, but he seems never to have recanted his antipathy to Brown. In 1972 he wrote in one of his columns: "I will go to my grave still convinced that Brown was bad law—a willful perversion of the clear meaning and intention of the Fourteenth Amendment."[13]

When one closely studies the complex and sometimes rough relationships between the various leaders and spokesmen of the South, one is drawn to the conclusion that their activities added up to a kind of ecosystem of counterrevolutionary leadership. The hallowed legacy of the saints and martyrs, the strategic initiatives of the tutelary geniuses, the tactical innovations of the charismatic demagogues, the expediential ploys of the pragmatists, and the rationalizing propaganda of the ideologues, all interacted and finally coalesced in a backlash synergism—constructive from the perspective of the white supremacists, destructive as far as the black man's hopes were concerned. None of these leadership elites, acting in isolation, could have stayed the prompt implementation of Brown. But acting in a loose sort of counterrevolutionary concert, they produced a total resistance effect that was greater than the sum of their individual effects. For almost two decades, their synergistic resistance would affect southern governments and society the way certain drugs temporarily increase the activity of vital processes and organs. And the regional hangover that followed the end of resistance rather closely resembled the after-effects of powerful stimulants.

5.

Popular Forces in the Movement

THE MASSIVE RESISTANCE ranks were a curious alliance of crackpots, honest conservatives, religious fanatics, visionaries, confused moderates, and simple thugs, often with not much more in common than a shared fear of the egalitarian revolution and a belief that the southern way of life was unique and worth preserving. Their numbers were probably never as large as their leaders claimed, and they were divided into warring factions almost from the start. Yet without the ranks, serried or otherwise, behind them, the demagogues would have been powerless to delay Brown's implementation. Knowing that, the South's leaders spent much of their time trying to organize, unite, and politicize the segregationist masses.

Contrary to what Marxists might argue, there is very little need for a strict "class analysis" in probing the mass politics of Massive Resistance. Leaders and followers came from all classes, parties, and groups of southern society, though it is no doubt true that the uneducated poor were more fanatical about white supremacy than their "betters." On the other hand, it was the educated segregationists from the middle and upper classes who seem to have had the deepest commitment to the myth of states'-rights federalism. Or at any rate, they were the ones who talked most about it.

While the politics of racial conflict never degenerated after 1954 into the politics of class conflict, the political analyst has the clear obligation to explain as best he can the role of at least the major popular forces behind the South's counterrevolution. At the start of such an explanation, it is well to emphasize that in the Massive Resistance backlash, the role of the segregationist masses was at once passive and negative. It was passive, for the masses were the manipulated majority, the anonymous audience cheering the demagogues and hissing the federal villains. It was also negative, for they were concerned only with destroying the egalitarian revolution, while giving little, if any, thought to ways of improving southern society and thus blunting the reformers' appeal. At no time were the white masses ever a disciplined, unified counterrevolutionary force, though, of course, that was just what their leaders had originally hoped to make them.

Of the scores of private groups that were organized to prevent Brown's implementation in the South, two were particularly important—the Ku Klux Klan and the White Citizens' Councils. It will, therefore, be necessary to analyze their contributions to Massive Resistance in some depth.

I. THE KU KLUX KLAN

THE KU KLUX KLAN was at once the most feared and the least respectable of the popular forces in the South's counterrevolution. Flaunting exotic rituals, secret oaths, and a vast paraphernalia of disguise, the Klan was fanatically determined to keep the black man "in his place"—by the rope, fagot, whip, and gun, if necessary. The more responsible Massive Resisters frowned upon the Klan's ruthless vigilantism, but that did not deter the Klan from creating and exploiting the kind of explosive atmosphere in which violence comes to be accepted as normal. Moreover, while they never publicly said so, the South's leaders were well aware that the Klan was aiding their cause in two ways. It frightened moderate whites into toeing the line of white supremacy, and it provided an organized, secret channel of violence for those segregationist zealots whose crusading zeal could not be restrained within the limits of legal resistance.

The origins of the Klan go back to the turbulent period of Reconstruction, when six veterans of the Confederate Army organized themselves at Pulaski, Tennessee, on Christmas Eve of 1865.[1] They chose their name from the Greek word for circle (*kyklos*), and as they grew they came to be known as the "Invisible Empire." From the start, their main goal seems to have been to keep the ex-slaves under the white man's control, but originally their activities seemed to be idealistic, even chivalrous.

In Nashville, Tennessee, in April of 1867, local Klan "dens" held a regional convocation at which they elected former Confederate Army General Nathan Bedford Forrest their grand wizard. They agreed to limit membership in the Klan to whites who opposed both the concept of racial equality and the radical legislation of the Reconstruction Congress. By the fall of 1868, Klan membership had reached 550,000. Then in early 1869, General Forrest suddenly announced that he had disbanded the organization, as it was no longer needed for "self-protection." However, this seems to have been nothing more than a public relations ploy, for new Klan dens continued to be formed, as their night-riding activities spread.

The formation of the Klan so soon after Appomattox was one of several signs that the white South was by no means ready to concede victory to the North in the Civil War. Its rapid growth was also a signal for the start of a campaign of "white terror" that made the Reconstruction era in the South a dangerous time for both blacks and non-conformist whites.[2] Though klansmen at first pretended to be engaged in pleasant social activities, they lost little time in assuming the role of the white South's chief protectors. By the end of the 1860's they were a force to be reckoned with all over the South, as they bullied the ex-slaves and intimidated whites who sympathized with them. Their campaign of white terror included the widespread use of torture and murder against blacks and various kinds of humiliation for non-cooperative whites.

Despite the fear and dread their terror tactics engendered among southerners of both races, the Klan never really took over the political or governmental machinery of any southern state. But if they did not dominate the white South, they became a tremendously important extra-legal force that politicians ignored at their peril. And in retrospect, it would appear that they achieved their power position more by the inaction of others than by their own initiatives. After a brief flurry of radical legislation right after the War, both Congress and the President lost interest in the plight of the freedmen in the South. Businessmen, North and South, were more interested in making money than promoting justice. Conservative forces in the North, like scheming politicians in the South, discovered that the Klan, for all its faults, could be of use in advancing their self-interest. And, perhaps saddest of all, the moderate silent majority of the South refused to attack the Klan openly for fear of reprisals, and collectively succumbed to a paralysis of will which further emboldened the Klan terrorists. The analogies between the Klan's white terror in Reconstruction days and the Massive Resisters' activities after 1954 are too obvious to need belaboring. But perhaps one point should be stressed: in neither case was it foreordained that the South and the nation should put up with such barbarous, extra-legal terror campaigns. The victories of the bigots in both instances were victories by default.

After suffering a general eclipse in the latter part of the nineteenth century, the Klan was reestablished at Stone Mountain, Georgia, in 1915 by a "Colonel" William Joseph Simmons. The new Klan gradually set up chapters or dens in virtually every state and before long had an enrollment of several millions. In a propaganda brochure, "Ideals of the Knights of the Ku Klux Klan," the Simmons group unblushingly proclaimed its racist ideology: "this is a White's Man's organization, exalting the Caucasian Race and teaching the doctrine of White Supremacy. . . . All of Christian

Civilization depends upon the preservation and upbuilding of the White Race."

In due course, Imperial Wizard Simmons added four new features that were propagated along with the traditional doctrine of white supremacy. These were nativism, anti-Catholicism, anti-Semitism, and free-enterprise materialism. On numerous occasions, Simmons stressed that the revived Klan was committed to "a pure Americanism, untrammeled by alien influences," and he also wanted it known that his group was "founded and operated by consecrated business brains."

By the mid-1920's the second Klan had evolved into a national organization and a political force of considerable importance in several states. It is even probable that in the Harding-Coolidge years the Klan rolls were larger in certain northern states (Indiana and Ohio, for example) than in any state south of the Mason-Dixon Line. Like its Reconstruction precursor, the Simmons Klan was credited with numerous cross-burnings, acts of harassment, dynamitings, kidnappings, floggings, bombings, and murders. But the Simmons klansmen harassed not only backs and white integrationists, they also flogged or otherwise humiliated Christian whites who were accused of gambling, selling liquor, peddling dope, or deserting a spouse. Southern vigilantes, it seems, have always had a strong puritanical side to their character.

In the 1940's the second Klan disintegrated as a result of a number of factors. These included World War II, their own internal power struggles, their ill-advised collaboration with American Nazis, as well as state and federal legal harassment. Officially the second Klan went out of business at an imperial "klonvokation" held in Atlanta on April 23, 1944. This disappearing act took place soon after the U. S. Bureau of Internal Revenue filed a lien for $685,305 in delinquent taxes against the organization.

The Klan experienced yet another renaissance in the mid-1950's, chiefly, it seems, because of the two Brown opinions. The first evidence of this was the 1955 chartering by Georgia of the U. S. Klans, Knights of the Ku Klux Klan, Inc. This group, whose Imperial Wizard was Eldon Lee Edwards, an Atlanta paint sprayer, set up branches in several southern states, but never succeeded in achieving much organizational cohesion.

Throughout the life of Massive Resistance, the southern Klans remained disunited and often quite antagonistic to one another. They included, among others, the Gulf Ku Klux Klan, Knights of the Ku Klux Klan of the Confederacy, the Association of Alabama Knights of the Ku Klux Klan, South Carolina Knights of the Ku Klux Klan, Inc., National Ku Klux Klan, Independent Knights of the Ku Klux Klan, Palmetto Knights of the Ku Klux Klan, and the Original Ku Klux Klan of the Confederacy. Given the anarchistic nature of the Klan movement, it is remarkable that the organization achieved the power and influence it did in the post-Brown years.

The Klan, more than any other group, brought a "warlike" character to the South's counterrevolution. This it did by fighting the egalitarian revolutionaries without any mutally observed normative rules and by stooping to physical violence when that was deemed necessary. Indeed, in some parts of the Deep South, the Klan's terror campaigns amounted to an undeclared guerrilla war against any and all southerners who supported Brown's implementation.

To be sure, the Klan was not responsible for all acts of violence that occurred in the South in the 1950's and 1960's. Yet most observers seem agreed that the organization perpetrated or inspired a substantial part of it. No less an authority than the House Committee on Un-American Activities has conclusively proved the Klan's complicity in quite a few of the acts of terrorism that became common in the late 1950's. For example, it is now pretty well established that the Klan was behind the wave of violence that erupted in Montgomery after the start of the black boycott of the city's buses. The climax of that episode was the bombing of four black Baptist churches and the homes of three of the bus boycott leaders. The state subsequently charged several klansmen with complicity in the bombings, but they brought only two to trial. Neither of those was convicted.

It has also been confirmed that the 1959 dynamiting of a home in North Carolina was the work of dissident klansmen known as "Chessmen" or "Black Shirts," all of whom were apprehended, convicted, and sentenced to prison. In the previous year, the attempted dynamiting of a black school near Charlotte was traced to the Klan, which resulted in prison sentences for the grand wizard of the National Christian Knights of the Ku Klux Klan and two of his henchmen.

The Klan's white terror was both a rural and an urban phenomenon. And while it affected the Piedmont area of the Southeast as well as the Deep South, the states of Mississippi and Alabama appear to have gone well beyond their sister states in tolerating Klan violence. This is perhaps best exemplified by the fact that juries in those states rarely if ever convicted klansmen charged with acts of terrorism.

In Alabama Klan strength seems to have been concentrated in Birmingham and in the counties of Jefferson, Shelby, Tuscaloosa, and St. Clair. The areas surrounding Mobile and Montgomery also became Klan redoubts. In Florida the Klan was strongest in the north and west, particularly around Jacksonville, Tampa, and Tallahassee. Georgia, which had fathered the post-Brown Klan, had considerable Klan activity in the vicinity of Atlanta, Macon, Savannah, Columbus, and Moultrie. Charlotte was the chief base for the North Carolina Klan, while in South Carolina the organization's strength lay in the cities of Greenville, Columbia, and Florence. It appears that at least a few Klan dens were set up in every southern and border state after 1954, though the great majority of these remained small and not very active.

As the lunatic fringe of the South's counterrevolution, the Klan was responsible not only for bombings, arson, floggings, minatory cross-burnings, and general intimidation of dissenters, but also for a number of murders, attempted murders, and acts of Gestapo-like torture. The full extent of the group's terror campaign will probably never be known. The Klan, unlike the Gestapo, kept very few records.

The most publicized act of torture was the castration of a black handyman in Birmingham, which seems to have been incidental to a Klan ritual ceremony. That act evoked memories of the antebellum South, where castration of rebellious slaves was sometimes used as punishment.

In the mid-1960's there were several sensational murders in the South, for which the Klan appears to have been directly or indirectly responsible. In 1964 Lemuel A. Penn, a black school administrator from the nation's capital, was fatally shot by klansmen as he drove through Georgia on his return from Army Reserve duty at Fort Benning. This was also the year that saw the brutal slaying of three civil rights workers—Michael H. Schwerner (23), Andrew Goodman (20), and James E. Chaney (21)—in the red clay hills of Mississippi's Neshoba County. Eighteen alleged klansmen were later indicted and tried on federal conspiracy charges stemming from the deaths. Seven of the defendants, including former Klan Imperial Wizard Sam H. Bowers Jr., were convicted and sentenced to federal prison. Eight were acquitted, and mistrials were declared in the cases of the other three. This seems to have been the first conviction ever in a Mississippi civil rights murder case.

In 1965 in the wake of the massive Selma-to-Montgomery march, a white civil rights worker from Detroit, Viola Liuzzo, was ambushed and killed on Highway 80 by a group of klansmen. At about the same time, three white Unitarian ministers were severely beaten in Alabama by Klan-inspired segregationists. One of these, the Reverend James J. Reeb, later died.

On January 10, 1966, night-riding terrorists burned the home of black leader Vernon Dahmer in Hattiesburg, Mississippi, and murdered him. Three men were convicted of his murder, one of whom—Charles C. Wilson—was a prominent Klan leader. In December 1972 Governor William L. Waller, who had been Wilson's trial attorney, released his former client from the state penitentiary under a work-release program.

Today most experts support the view that the bulk of the Klan's counterrevolutionary terrorism in the Massive Resistance era was not perpetrated by rank-and-file members but by super-secret "action groups." These groups usually included less than a dozen members each and, like urban gangster organizations, they often committed their terrorist acts away from their home areas. Congressional investigators have revealed that the members of these hard-core, carefully screened groups were given military and para-military training, which included instruction in judo, karate, and the use of explosives and incendiaries. Exposing such groups seems to be beyond the power of most southern police departments, to a great extent because klansmen are notoriously addicted to that old Mafia disease—lockjaw. The secrecy that protects the Klan's terror campaigns is maintained not only by the group's secrecy oath, but also by closely guarded meetings, the use of covert intelligence operatives, and the wearing of hoods and masks when permitted.

Another factor contributing to the immunity of the Klan from prosecution is its widespread infiltration of government agencies in the South. Stealing an old communist ploy, the Klan concentrated its infiltration efforts on police forces, sheriffs' departments, highway patrols, conservation bodies, and organizations of justices of the peace. Since all of these agencies are directly or indirectly involved in law enforcement, it is obvious why the Klan sought to infiltrate as many of them as possible.

In addition to infiltrating law enforcement agencies, the Klan spent a lot of time and money courting the favor of southern governors and other high officials by politicking for them. In Alabama, Governor John Patterson, who succeeded the moderate Folsom, came very close to openly soliciting Klan support in his campaigns. The Klan appreciated his tacit approval, and Imperial Wizard Robert M. Shelton, Jr., of the United Klans vigorously campaigned for him. Shelton was the man who once announced that the Klan had declared open war "against the evils of Negroism and Jewism and the Jewish Communists."

The relations between Alabama's George Wallace and the Klan have long been a matter of interest and speculation to students of southern politics. It is a matter of record that in 1958, when Patterson and Wallace met in the Democratic gubernatorial primary, Wallace mildly criticized the Klan and refused to speak at Klan rallies. On election day Patterson beat him badly. After that experience, Wallace moved quickly to improve his relations with the Invisible Empire—apparently to the benefit of both. Shelton became a friend of Wallace as he had been of Patterson, and before long he was a leading fund-solicitor for the Wallace campaigns. When questioned about the Klan support of his candidacy, Wallace's stock reply was, "I'm glad to get support from anyone except gangsters and communists." Although Alabama's Attorney General Richmond Flowers proposed investigating Klan terror in the mid-1960's, Wallace was rather less than enthusiastic about the idea.

In 1964 the U. S. Bureau of Public Roads shocked a lot of people by charging the Wallace administration with coercing an engineering firm to hire Shelton as an "agent" for $4,000. Not long after that, it was revealed that Wallace had employed the Klan's Bureau of Investigation chief to make an inquiry into the Klan's activities in Alabama. This, of course, had nothing to do with the serious investigation proposed a little later by Flowers.

According to Robert Sherrill, Wallace revealed his pro-Klan leanings in a number of other ways. He paroled the klansman who had been convicted in the notorious castration case. He helped to defeat in the Alabama senate a bill that would have restricted the sale of dynamite in the state. He allowed his police chief, Al Lingo, to sit on the same platform with Klan speakers and be introduced by them as "a good friend." He maintained close relations with Asa (Ace) Carter, who in the 1950's had formed his own Birmingham Klan, and who had once been charged with shooting another klansman. And in 1968, when Wallace ran for President, he got the support of nearly all the Klan leaders. Gerald L. K. Smith, a long-time fellow traveler of the Klan, strongly supported him. The Imperial Wizards of the Maryland and Virginia Klans also announced that they were supporting him "100 percent." Robert Shelton is supposed to have claimed, "We made him Governor and we must make him President." And, as was expected, the Klan paper, *The Fiery Cross*, editorialized in favor of the Wallace candidacy.[3] So far as is known, Wallace never disavowed any of his Klan supporters—presumably because they were not "gangsters" or "communists."

Though Shelton's United Klans of America, aided by Wallace's benign toleration policy, gained the greatest political influence in the counterrevolutionary South, it was the unaffiliated Mississippi White Knights of the Ku Klux Klan who were the chief source of violence against white and black desegregationists. After the "long hot summer" of 1964, federal authorities arrested no less than thirty-six White Knights and charged them with seven murders and related felonies. In 1966 the chief of the NAACP's Hattiesburg chapter was fatally shot and his home fire-bombed, apparently by carloads of White Knights. The next year, the chief of the NAACP's Natchez chapter was killed by a bomb that had been planted in his car, and again it appeared that the Knights were the culprits. As though this record were not gruesome enough, the White Knights were also suspected of having burned more than seventy-five churches of various denominations. It was no coincidence that the Klan's reign of terror reached a peak of barbarism in Mississippi, for traditionally Klan violence has been most brazen and common where state and local officials are most understanding and tolerant. In states like North Carolina and Virginia, where public officials were generally dead set against the Klan, the organization's terror campaigns never got very far.[4]

It is tempting in an analysis such as this to attribute the rise of Massive Resistance solely or mainly to conspiratorial action by the various Klans. Yet an unqualified conspiracy theory of the movement does not seem substantiated by the empirical evidence. Klan conspiracies there certainly were—hundreds of them. But more often than not, the hooded conspirators of the Klan were doing little more than turning the flintwheel in volatile situations which they made worse but did not create. Of course, they lost little time in turning all such inflammatory situations to their advantage, but that is another story.

From the Massive Resisters' perspective, the worst thing the Klan did was to bring about a degradation of the South's traditional conservatism by equating tradition with mindless fanaticism and total reaction. In the end, the klansmen came to espouse, implicitly, a kind of ultra-conservative nihilism. This was manifested by their overlooking the obvious aspects of unreason and injustice in the South's treatment of blacks in order that they might give full (perhaps overcompensating) assent to the abstraction they called the southern way of life. There is no better word than nihilism to describe their utter refusal to concede that bigotry, racism, and social injustice existed in the South or ever had existed there.

It has not been the purpose of this discussion to suggest that the Klan "caused" Massive Resistance or totally dominated southern politics in the post-Brown years. Rather the purpose was to show that the Klan, despite its limited membership of perhaps ten or fifteen thousand, was a key popular force in preventing the peaceful implementation of Brown when the initial southern reactions to that decision suggested this was possible.[5]

II. The Citizens' Councils

WITH THE FORMATION of the first Citizens' Councils in Mississippi in July 1954, the South's counterrevolution—inchoate though it was—began to gather mass and momentum. The Councils were both cause and effect of the steady hardening of southern racism that followed Brown, and they seemed hell-bent on destroying what C. Vann Woodward has called the "New Reconstruction."[6]

Though the Councils have often been linked with the Klan through such epithets as "white-collar Klan," "uptown Klan," "button-down Klan," and "country club Klan," they usually disdained the cruder forms of lawlessness perpetrated by the Klan and preferred subtler forms of resistance. They have refused to open their membership records to scholarly researchers, but the best estimate is that in their heyday, around 1957, the Councils had about 250,000 members. Included among their members were bankers, industrialists, lawyers, doctors, judges, congressmen, and governors. And because of their prestigious membership rosters, they had a good deal more success than the Klan in achieving respectability and in politicizing the segregationist masses. While only a minority of white supremacists ever joined the Councils, it would appear that a majority of southern whites approved their goals and tactics.

The Mississippi Plan of 1890 had brought about Southwide disfranchisement of blacks, and the Mississippi Plan of 1954 created the Citizens' Council movement. It quickly snowballed, and by the end of the year, the Mississippi Association of Citizens' Councils was recruiting in several other southern states and was taking credit for the victories of segregationists in two political campaigns.[7] In the following year, the Association began to put out its own monthly journal, *The Citizens' Council*, with William J. Simmons as editor, which in 1966 became *The Citizen*.

Eventually the Councils were firmly established in the states of Mississippi, Alabama, Louisiana, South Carolina, Florida, Texas, Virginia, Arkansas, and Tennessee. But though they had chapters in most parts of the South, the Councils, like the Klan, were most successful in the Deep South, especially in Mississippi and Alabama. Indeed, by the late 1950's they had become the single most powerful political force in Mississippi. And once Ross Barnett became governor, the Councils and the Mississippi state government became virtually indistinguishable.

After 1956, the Alabama Councils experienced an extraordinary growth. It was not surprising that this growth was most marked in the black belt areas of the state, since Alabama's first Council had been organized in Dallas County, which is in the center of the black belt. The most influential leader of the Alabama Councils was State Senator Sam Engelhardt, a feudal-type planter from Macon County and a charismatic demagogue, whose popularity rivaled that of George Wallace for a time. Asa Carter, who also dabbled in Klan activities, was a Council leader for a brief period.

Near the end of 1955 the Montgomery bus boycott got underway, followed a few weeks later by an outbreak of violence at the University of Alabama over efforts of Autherine Lucy to desegregate the university. It was largely these events, headlined across the nation, that accounted for the rapid increase in the Alabama Councils' membership and made Montgomery a citadel of Council power. After the blacks won their fight to desegregate the Montgomery buses, membership in the Councils began to fall, and their center of influence shifted from Montgomery to Selma.

In Louisiana the Councils enjoyed a close working relationship with the state's Joint Legislative Committee to Maintain Segregation. This relationship was strengthened when the Committee's chairman, State Senator William M. Rainach, became president of the Association of Citizens' Councils of Louisiana. Senator Rainach and the irrepressible Leander Perez were Louisiana's leading charismatic demagogues in the Massive Resistance years. And it was because of support from such public figures as Rainach and Perez that the Louisiana Councils became a political power, most notably in the Protestant up-country.

In the summer of 1964 the editor of the Mississippi Councils' official paper spoke at the organizational meeting of the Greater

Los Angeles Citizens' Council. In his address on that occasion, the editor put the Councils solidly behind the two basic myths of the Massive Resisters' ideology.[8] According to Simmons, the original goal of the Councils was twofold: to halt racial integration and slow down the growth of a tyrannical federal establishment. Both these "evils," he believed, had sprung from the same source—the egalitarianism that had been insidiously propagated through our educational system since World War I. Simmons went on to argue that since the days of the New Deal, the United States had been managed (or mismanaged) by elites from Harvard, with ideological assistance from Columbia. He was thus implying, if not quite saying so explicitly, that the egalitarian revolution threatening the Jim Crow system had been caused less by the Supreme Court than by the collusion of Harvard, Columbia, and the New Deal.

Though the Councils shared a common philosophy and vision of reality, their tactical gambits differed from state to state. In Alabama they spent much of their time legally and otherwise harassing the NAACP. In Florida they tried to force Florida State University to expel all "pro-integration students," and at Tallahassee they spearheaded a drive to remove "communist and integration books" from public libraries. In New Orleans they aroused white parents by warning that "subversive" history books were about to be adopted for school use. And in Texas they picketed liberals and racial moderates, such as Governor Clement of Tennessee, and bitterly fought the integration of the first grade in the Port Arthur elementary school. These actions, of course, constituted but a tiny part of the Councils' input to the chaos, disorder, violence, and bigotry that Massive Resistance eventually became, but they suggest the scope and variety of Council resistance.

From this brief analysis of the Citizens' Councils, one can draw at least eight generalized conclusions:

    1. Despite their success in influencing the attitudes and behavior of southern political elites, the Councils never became a genuine grass-roots popular force in terms of membership.

    2. The Councils, unlike the Klan, enjoyed a relatively high community status, and in the Deep South were eminently respectable.

    3. The Councils rejected (at least publicly) the kind of

violence perpetrated by the Klan and concentrated instead on pressure group politics, bloc voting, economic harassment, and mass media saturation propaganda.

4. Though the Councils were unable to roll back the egalitarian revolution, they were probably more effective than the Klan in silencing white moderates and preventing a rationally planned transition to a new social order.

5. When the South's counterrevolution was at its peak, political power in much of the region lay in the hands of interlocked oligarchies, in whose ranks the Councils had significant representation.

6. A substantial part of the pro-segregation legislation that made up the public policies of Massive Resistance was either drafted or inspired by Council members and their legislative fellow travelers.

7. The Councils were not only anti-black and anti-integration, they also were a reactionary political force whose tactics and general philosophy potentially threatened the rights of union labor, Catholics, Jews, and all progressive or liberal minority groups.

8. The Councils, for all their bigotry, never quite realized their full potential for mischief. Had they chosen to be as unscrupulously violent as the Klan, they might conceivably have delayed token integration for a longer time than they did. But in the process they would probably have accelerated the federalization of civil liberties in the South—something they sought to avoid at all cost. Viewing southern history through a rearview mirror, the Councils were clearly pursuing an "impossible dream"—the dream that desegregation would not come to the South and that segregation was destined to last forever. It was an illusion which almost all Massive Resisters shared, especially in the late 1950's. And as somebody so wisely said long ago, it is easier to slay a dragon than an illusion.

As a final point, it might be said that what the Klan sought to achieve through violent mob action, the more cautious Councils sought to achieve through appeals to states' rights, southern regionalism, and obstructive legislative tactics. All of which means that while the Klan was the voice of southern nihilism, the Councils were the voices of southern political reaction.

III. OTHER RESISTANCE GROUPS

F OR ALMOST A DECADE, the Klan and the Citizens' Councils were the most influential popular forces in the South's counterrevolution. But a number of other groups, especially prominent in the upper South, also aided and abetted the southern governments' resistance efforts. Some of these were loosely linked to the Councils, others were wholly independent.

In Virginia it was, of course, the Byrd machine that led the forces of Massive Resistance. But the Byrd people were supported by a number of segregationist groups, the most important of which was the group known as the Defenders of State Sovereignty and Individual Liberties. The Defenders were particularly strong in the state's southside black belt, which had always given Byrd-backed candidates overwhelming support. Their principal contribution to Virginia's Massive Resistance was to set up in May 1958 an organization called the "Virginia Education Fund," whose purpose was to promote segregated private-school projects.

In Georgia, as in Virginia, the Citizens' Councils of America, Incorporated, were relatively insignificant. But there was a group in the state, the States' Rights Council of Georgia, that had a very close working relationship with the Councils. This organization was largely the brainchild of Governor Marvin Griffin and Roy V. Harris, two of the state's leading charismatic demagogues. Its origins are usually traced back to a meeting in Augusta in December 1954. But it was not until the fall of 1955, when Griffin and Harris sponsored an Atlanta meeting of Georgia's political leaders, that the States' Rights Council emerged as a potent antiintegration force. The Atlanta meeting picked R. Carter Pittman, an attorney and segregationist firebrand from Dalton, to be president of the Council. William T. Bodenhamer, a Baptist minister who sat on both the state board of education and the Georgia

Baptist Convention's executive committee, was made executive secretary. After 1955 Georgia's most influential proponents of Massive Resistance were the state government, county and local governments, the prestigious Commission on Education, and the States' Rights Council. The influence of these agencies was enhanced by the fact that they all had overlapping membership.

The Patriots of North Carolina, Inc., made a determined effort to energize the white masses of the Tar Heel state. Established in August 1955, the Patriots picked Wesley C. George (research professor at the University of North Carolina Medical School) to be their president and A. Allison James (Winston-Salem druggist and ex-employee of the U.S. Treasury Department) to be their executive secretary. They were strongest in the Piedmont area around Greensboro, and Piedmont textile officials seem to have been the chief economic group among the original officers.[9]

Like the States' Rights Council of Georgia, the Patriots initially attracted a number of big names to their banner. As the *Charlotte Observer* noted on May 18, 1956, "Some of the most respected men in North Carolina became charter members of the Patriots." In addition to Dr. George (former president of the North Carolina Academy of Science), charter members included three ex-speakers of the state house of representatives, a University of North Carolina trustee, a state senator, two state representatives, and a former Democratic national committeeman. Unlike most resistance groups in the post-Brown era, the Patriots flourished in the upcountry west of the fall line instead of in the Black Belt or old plantation counties of the Tidewater, where most of the state's blacks lived. In fact, it was estimated that more than ninety percent of the Patriots' charter members came from Guilford County.

Despite their auspicious beginning, the Patriots turned out to be about the least durable of all the south's major resistance groups. In 1956 they helped to defeat Representatives Charles B. Deane and Thurmond D. Chatham, two of the three North Carolina congressmen who refused to sign the Southern Manifesto. But after that their star waned, and by the middle of 1958 they had disappeared from the Tar Heel political scene.

The successors of the Patriots were another Piedmont group —the North Carolina Defenders of States' Rights. The Defenders, who included many ex-Patriots, were fanatical about white supremacy, and their chief spokesman was the Reverend James P. Dees, a charismatic demagogue and rector of Statesville's Trinity Episcopal Church until he resigned to set up an independent congregation. The Defenders were also short-lived and had to share the spotlight with the followers of I. Beverly Lake, former Wake Forest law professor and 1960 gubernatorial candidate. In the Tar Heel state, in short, Massive Resistance had become a massive illusion by the late 1950's.

In listing the popular forces of the South's counterrevolution, one must not fail to include the Democratic and Republican parties and, in the late 1960's, the Wallace party. For it was, after all, the region's political parties—particularly the dominant Democrats—that bore the chief responsibility for politicizing the segregationist masses and getting them to the polls on election day to vote for anti-integration candidates. Furthermore, since membership in southern parties overlapped with membership in the Klan, the Councils, and other resistance groups, it appeared for a time that the segregationists would get a stranglehold on policymaking in the racial area, and prevent even tokenism. That this never quite happened was more a testimony to the centrifugal nature of the forces in the Massive Resistance movement than a sign of lack of desire.

Clearly the disparate popular forces that made up the South's counterrevolution—like the leaders who gave them their cues— were self-confessed practitioners of the politics of conflict with no hesitation about spreading their sails to the winds of racist hysteria. For a few months, enthusiasm among the ranks was high, and in 1956 it burgeoned into euphoria with the proclamation of the Southern Manifesto and the doctrine of interposition. But unlike genuine Jeffersonian conservatives, none of the Massive Resistance groups ever learned to walk with grace the delicate line between tradition and transition. It was, therefore, hardly surprising that when the showdowns finally came at Little Rock and other cities, the Gadarene herd of euphoric counterrevolutionaries hurled themselves—blindly as it were—down the Massive Resistance slopes and into a sea of utter futility. Their myth of "Never" shattered, they groped piteously toward a past that had now become yet another lost cause.

IV. A Typology of Resisters

JUST AS ONE CAN DISTINGUISH, analytically and empirically, different types of Massive Resistance leaders, one can distinguish different types of individual Resisters in the ranks. The differences among the rank-and-file, like those among leaders, were primarily differences of attitudes and methods, and though they are given slightly different labels here, they come down pretty much to the same thing. Such categorization in a study of this kind seems to be justified for at least three reasons. It emphasizes the fact that rank-and-file segregationists did not constitute a monolithic group in their attitudes toward blacks and their reactions to change; it suggests some clues as to the kinds of whites one might expect to find in the various categories; and it offers a few conjectures about the purposes and objectives of the different groups.

The most extreme and ultra-reactionary Massive Resisters may aptly be described as the "zealots" of the South's counterrevolution. Manifesting the usual traits of fanatics, true believers, and mindless stand-patters, the zealots acted from a blazing certitude of their own virtue and of the total depravity of their opponents. Visceral rather than cerebral, more dogmatic than pragmatic, they were like the zealots of earlier counterrevolutions in their bondage to fear, anxiety, insecurity, frustration, and simple hate.

In the Massive Resistance movement, the zealots were conspicuous, if not dominant, in such groups as the Klan, the North Carolina Patriots, and J. B. Stoner's lesser known but equally bigoted National States' Rights Party. They also surfaced from time to time in isolated groups of unorganized whites. As uncritical defenders of the status quo, the segregationist zealots were the vanguard of the Massive Resistance masses as the charismatic demagogues were the vanguard of the leadership elites. It was the zealots who kidnapped a young black man in Florida and beat him with a machete in the belief (fallacious) that he had been intimate with a white girl. And it was Klan zealots who murdered Lemuel Penn and Viola Liuzzo. When torture or murder was called for, it was the zealots who were "contracted" to do the job.

Short of psychoanalyzing each and every one of them, one can only conjecture about the ultimate motivations and goals of the zealots. In some cases their impulses toward aggression and violence appear to have derived from frustrated aspirations. In other cases they probably originated in a deep ambiguity about individual and group identity. Be that as it may, the zealots clearly hoped to gain from membership in extremist groups a sharper sense of identity along with more meaningful social relationships that would legitimate the use of violence. It seems plausible to assume that many if not most of the South's zealots did in fact attain these goals by joining such groups as the Klan and the Patriots.

As regards the sociology of the zealots, it is generally assumed that the great majority of them came from those groups that have traditionally been the most culturally and economically deprived. Thus they were prominent among small-town poor whites, religious fundamentalists, marginal small businessmen, and unskilled and semiskilled workers in the textile, construction, aircraft, coal, and steel industries. But again it must be stressed that Massive Resistance was not exclusively a lower-class movement, and there were middle-class zealots as well as lower-class ones, though probably not as many.

A second group of Massive Resisters might be denoted "opportunists." Like their pragmatic self-aggrandizing leaders, they were motivated by opportunism rather than by principled bigotry. And as the zealots had a positive passion for anachronism and seemed mesmerized by the past, the opportunists had a passion for timely expediency and a habit of hopping on any bandwagon that seemed to be riding high. Also it might be said that whereas the zealots were committed to an anti-rational romanticism, the opportunists were committed to a Machiavellian amoralism.

Southern whites who became opportunistic Massive Resisters

doubtless did so in the belief they were doing the "in" thing and in the hope they would thereby enhance their status, reputation, or career. As a rule, the white opportunists held no deep-seated fear or hatred of blacks, and in private they often spoke well of black people. However, once the charismatic demagogues solidified southern opinion against desegregation, many of the opportunists began sounding more "ultra" than the zealots. They apparently felt that such a posture was necessary to avoid having their loyalty to the southern way of life impugned.

Opportunistic Massive Resisters were most common in business, politics, and the professions. They were generally better educated than the zealots, and on the average enjoyed a higher socioeconomic status. Furthermore, since they were more interested in maximizing their own fortunes than in guaranteeing the survival of Jim Crow, they did not view the ultimate demise of Massive Resistance as the apocalyptic tragedy the zealots took it to be.

The third category of white counterrevolutionaries can best be described as "traditionalists." Closer in most ways to the opportunists than to the zealots, the traditionalists were semi-passive camp-followers of Massive Resistance, who resisted desegregation only when there seemed to be no honorable or safe way of avoiding resisting. They were thus motivated not by fanaticism or crass opportunism, but by a don't-rock-the-boat philosophy.

During the fifties and sixties, the traditionalists dutifully obeyed the laws and etiquette of southern "apartheid" without feeling any deep emotional attachment to the system's values. Generally conciliatory by nature, they rested their obedience to the imperatives of the status quo on a simple faith in the rightness of custom and on a desire to avoid unnecessary trouble. In short, they did not want to get involved—neither with reform nor with reaction. What disturbed them most was the violence that marked so many showdowns between revolutionaries and counterrevolutionaries. And in time, most of them came to fear the zealots' reign of terror even more than the integration of public facilities.

The traditionalists were prominent among young people, academicians, religious leaders, and the more forward-looking business and professional people. They also seem to have been numerous in journalistic circles, especially in the upper South and border states. If one can judge from the evidence available today, it seems probable that a majority of white southerners were only traditional segregationists in the early months after Brown, though by 1956 most of them had become zealots or opportunists.

Except for the zealots, the Massive Resistance ranks never resisted Brown's implementation in the South quite as enthusiastically as their leaders hoped they would. All too often, they simply went through the motions of resistance without genuine conviction. There were many reasons for this failure of the ranks to wage "total counterrevolution." In retrospect, three appear to have been crucial: the lack of an appealing cause, the failure to evolve a coherent philosophy of reaction, and the absence of truly creative leadership of the first order.

6.

The Iconography and Demonology of Massive Resistance

I. Segregationist Icons and Symbols

WHILE IT IS OBVIOUS, at least to experts, that an enormous variety of objective conditions can create counterrevolutionary potential, it is not so obvious that the manipulation of myths and symbols by mass-movement elites is among the most important of such conditions. Yet it almost certainly is. And that being the case, the student of Massive Resistance who neglects the symbolic environment of that movement will fail to grasp one of its crucial dimensions.

The mythology of Massive Resistance included not only a pantheon of saints and martyrs and verbalized propositions such as white supremacy and states'-rights federalism, but also a vast panoply of symbols, icons, emblems, totems, taboos, scapegoats, and stylized rituals. Many of these were deeply embedded in the southern character and culture, and their ceaseless manipulation after 1954 unquestionably strengthened the tendency toward "orthodoxy" on the part of southern whites. Professor Whitehead, alarmed by the ubiquity of symbolization in human behavior, warned some years ago that "the life of humanity can easily be overwhelmed by its symbolic accessories." Though this may sound like an alarmist view to some, a number of social scientists have warned of the same danger.[1]

The student of southern politics is less interested in labeling a particular southern myth as "good" or "bad" in moral terms than in discovering how effectively it does what conservative and counterrevolutionary myths are meant to do—viz., exalt the past, glorify the status quo, promote social cohesion, indoctrinate the young with the merits of prescription, and prevent radical change. Aware of all this, the leaders of Massive Resistance consciously manipulated their myths to "fuse the real and the imaginary into a blend that becomes a reality itself, a force in history."[2] And on balance, the South's myth structure seems to have been, for a few years at least, an effective goal-maximizer, even though—or because—some of the component myths institutionalized and masked abhorrent realities.

The segregationists' myths even served a quasi-religious function. This can be seen from the fact that they helped to harmonize and unify the conflicting experiences of southerners very much as the Resisters' evangelical faith did. Many of the segregationists, especially the zealots, had little formal education, and thus their racial mythology—even more than their religion—was an instrument for making their experiences intelligible to themselves and to one another. And, of course, both the racial and religious mythologies of white southerners were (and are) an amalgam of traditional values, prejudices, frustrated hopes, and ideals.

Before looking at some of the icons and mythic symbols that were conspicuous in the politics of Massive Resistance, it will be well to make one additional prefatory point. That point is the fact that from the outset the South's counterrevolutionaries suffered from the handicap of having their opponents preempt virtually all the national historic symbols of the United States. Among the symbols preempted by the egalitarians were Old Glory, the Declaration of Independence, the Constitution, the Bill of Rights, constitutional democracy, the Jeffersonian concept of equality, and the mystique of the Great Emancipator. As a result of this wholesale preemption, the South's leaders found themselves at a distinct disadvantage in the vital political art of myth-manipulation, for all they had left to manipulate were regional myths and icons discredited by the Great Rebellion.

As used in this analysis, the word "icon" simply means any object of uncritical and emotional devotion that is venerated by the ranks in a mass movement as a concrete symbol of some guiding ideal or belief. "Icon-waving" has long been one of the most prevalent and visible means of political symbolization, and it proved to be a useful tool in the Massive Resisters' bag of tricks. Icon-waving, of course, was a two-way street in the post-Brown era, and the egalitarian revolutionaries did their share of manipulating myths and icons. But in terms of sheer quantity of symbolic images, the South's counterrevolutionaries probably outdid their antagonists.

Of all the South's icons, the most visible was the Confederate flag. While this symbol of the "lost cause" had never quite vanished from the southern scene after Appomattox, it sprang up everywhere in the mid-1950's and replaced Old Glory in much of the South. At first it was mainly confined to football games and dormitory rooms of southern college students. But in the wake of Brown it became increasingly prominent on automobiles, in the windows of homes, on flagpoles in front of public buildings, and on the clothes and uniforms worn by many white southerners. And, for a time, it was reportedly flown above our national emblem on the Alabama statehouse flagpole. The South's charismatic demagogues seemed proud to have their speakers' platforms decorated with the Confederate flag.

An almost equally ubiquitous icon of the segregationists was an aural one—the song *Dixie*, which has been described, with good reason, as the national anthem of the white South. *Dixie*, which symbolizes to segregationists the glories of antebellum days and the charms of cavalier-life on the old plantation, was played at nearly every rally of the Klan and the Citizens' Councils in the heyday of Massive Resistance. It also became the chief marching song of innumerable southern high schools and colleges. In the late 1960's, blacks in the South's integrated schools increasingly took exception to using *Dixie* as a school song, but many schools continued to feature it despite black protests.

The Confederate flag and *Dixie* were particularly prominent at fall football games in the South—another of the segregationists' icons. Indeed, the mystique of southern football in the post-World War II years included resonances, nuances, and an intensity of emotion found in few other places in the country. In the Massive Resistance era, southern football, which continued to be exclusively white save for the region's black colleges, attained a place in society that resembled in many respects the antebellum dueling tradition. Perhaps the fact that the South has always been short of organized entertainment as well as of wealth and industry has been a factor in making its pursuit of football excellence a matter of fanatical dedication.

To tens of thousands of southern football fans, the football season has traditionally been a frenetic succession of riotous Saturdays and punch-drunk Sundays, all providing a temporary escape from the tedium of southern life. To be sure, it is a ritual that has never been overtly racist, except in its exclusion (until recently) of black players. Yet, when accompanied by the playing of *Dixie*, the frantic waving of Confederate flags, and the violent encounters on the playing field, southern football becomes a stylized ritual and an integral part of the non-verbal mythology of white racism. There is—or used to be—no racial or other ambivalence on the football field. It's simply a case of "them" against "us." And if southerners in 1954 had opposed racial integration for no other reason, they would have done so because of the threat it posed to the ritualistic—and racial—purity of southern football.

Moving on to a different field, we should not neglect to mention the King James Bible as a Massive Resistance icon. To be sure, not all the South's segregationists were Protestants who accepted this version of the Bible, but the great majority of them were. And this was especially true of those who held public office. Even before the 1950's, the South's charismatic demagogues were tracing segregation all the way back to God, and in the process making the King James Bible the chief legitimating authority for the Jim Crow system. Even the Klan, whose white terror against blacks and liberals would seem to have had little in common with the Gospel message, publicly revered the Bible—and the Christian cross as well.

Towering over the total structure of Massive Resistance iconography was that ubiquitous abstraction known as "the southern way of life." That mythic concept, which revealed the banality of the South's metaphysic, achieved an almost religious status in the post-Brown years. Eventually, though, it came to be tinged with a sentimentality that became steadily more sickly as it became more and more divorced from reality. But even so, it never lost its appeal to white southerners and continued to embrace a wide variety of things, including Jim Crow, white supremacy, states' rights, agrarianism, religious fundamentalism, a cuisine featuring fried foods and corn dishes, a languorous life-style, and the extended family concept. It is also well known that it was much used after 1954 as a code phrase for illegal discrimination against blacks in the same way that "law and order" was used by conservatives in the 1968 presidential campaign. It sounded both nobler and more altruistic to say one was fighting for the southern way of life rather than for white supremacy.

If the "southern way of life" was the most comprehensive of the South's symbolic slogans, it was by no means the only one. Other talismanic words and phrases used to advance the cause of Massive Resistance were "rebel," "race purity," "freedom of choice," "the neighborhood school," "southern maid," "states' rights," and the exclamation, "Never!" Among the segregationists' pejorative epithets used to discredit the egalitarians were "nigger," "nigger-lover, "Mixiecrat," "outside agitator," and "bleeding-heart liberal." A semanticist might say, and justly so, that the Massive Resisters' verbal icons constituted a sacred "in-language" like the languages of children, poetry, and religious sects. The more ambiguous slogans, such as "southern way of life" and "freedom of choice," had a kind of double life in southern mouths, at once luminous and obscure, and they both revealed and concealed reality. They were words that said nothing and said everything. But as symbolic icons, they were—for segregationists —definitive and categorical, whatever their seeming ambiguities.

Like the ghetto language of the northern cities, the South's "fighting words," with their aggressive, electric syllables, resembled the flash given off by a knife when it strikes a hard opaque body. In a curious way, they condensed all the racists' appetites, all their hatreds and enthusiasms, all the longings that raged unexpressed in the depths of the southern psyche. Finally, these totemic words were the sign and seal of Massive Resistance, and in a very real sense they were a way of affirming the user's counterrevolutionary identity.

A final category of southern iconography that indirectly aided Massive Resistance was the group of concepts, slogans, symbols, rites, and emblems focusing on that most obsessive of southern cults—the Lost Cause of the late Confederacy. Central to this category, as noted above, was the widespread veneration of the Confederate flag. But it extended far beyond mere flag-waving, and, indeed, to all the historic memories of southerners, whose memories are longer than those of most Americans. It included a revival of the mythic image of a chivalric and gallant war-torn South. It also included the numberless statues to "our glorious Confederate dead," the numerous schools and other institutions named for Robert E. Lee and Jefferson Davis, the panoply of books glorifying the Lost Cause à la *Gone With the Wind*, the phenomenon of the "Confederate Colonel," the Kappa Alpha "Old South" fraternity—a solid bastion of counterrevolution, and last, but by no means least, the vestal virgins of Confederate nostalgia—the redoubtable ladies of the United Daughters of the Confederacy. Rarely has a Lost Cause in modern times been kept so "cultishly" alive as the Lost Cause of the Confederacy, and few have done more to make that a reality than the ladies of the U.D.C., almost all of whom were ardent proponents of Massive Resistance. And as long as the U.D.C. exists, the memory of the 1860's exercise in Caucasian fatuity will not perish from the land of Dixie.

When one approaches the iconography of the Massive Resisters with the objectivity of the scholar instead of the passion of the true believer, one cannot escape the conclusion that it was quite naive, stridently parochial, and hyper-defensive. The segregationists' totemic veneration of the icons of the Lost Cause, their insistence that the South is God's country, their preference for rhetoric over reason, all seemed to suggest a deep malaise in the southern mind. Specifically, they suggested a kind of spiritual *Angst*, a penchant for romantic escapism, a fascination with utopian abstractions, and a growing, gnawing realization of both individual and regional vulnerability. In short, the southerners' massive resort to symbolism was in itself a kind of sickness.

But one must not go overboard in stressing the negative side of southern symbolism and mythology. It was a useful weapon in the hands of the charismatic demagogues. It did for a time increase cohesion in the white community. And, until the advent of token integration, it even seemed to be in tune with reality. So, though one cannot say that the Massive Resisters' symbolism was a smashing success on the battlefields of the fifties and sixties, it was a weapon whose tireless manipulation constantly gave trouble to the egalitarians. Paraphrasing the younger Mill, one is led to assert that a single counterrevolutionary with an arsenal of icons and myths at his disposal is a social power equal to ninety-nine who have only material interests motivating them. Like the Irish, southerners have always had a plethora of icons, and also like the Irish they have done rather well to have been stuck with so many Lost Causes.

Perhaps the best thing one can say in retrospect about the counterrevolutionary South's myths and symbols is that they had marked success as tactical slogans but created insuperable difficulties when public officials tried to use them as the basis of public policy. Only then did their intellectual and moral poverty rise clearly to the surface.

II. DEMONS AND SCAPEGOATS

IN THE CALCULUS of Massive Resistance mythology, demons and scapegoats played quite as big a role as icons. This was to be expected, for mass movements have traditionally propagated a Manichaean view of reality, which inevitably leads to the politics of polarization. The South's demons were excoriated for two reasons. They were heroes to the egalitarians, and they were seeking to expose the "false ideology" of the Massive Resisters. Like myth-makers everywhere, the segregationists feared the intrusion of reason into their belief system, for as Bertrand Russell once wrote, "Men fear thought as they fear nothing else on earth—more than ruin, more even than death. Thought is subversive and revolutionary, destructive and terrible."

High on the list of Massive Resistance demons was the United States Supreme Court, particularly two of its most famous members—Chief Justice Warren (author of Brown) and Mr. Justice Black (a "turncoat" southerner). The abuse which the South's demagogues heaped upon the Warren Court after 1954 was as merciless as it was outrageous. Day in and day out southern politicians, grinding the axe of racism, denounced the justices as nigger-lovers, communists, sex perverts, and traitors to both the American and southern way of life. In the either-or rhetoric of the segregationists, no accusation was too bizarre to hurl against the Court, no polemical attack too extreme.

Another of the South's demons was Dr. Martin Luther King, Jr., who, like the Supreme Court, was endowed with demonic qualities by segregationist orators. Though it was not obvious at first, it now seems probable that the South's relentless excoriation of Dr. King stemmed as much from a deep-seated fear of his charisma and moral influence as from his overt actions against the Jim Crow system. It will be recalled that Dr. King did not become a major opponent of the Massive Resisters until his successful leadership of the Montgomery bus boycott. But after that victory, he became the most tireless goader of the southern and national conscience. Among other things, he became the chief spokesman for the Southern Christian Leadership Conference. He helped to inspire and direct numerous civil rights demonstrations in the 1960's. He spoke constantly to national and international audiences about the immorality of segregation. He insisted with passion that an unjust law is no law at all. And, more important still, he brought Gandhi's idea of non-violent resistance to evil to the attention of the American people in a way that had not been done since Thoreau's crusading against slavery. It is not unlikely that thousands of Massive Resisters breathed a sigh of relief when Dr. King was assassinated in 1968, for now the King was dead—literally and symbolically. Unfortunately for the segregationists, however, the egalitarian revolution kept rolling right along.

Among national political leaders, the white South chose to vent its deepest hate on the Kennedys and Hubert Humphrey. Southern dislike of the Minnesotan went back to the 1948 Democratic Convention when Humphrey took the lead in the fight for a strong civil rights plank in the Democratic platform of that year. Southern antipathy to the Kennedys was of more recent origin and seems to have stemmed from three things. The Kennedys were vigorous proponents of civil rights laws in the 1960's; President Kennedy sent federal troops to desegregate Ole Miss; and Attorney General Robert Kennedy took an extremely tough line against the whole Massive Resistance movement. The segregationists also believed (and said) that the Kennedys and Humphrey had bartered away venerable constitutional principles for black votes in a cynical "sellout" to Dr. King and the NAACP.

Demons, of course, may be non-human as well as human, and the South had the non-human kind too. Chief among these were such "horrors" as the two Brown decisions, the fourteenth amendment (especially its equal protection clause), all the writings of Gunnar Myrdal, most TV coverage of the post-Brown crises in the South, the concepts "equality" and "freedom now," such leftist ideologies as Marxism and socialism, and the entire corpus of modern social science. Since these things were "horrors," the Massive Resisters did all in their power to extirpate them from the southern scene before they could fatally contaminate Caucasian minds and the southern way of life.

In addition to a mixed bag of human and non-human demons, the South's mythology included numerous scapegoats. It is true, of course, that all scapegoats of a given mythic system are also demons, but the converse is not always true. It is not always true, that is, if one defines scapegoats as a species of demons that are used by a social group as symbolic whipping-boys upon which all the group's faults and failures are thrust. That is the sense in which the term scapegoat is being used here.

Long before most people in the South had ever heard of such

"demons" as Dr. King, the Kennedys, or Hubert Humphrey, the NAACP's lawyers and organizers had achieved the full status of incubi in southern folklore—demonic spirits that tormented and oppressed white people like a nightmare. The southern demagogues, for a number of reasons, found it more convenient and tactically effective to blame the NAACP for their post-Brown problems and mistakes rather than themselves or the Founding Fathers who wrote the Constitution. Everything bad that took place in the South—whether it was riots, bombings, boycotts, or demonstrations—was blamed on the conspiratorial machinations of the NAACP. One of the more interesting features of the South's scapegoat strategy was to propagate the "fallacy of the false equation"—i.e., the argument that the NAACP was as extremist on the left side of the political spectrum as the Klan was on the right, and therefore they were equally to blame for whatever violence occurred. Klansmen, or course, never propagated such an "equation," for they felt infinitely superior to all black protest organizations, and probably did not wish to share the "blame" for violence with them.

In seeking to besmirch the fine national reputation of their symbolic enemy and whipping-boy, the Massive Resisters employed a wide and varied range of weapons—legislative, judicial, political, propagandistic, and terroristic. Among the most publicized anti-NAACP ploys were rules against state employees joining the organization, legislative investigations of its leaders, confiscation of its records, laws requiring publication of its membership lists, and the imposition of strict legal controls on its activities in behalf of civil rights.[3]

One might have thought that since the NAACP was such a handy scapegoat, the South's counterrevolutionaries would not have tried to destroy it. But since they were more committed to ideology than to strategic rationality, they bent every effort to wipe the organization from the face of Dixie. Obviously the South's concerted assault on the NAACP raised a number of grave constitutional questions, the most important of which was the degree to which the first amendment protects militant civil rights groups. Eventually most of the South's anti-NAACP statutes were invalidated by federal courts. But for a time in the late fifties, it was touch and go as to whether the NAACP would be able to survive in the South except as a historical symbol.

Though white southerners detested just about everything about the NAACP, it was the organization's Legal Defense and Educational Fund, Inc. (L. D. F.) that particularly aroused the ire of the Massive Resisters. Founded in 1939, the L. D. F. first had but one attorney, Thurgood Marshall, but by the late 1960's it had twenty-five, about half of whom were black. As the legal ramrod of the NAACP, the dedicated lawyers of the L. D. F. defended the rights of blacks in thousands of court cases, including Brown. In 1968 they argued more cases before the U. S. Supreme Court than any other agency except the Justice Department. The Massive Resisters were well aware of this ceaseless activity on behalf of black rights, and it served to harden their hatred of the NAACP.

Tactically speaking, the South's use of the NAACP as a universal whipping-boy was both clever and unclever. It was clever in that the NAACP was a highly visible, unified organization, and being composed almost wholly of blacks and white liberals, was not much admired by the average white southerner. It was unclever in that the NAACP had a very positive national reputation, was backed by some of the best legal talent in the country, and had the mythology of the Declaration of Independence and the Constitution solidly on its side.

Typical of the scapegoating rhetoric of the Massive Resisters in their anti-NAACP campaign was a speech made by Georgia's Attorney General Eugene Cook, which he called "The Ugly Truth About the NAACP." As Cook saw it, the NAACP had "allowed itself to become part and parcel of the Communist conspiracy to overthrow the democratic governments of this nation and its sovereign states."[4] Cook also professed to believe that the NAACP was not sincere in its public solicitude for the welfare of blacks but rather was cynically using the racial issue as "a convenient front for their more nefarious activities and as one with which they could dupe naive do-gooders, fuzzy-minded intellectuals, misguided clergymen and radical journalists to be their pawns."[5] Should the NAACP leaders be allowed to continue their revolutionary activities unmolested, Cook predicted that they would eventually deliver "this nation into the hands of international Communism."[6]

Next to the NAACP, the chief scapegoats of the Massive Resisters were all those white and black civil rights activists who were usually labeled "outside agitators." No effort was ever made to supply an objective definition of that code phrase, but that was hardly necessary since all segregationists knew exactly what it meant. Though most of the troubles in the post-Brown South were blamed on the NAACP, "outside agitators" came in for a good share of the blame too. And just as the South's leaders impugned the sincerity and integrity of the NAACP, they likewise attacked the "outside agitators" for being morally corrupt, politically subversive, and opportunistic pseudo-liberals in search of publicity and financial gain. In fact, they were considered such a serious threat to the southern way of life that it was proposed by the South's spokesmen that they be forbidden to cross state lines to agitate for civil rights. In 1968 something very close to that proposal was adopted by Congress.

To even the elementary student of psychology it is obvious that scapegoating, as practiced by the Massive Resisters, was an overt manifestation of a deep-seated prejudice against blacks and liberals.[7] True, the segregationists were neither original nor unique in their objectification and institutionalization of fear-hate reactions, since this is an old American as well as a general human behavioral trait. But if they were not original scapegoaters, they were among the most persistent practitioners of the art in modern times.

In functional terms, scapegoats are analogous to witches, and witchcraft is probably as old as the human race. It seems clear that the segregationists viewed the NAACP's leaders and "outside agitators" as New England Calvinists viewed witches in the seventeenth century: as fiendishly demonic beings endowed with "evil eyes" and the power to mesmerize innocent people by a kind of magic brainwashing. Extending the analogy, one might say that such happenings as the Klan's big rallies with their ceremonial cross-burnings stood in the tradition of the ancient Chinese bonfires which sought, through stylized rites, to exorcise evil spirits and thereby maximize community peace and harmony. Whatever else it is, scapegoating comes down to a kind of conspiratorial fantasizing, which Richard Hofstadter has called the "paranoid style of politics."[8] And while this phenomenon is doubtless characteristic of all mass movements, whether of the left or the right, it would appear that counterrevolutionaries excel in its practical application.

In the Kantian world of counterrevolution, reality is what resisting leaders, steeped in myth and symbolism, perceive (or believe) it to be. It logically follows, therefore, that the Massive Resisters' icons, myths, demons, and scapegoats were apocryphal to the degree that they were reality-distorters, but at the same time canonical in the sense that they became institutionalized as the hard core of the true believers' faith.

Today only an innocent from another world would deny that myths and symbols play a crucial role in structuring our patterns of social and political behavior, particularly in the "negative" directions of confusion, mystification, and distortion. If the full truth is ever known, it may well be that all right-wing, backlash movements will stand revealed as metaphors representing man's search for his primordial roots and his foredoomed efforts to retrieve a golden past that never was, save in the imaginings of the backward-looking mind.

7.

Massive Resistance Programs

I. OVERALL STRATEGY

POLITICAL COUNTERREVOLUTIONS such as Massive Resistance do not develop neatly in straight lines. They move forward, then backward, and quite often sideways as their leadership elites maneuver for tactical advantage. During the course of their history, they achieve sudden triumphs and equally sudden reversals. At any given moment their pace and direction will be determined by three things: the actions of their revolutionary antagonists, their own initiatives and momentum, and the accidents of chance. But throughout they are characterized by one dominating theme— the effort to bring about a restoration of a collapsing social system. In the case of Massive Resistance, that meant the pre-1954 Jim Crow system, when white supremacy in the South was still legitimate and morally respectable.

While the South's tutelary geniuses had provided the basic anti-Brown strategy in the Southern Manifesto, it remained for the region's governors, attorneys general, state legislators, and city councilmen to make supplementary strategy decisions that would transform the Massive Resistance idea into a viable counterrevolutionary policy. This they proceeded to do—with an Old South panache—in a series of legislative enactments, city ordinances, legal decisions, and executive orders. Once the leaders had clearly defined the movement's strategy and tactical programs, it fell to the South's policemen, sheriffs, constables, state troopers, local judges, school officials, lower-echelon bureaucrats, and agency attorneys to implement and defend these against attacks by the egalitarians.

The Massive Resistance strategists and tacticians were seeking to reestablish a static world, based upon the mythic—and thus "sacred"—principles of tradition and legitimacy. In the case of the South, this obviously meant trying to revitalize the myths of white supremacy and states'-rights federalism. The disagreements that arose within the movement were largely over tactics—over how and where they should confront the forces of the egalitarian revolution. And though they never said so publicly, the strategists of Massive Resistance clearly adhered to the principle that the end—saving Jim Crow—justified any means.

The closer one studies the historical record, the more one is compelled to concede the cleverness of the tactical ruses concocted by the segregationists. The tragic thing about all this is that their innovative ingenuity might better have been used to grapple with the *real* problems—such as poverty and inequality—that faced both the South and the nation in the fifties. Only in the past few years have the South's leaders begun to deal with these in a serious way.

II. 1956 TACTICS

B Y 1956, when most of the South's legislatures were meeting in their second post-Brown sessions, the pace of events had radically altered the southern *Zeitgeist*. Massive Resistance was in the process of becoming a flesh-and-blood reality, not just an abstraction, and signs of mounting defiance were visible on every hand. That defiance, still for the most part legal, was symbolized by the numerous anti-integration laws that southern legislatures were now racing to adopt.

Alabama's legislature approved a "freedom of choice" bill and set August 28 as the date for a referendum on a series of constitutional amendments that would permit abolition of the public schools in certain circumstances. It likewise adopted an interposition resolution as well as a memorial petitioning the Supreme Court to modify its desegregation holdings so that violence might be averted.

Georgia's general assembly, not to be outdone by Alabama, also passed an interposition resolution. At about the same time it enacted into law bills that enabled the governor to close schools under desegregation orders, allowed the lease of school property, permitted teachers to receive retirement benefits if they transferred to private schools, forbade entry into state-owned property closed by state officials, required all law enforcement agencies to enforce segregation laws, and authorized state legal counsel to represent state officials who might be sued for enforcing segregation laws.

Keeping in step with Alabama and Georgia, Mississippi's solons passed an interposition resolution as well as resolutions commending the state's congressional delegation for opposing school desegregation. In addition they established a State Sovereignty Commission to resist "federal encroachment," forbade public officials to comply with court integration decrees, repealed compulsory school laws, made it obligatory for teachers to list the organizations they belonged to, and, with the NAACP in mind, outlawed the fomenting or solicitation of litigation.

As in 1955 the South Carolina legislature was quite active in the field of anti-integration policy making. Among other things, it adopted an interposition resolution, forbade the spending of tax monies on integrated schools, authorized county sheriffs to make school assignments in emergency situations, prohibited NAACP members from holding state or local government jobs, set up a commission to investigate NAACP activities at the state's black colleges, and extended the life of an agency set up in 1951 with the task of studying all phases of the school crisis.

In its 1956 regular session the Virginia general assembly's major action was the adoption of an interposition resolution, which denounced the Supreme Court's "illegal encroachment upon our sovereign powers," and urged other states to "check this and further encroachment by the Supreme Court, through judicial legislation, upon the reserved powers of the states." Two days after the general assembly adjourned, the Southern Manifesto was introduced into Congress, giving an authoritative imprimatur to the strategy of Massive Resistance. The Virginia counterrevolutionaries quickly laid plans for a special summer session of the legislature to construct Massive Resistance dikes throughout the state.

Louisiana's legislature met in late May and became the sixth southern state to adopt an interposition resolution. As a footnote to that action, it is interesting that not one of the twenty sponsors of the resolution was a "Long man"—i.e., a supporter of the incumbent governor, Earl K. Long. Moreover, though no votes were recorded against the resolution, nine representatives and two senators abstained from voting.

The 1956 session of the Louisiana legislature was literally swamped with anti-integration bills, most of them masterminded by one of the state's leading charismatic demagogues, Senator William Rainach. The legislators eventually passed ten segregation bills that directly affected the operations of the public schools, of which three were considered of more than passing significance. One suspended the compulsory attendance law for students affected by school integration. A second made it easier to dismiss regular employees of the school system. A third had as its object the freezing of segregation in the schools of New Orleans.

In 1956 the states of Florida, North Carolina, and Virginia held special summer legislative sessions to shore up their segregation defenses. The Florida legislature approved a five-point program, which Governor LeRoy Collins, a moderate pragmatist, predicted would allow the state to keep its school system segregated indefinitely. Most of the drafting of the Florida bills had been supervised by Attorney General Richard W. Ervin, who, like Attorney General Cook of Georgia, served as his state's chief legal officer throughout the first decade of Massive Resistance. Ervin's bills were based on a series of recommendations put forth by the so-called Fabisinski Committee, a group of retired lawyers and judges appointed by Governor Collins to propose new anti-integration legislation. The report produced by the Fabisinski Committee (the chairman was a retired circuit court judge from Pensacola) revealed the extent to which the leading lawyers of Florida and her sister states had cast aside their role of moral educators of their people to head down the low road of militant backlash.[1] It would be hard to overemphasize the fact that when the "best people" of an area defy the law of the land, they in effect give to the "lower classes" a green light to go on a rampage of law-breaking and civil disorder. It is more than a little ironic that those white southerners who in the 1960's screamed loudest for "law and order" were precisely the ones who in the previous decade had contributed most to the erosion of both.

North Carolina's general assembly met in special session for less than a week, from July 23 through July 27, and generally disappointed the zealots and charismatic demagogues. The shortness of the session was a tribute to the political leadership and pragmatic moderation of Governor Luther Hodges and his Advisory Committee on Education. The legislators did approve the so-called "Pearsall Plan," which was a series of constitutional amendments (approved by the voters on September 8) providing for a private tuition payment system and "local option" elections on the issue of closing schools under court integration orders.[2] The legislators also adopted a "resolution of protest" against the Supreme Court but defeated efforts to transform it into a resolution of interposition.

In its 1956 month-long special session, the Virginia general assembly passed more than a score of new anti-integration measures, all of which were signed into law by Governor Stanley, a recent convert to all-out Massive Resistance. The Virginia laws were designed to provide a four-line-defense-in-depth against school desegregation. The first defensive line would be a new pupil placement board, to be appointed by the governor, which would relieve local school boards of the responsibility of assigning pupils to specific schools. The second line was to be the automatic closing of any school which local officials, voluntarily or involuntarily, might seek to integrate. The third line involved the making of tuition grants to pupils attending private schools. And the fourth and final line would be the complete shutting off of state funds to any locality that integrated its public schools. There was a good deal of sentiment at the session for a "local option" program of the kind North Carolina had adopted. But Governor Stanley insisted on a uniform statewide policy as the best way of avoiding *any* desegregation, and his wishes prevailed.

There was a clear counterrevolutionary philosophy underpinning the new Virginia program, which was made quite explicit in this provision in one of the laws:

> *Every action authorized and taken in conformity with the provisions of this act shall be and is hereby declared to be the act of the General Assembly of Virginia and an act of the governor of Virginia and an act taken on behalf of the sovereign [sic] commonwealth of Virginia, and if any suit . . . be instituted relative thereto, the same shall be regarded and is hereby declared to be a suit . . . against the commonwealth of Virginia.*

A close scrutiny of the South's 1956 legislative record permits at least three general conclusions. One, most of the southern legislators in 1956—all of whom of course were white—were literally obsessed with the politics of backlash, and showed no intention whatever of facilitating Brown's implementation. Two, almost every one of the tactical ploys used by the Massive Resisters first surfaced in 1956. And three, while there was no regional planning of state legislative programs to combat integration, there was a close similarity among the programs adopted by the various states.

Few of the South's 1956 tactical ploys would survive review by the federal courts, but that did not prevent their achieving an enormous popularity among white southerners. Among the most popular were special committees set up to plan anti-integration legislation, withdrawal of a state's consent to be sued, abolition of compulsory school laws, harassment of the NAACP, providing tuition grants for "private" schools, pupil placement laws in which the racial factor was concealed, adoption of interposition resolutions, and legislative legitimation of "segregation by choice." Though interposition became the most widely touted tool in the

Resisters' 1956 kit, it is not clear that it was the most effective obstacle to school desegregation.[3]

One could make a very good case for the proposition that the most effective anti-Brown tool of the South was not interposition but the various commissions and committees which the southern states set up in the mid-1950's to study ways and means of evading compliance with Brown. These public bodies bore a variety of names, but they had a common purpose: to lay the foundations for the lawful avoidance of public school desegregation. South Carolina set up one of the first of these bodies, called the Gressette Committee, which published a number of reports suggesting new segregation laws. Georgia created a Commission on Education in 1953, and its powers to prepare legislation were extended in 1957. As noted earlier, Florida had a Special Advisory Committee (the so-called Fabisinski Committee), which rendered its report on July 16, 1956. North Carolina and Arkansas also created important Advisory Committees on Education which had the power to make recommendations for official action with respect to the public schools. The governor of Texas, just a few weeks after Brown II was announced, appointed a Texas Advisory Committee to find ways of preventing "forced integration." In 1956 the Louisiana legislature extended the life of the influential Joint Legislative Committee (created in 1954) for the purpose of "carrying on and conducting the fight to maintain segregation of the races" by drafting appropriate legislation and compiling relevant data. Virginia had its "Gray Commission," whose recommendations strongly influenced the course of legislation in that state. Mississippi and Arkansas had what were called State Sovereignty Commissions, and the Mississippi Commission may well have been the most significant of all these planning bodies. It is not stretching a point to say that virtually all the Massive Resistance programs which the southern states set up after the mid-1950's were either suggested or directly developed by these committees.

One further tactical development in 1956 merits mention here. That was the special investigation of the District of Columbia's integrated schools which a subcommittee of the House District of Columbia Committee began in the fall of 1956. Mississippi's John Bell Williams, a subcommittee member, seems to have suggested the inquiry, and James C. Davis of Georgia was the subcommittee's chairman. Chief counsel for the group was William E. Gerber, who would later insist, according to the *Arkansas Gazette*, that blacks are definitely inferior to whites. Of the six subcommittee members, four were southern segregationists.

The subcommittee released its report in December 1956. The report turned out to be little more than a propaganda broadside against the goals of the egalitarian revolution and a strong brief for segregated education. Central to the findings of the investigators was the conclusion "that the integrated school system in the District of Columbia cannot be copied by those who seek an orderly and successful school operation."[4] The four southerners went further and asked "that racially separate public schools be reestablished." The report was only a minor setback to the egalitarian cause, but it created quite a stir in the South, where the slightest pro-segregation propaganda had a way of becoming holy writ overnight.

III. 1957 TACTICS

DURING 1957 southern legislatures passed around fifty new bills, with local or statewide application, whose purpose was to prevent or at least limit school desegregation. This harvest of new laws brought to more than 140 the number of anti-integration measures that the counterrevolutionary South had adopted since May 1954. A total of thirteen southern and border-state legislatures were in session during the first part of 1957, but five of those failed to pass additional segregation bills.

Actually most of the 1957 enactments were variations on now familiar themes, though a few were more or less original. Thus, in Florida, the legislature passed a local act forbidding teachers of one race to instruct pupils of another. In neighboring Georgia a resolution was approved calling for the impeachment of six justices of the U. S. Supreme Court. Tennessee's legislators approved bills authorizing sexual segregation in public schools and adjusting transportation, pupil transfer, and school consolidation laws in order that the state would have more up-to-date laws to deal with new situations. And in Texas the legislature enacted a strong measure absolutely forbidding desegregation at any school without the express approval of a majority of the voters in whatever school district might be slapped with a court order to desegregate.

"Non-racial" pupil placement laws continued to be popular, as Tennessee and Texas joined the list of states that had adopted them. Arkansas in 1957 released any student from enrolling in or attending any school that enrolled white and black children. This was really a copy of a Virginia law that had been passed in the previous year.

Georgia and South Carolina, like several other southern states, used the pocketbook method of closing schools faced with imminent desegregation. The Georgia General Appropriations Act for the fiscal year 1957 provided that no tax funds should be used for any public educational facility that did not segregate the races, even if court orders forbade such segregation. A few months earlier South Carolina's legislators had passed a law providing for the stoppage of funds to schools under desegregation orders, and further providing that funds would be restored to such schools only when segregation had been restored.

By the end of 1957 more than half the southern states had modified their compulsory school attendance laws in order to legalize the closing of any public schools that might be integrated. Georgia's approach was fairly typical, when the legislature in 1957 authorized the governor to suspend the state's school attendance law whenever he deemed such action necessary because of rioting, insurrection, public disorder, disturbance of the peace, natural calamity, or disaster. Also in 1957 Florida and Texas provided for the closing of their public schools if federal military force were used in the vicinity of a school. Florida's law-makers went further and provided for local boards to supervise the reassignment of pupils in the event of such a closure.

In five states that had rejected total Massive Resistance in favor of token desegregation—Arkansas, Delaware, Texas, Oklahoma, and Tennessee—the legislatures adopted additional measures aimed at circumscribing school desegregation. Florida's legislature, on the other hand, rejected more pro-segregation bills than it approved.

North Carolina in 1957 became the first of the South Atlantic states to accept token desegregation. This took place in the cities of Greensboro, Winston-Salem, and Charlotte. Meanwhile the Tar Heel legislators refused to expand the anti-integration programs adopted in the two previous years.

The high point of 1957 was the confrontation at Little Rock, which occurred at the opening of the new school year. Though Massive Resistance lost at Central High, the shock waves from that showdown gave a new impetus to the South's counterrevolution and led to the enactment of a rash of "Little Rock bills" in a number of southern states, the purpose of which was to prevent further federal "usurpation" of states' rights.

As the officials of Mississippi and Alabama dominated the news in the Deep South, the politicians of Virginia held center stage in the upper South. No public school desegregation took place in Virginia in 1957, but the voters were treated to a spirited gubernatorial election in which Massive Resistance was virtually the only issue. The Democratic candidate was Attorney General Lindsay Almond, Jr., who had played a big role in helping school districts fight desegregation suits. His opponent was Ted Dalton, who had almost won in 1953 and who campaigned for local option in the belief that the courts would strike down the state's Massive Resistance laws. Judge Walter Hoffman did, indeed, strike down as unconstitutional Virginia's pupil placement law in the midst of the campaign, but Almond won the election. His victory was assured by two things—all-out support from the Byrd organization and President Eisenhower's dispatch of federal troops to Little Rock.

IV. 1958 Tactics

THE SOUTH's 1958 harvest of anti-Brown legislation included a number of strictly local acts, fourteen major statutes, five resolutions, and two constitutional amendments. The bulk of the

year's legislating was done by five of the most defiant states—
Georgia, Louisiana, Mississippi, South Carolina, and Virginia.
The new measures, added to those approved earlier, brought to
more than 190 the number of pro-segregation bills passed by
southern legislatures since 1954.

The most popular, and extreme, measures adopted in 1958
were contingent school closing laws. The legislatures of Louisiana,
Mississippi, and Virginia passed such laws. The Louisiana law
stated flatly that the governor could close any racially mixed public school or any school that was under court orders to integrate
its facilities. Furthermore, the law provided that parish and city
school boards could transfer the property of a closed school to
a private agency for the operation of a private nonsectarian
school.

Mississippi's school closing law authorized the governor to
close institutions of higher learning or public schools when he
believed such action would be in the state's interest or would
promote public peace and tranquility. By the end of the year, at
least seven southern states had approved some kind of legislation
facilitating the closure of integrated schools. Most of the school
closing laws were a direct consequence of the 1957 Little Rock
crisis.

South Carolina's legislature, one of the bastions of Massive
Resistance, approved but one new act in 1958 directly relating to
the segregation crisis. This act authorized the state's attorney general to inspect periodically the records of non-profit organizations
that did business within the state. The NAACP, though not specifically mentioned in the act, was clearly the main organization the
legislators had in mind. The South Carolina legislators made a
tactical blunder when they wrote into the educational section of
their general appropriations act an old racist provision to the effect that appropriated funds were to be spent "for racially segregated schools only." This language, of course, had long been
common in the southern states, but its continued use after Brown
was *prima facie* evidence of an intention to defy the law of the
land, as subsequent litigation would demonstrate.

The Virginia general assembly did not make a lot of dramatic
news in 1958 but it added seven new laws to the more than twenty

Massive Resistance measures already on the statute books. The new legislation reflected a hardening of counterrevolutionary sentiment in "Byrdland" and a heating up of the politics of conflict. Among other things, the legislators created a commission on constitutional government, amended the state's pupil placement law, authorized the contingent closing of public schools, established a new Committee on Offenses Against the Administration of Justice, and required the filing of information about membership rosters and financial standing by non-profit organizations "engaged in the unauthorized practice of law."

The legislatures of Mississippi and Louisiana adopted constitutional amendments in their continuing fight to save segregation. The purpose of the Louisiana amendment was to expand the legislature's authority in the field of education to cover private as well as public schools. Mississippi's was a technical amendment intended to simplify somewhat the constitutional amending process.

The legislatures of Georgia, Mississippi, South Carolina, and Virginia adopted resolutions in 1958 that were broadly anti-integration. Georgia's took note of violent incidents in New York schools and expressed the hope that local authorities there would be allowed to handle their own problems. South Carolina's condemned the dispatch of federal troops to Little Rock. Virginia's, taking aim at the NAACP, requested "the Virginia Bar Association to take certain actions relative to the unethical and unauthorized practice of law . . . [in the case of] desegregation suits." The Mississippi legislature passed a couple of resolutions, one calling for a legislative investigation of the NAACP, the other requesting the state health department to make a study of diseases believed unique to whites and blacks. Presumably such a study would reveal significant genetic differences between whites and blacks and thus buttress the basic premise of white supremacy.

Despite the unparalleled efforts which the South's legislators and executive branch officials had made in the four years since Brown I to devise effective anti-integration programs, the foundations of the Jim Crow system were continuing to give way as 1958 drew to a close. The University of Florida was finally segregated in 1958 as a direct result of an NAACP suit. And at the public school level, it was estimated that 400,000 black students attended desegregated schools, as compared to 350,000 in 1957. It was also reported in 1958 that 790 of 2,890 southern and border-state school districts had desegregated their facilities. This still, however, was only token integration, since more than two and a half million black children remained in Jim Crow schools. But the important thing was that the elaborate dikes of segregation were not holding back the egalitarian revolution.

V. 1959 TACTICS

THE DECLINE in the quantity and quality of backlash legislation that began in 1957 continued through the end of the decade. The zealots in southern legislatures introduced about as many pro-segregation bills as in previous years, but most of them failed of adoption.

On January 28 Virginia's general assembly met in a special session, which had been called by Governor Lindsay Almond as a result of pressure from the Defenders of State Sovereignty. Since Arlington County was then under a court order to admit four black pupils to its Stratford Junior High School on February 2, the segregationist legislators faced a crucial policy decision. Should they pursue their policy of total Massive Resistance to the bitter end or should they accept token integration as inevitable? As President Eisenhower described the Virginia showdown at a press conference, "it comes down to the question of whether any citizen, either in official or civilian life, is ready to obey the laws of his state and his nation."

Governor Almond addressed the general assembly on Wednesday, January 28, and his speech turned out to be a milestone in the history of Massive Resistance. The speech, of course, contained the ritualistic standbys of southern oratory—condemnation of the Supreme Court, assertion of state sovereignty, comments on the evils of race mixing—but these were not the heart of the speech. The heart was a surprising admission that total Massive Resistance was no longer possible in Virginia for the reason that most of the state's anti-integration programs had been invalidated either by federal courts or the Virginia Supreme Court of Appeals.

Almond rejected pleas from the zealots and extremists for a last-ditch fight against Brown's implementation by saying:

> The police power cannot be asserted to thwart or override the decree of a court of competent jurisdiction, state or federal. . . .
>
> Contrary to the opinion of some, I cannot conceive how the Pupil Placement Act can be asserted . . . as a buffer . . . between the . . . superior power of the federal government and the operation of a segregated school. That which the state is powerless to do it cannot confer upon an administrative agency.[5]

Concerning legislative proposals, the Governor warned against new segregation laws and simply recommended that the legislators "enact the emergency measures which I shall submit, and then stand in recess to receive further recommendations" from a new commission the Governor would appoint.

Against the wishes of the zealots, the 1959 special session of the Virginia legislature in effect repealed the state's panoply of Massive Resistance statutes. The legislators also provided for compulsory attendance without mention of race, for return of control to local school boards, and for the financial structuring of local boards. All of these actions became virtually inevitable after a United States District Court completely undermined Massive Resistance by holding that Virginia could not close its public schools to avoid the effect of the law of the land as interpreted by the Supreme Court.

In February 1959 fifty-three black pupils were admitted to eleven formerly all-white schools in four Virginia communities. In some instances, however, white students withdrew from desegregating schools and finished the 1958–59 school year at segregated private schools that were now springing up all over the state.

The collapse of Massive Resistance in Virginia in 1959 was a decisive event in the history of the South's counterrevolution. And it is well to recall that the admission of black pupils to white schools, though doubtless resented by a majority of whites, took place without any mob violence or abuse of black pupils. The Almond administration had made it plain that violence would not be tolerated, and none broke out. Violence may also have been avoided by the fact that school desegregation occurred in large communities with adequate law enforcement agencies.

Down in Arkansas, the legislature, still smarting from the frustrations of Little Rock, passed additional bills, all approved by the Faubus administration and all designed to confine school desegregation to the narrowest possible scope. The most significant of these bills was an amendment to a 1958 law which, following the outlines of a recently enacted Virginia bill, authorized tuition grants to students enrolled in private schools. Arkansas and Virginia thus joined four other southern states which by the end of the fifties had approved this increasingly popular Massive Resistance program. The other states were North Carolina (special session, 1956), Louisiana (1958), Georgia (1956), and Alabama (special session, 1956). When a federal court invalidated the Arkansas Tuition Grant Act later in the summer of 1959, it became evident that this ploy of the segregationists would be no more than a temporary (but costly) obstacle to Brown's implementation.

Georgia's legislators continued to be enthralled by the mythology of Massive Resistance, and in their 1959 session they adopted six new major segregation bills. Governor Vandiver had requested these. And though he would later become a racial moderate, at this point Vandiver was still proclaiming that Georgia would tolerate *no* amount of desegregation—token or otherwise. Two of the Georgia bills dealt with higher education, where desegregation appeared to be most likely. One empowered the governor to close any unit of the university system when necessary to preserve "peace, dignity and good order in the state." The other required college applicants to be under 25 if they were to be eligible for admission to state institutions without special permission.

The 1959 retreat of the border states from Massive Resistance was dramatized by the Maryland general assembly's ratification by joint resolution of the fourteenth amendment to the U. S. Constitution. Though of no practical significance, this action was symbolically important, for it evidenced Maryland's determination to accept peacefully whatever degree of desegregation might be required in the state. This seems to have been the first *pro*-integration measure adopted by the state's legislators since 1951.[6]

Elsewhere the political counterrevolution was moving in fits and starts. Florida's solons adopted a bill providing for the mechanics of a private school system. Segregation leaders in Louisiana thwarted a move by state administration forces to ease the state's voter registration laws, as moderate Governor Earl K. Long won his freedom from a state mental institution. The Alabama legislature, in almost continuous session during the year, adopted several new anti-integration bills, including one to hinder the mass registration of blacks. But in Strom Thurmond's home state, the general assembly failed to pass any new pro-segregation laws.

Looking back on 1959 and the decade of the fifties, one cannot avoid the conclusion that the towering edifice of Massive Resistance which the South's counterrevolutionaries constructed with an inspired ad hockery strategy came down in the end to little more than a briar patch of futility, frustration, and byzantine complexities. Certainly Virginia's rejection of Massive Resistance in favor of "local option," belated though it was, portended the eventual collapse of the entire movement. The segregationists continued to oppose even token integration, but it was now plain that tokenism, not Massive Resistance, would be the wave of the future.

VI. TACTICS OF 1960's

By 1960 well over 200 pro-segregation statutes, resolutions, and constitutional amendments had been adopted by the counterrevolutionary South in the desperate hope of delaying as long as possible the full implementation of Brown. And though southern legislatures, particularly those in the Deep South, continued for a few years to legislate against integration, they rarely came up with any gambits that had not been tried in the fifties.

In 1961, when twelve southern and border-state legislatures were in session, segregation was the dominant issue in only two states. Those states were Georgia and Louisiana, and in both states the main thrust of new racial legislation was to soften the earlier "segregation or no schools" stand. For the first time since 1957, Arkansas' legislators convened in 1961 with segregation only a very minor issue, though Governor Faubus did propose two constitutional amendments on the subject. It is also worth noting that the 1961–62 school year was the first without racial violence in the South's schools since 1954.

Those southern legislators and executive officials who began to change their attitudes in the 1960's may well have been consciously reacting to a decline in extremism reported in public opinion polls. Thus the Gallup Poll reported in early 1961 that 76 per cent of southerners "believe now that the day will come when white and colored persons will generally share the same public accommodations in the southern states." The comparable figure had been 45 per cent of those interviewed in 1957 and 53 per cent in 1958. A large majority of white southerners, however, still opposed the Brown decision.

One of the South's most cunning and devious tactics of the 1960's was to integrate whatever schools the courts ordered integrated and then to punish black teachers and principals by easing them out of their jobs in the integrated schools. This violation of the spirit of Brown was nothing less than a tragedy for those well educated members of the South's "black aristocracy" who had found a niche in the semi-autonomous black schools of the old Jim Crow system. For despite the disadvantages of "Negro Education," the system had provided reasonably pleasant employment and security for tens of thousands of black educational professionals over several generations.

By the mid-1960's there was almost a one-to-one relationship between the number of southern schools desegregated and the number of black principals eliminated from the school systems. In quantitative terms black teachers were hurt more than black principals since there were more black teachers to begin with. But because of the principals' demonstrated talents and high standing in the black communities, their ruthless elimination was a severe setback for the entire black community and for the hopes of integrationists. Moreover, since the hiring and firing of teachers in most southern schools has traditionally been handled by principals, the reduction in the number of black principals inevitably led to a decline in the recruitment of new black teachers. These developments were taking place at a time when the South's young blacks desperately needed the image of hope, authoritative leadership, and respectability which the black principals and teachers had effectively provided.

A few statistics about the workings of this displacement will illustrate the mischief caused by this tactic of the Massive Resisters. According to a 1965 National Education Association Task Force Report, Kentucky had 1,440 black teachers in 1955 and 39,788 black students. Ten years later the state's public school system had 1,399 black teachers and 55,215 black students, which means that during the decade black teachers were decreasing by 3 per cent as black student enrollment was increasing by 15 per cent. Furthermore a survey of the Kentucky State Department of Education revealed that in the 1969–70 school year there were only thirty-six black principals left in the entire state—twenty-two of whom were in the Louisville system—compared to around 200 in 1954.

In Maryland, another border state, a similar development was taking place. In the year of the Brown decision the Maryland school system had forty-four black high school principals and 167 white principals. In 1968 the number of black principals had declined to thirty-one while the number of white principals had increased to 280. It also appears that there was a decline in the number of black principals in all eleven counties where there was an increase in the number of high schools. In addition, seven of the twenty-four Maryland school districts phased out *all* their black principals in elementary schools between 1954 and 1968. True, Baltimore increased its black elementary principals in this period, but the new principals were assigned to schools wholly or largely black.

The situation in the Deep South in the 1960's was even more

uncongenial to black administrators. In May of 1969, for example, the Georgia Teachers and Education Association reported that in thirty selected school districts the number of black principals declined from 16 per cent of the total in 1963–64 to seven per cent in 1968–69. In Florida's Dade County (Miami), the only black high school principal left in the school system was to retire in the early 1970's. And in Alabama, Mississippi, and Louisiana, black teachers and principals were often phased out completely when unitary school systems replaced dual ones.

The future of the "redundant" black principals did not seem bright in the 1960's. Usually they were not fired outright, but if they did not retire they were forced into jobs that were really demotions. These included assistant principalships (under white superiors), classroom teaching, counseling, and supply and maintenance work. Their position seemed even more desperate when it became obvious that the federal government intended to do little if anything to ease their plight.

Another well-known ploy of the Massive Resisters in the sixties was to set up publicly aided private schools for whites while abandoning the integrated public schools to the blacks. This, of course, meant that the blacks found themselves segregated again—this time in formerly all white schools. The counterrevolutionaries made this ploy feasible by the numerous bills they got southern legislatures to pass in the fifties which provided "tuition grants" from tax funds to students enrolled in private schools. Eight states eventually passed such bills.

Statistical data concerning the number of white students attending the new quasi-public "private" schools in the 1960's were hard to come by, but it seemed to be increasing throughout the decade. The best estimate was that more than 450 private schools had been set up in the South by 1970 with the sole purpose of helping white students avoid integrated school situations. The Citizens' Council School Foundation alone had 500 white students in its three "segregation academies" in 1969 and 5,000 in 1970. It was also learned in 1970 that a group of Mississippi banks, two of which were headed by members of a presidential advisory committee on school desegregation, had loaned the Citizens' Council $600,000 to operate segregated schools in the Jackson area. Even the U. S. Internal Revenue Service seemed to be cooperating with the private schools when it announced that it would grant tax-exempt status to any school that would declare an open-admissions policy, whether or not the policy were subsequently implemented. By 1970 most of the private schools had made such a policy declaration—knowing it to be meaningless—and thereby gained tax-exempt status.

Not surprisingly the "segregation academies" were most popular in the Deep South, notably in those districts where blacks have traditionally outnumbered whites. Experience seemed to suggest that once black enrollment passed 35 per cent, all or most whites would soon forsake the integrated schools. The greater the white exodus, the less willing white legislators were to vote adequate appropriations for the nearly all-black public schools.

There were, however, serious problems attending the carrying out of this Massive Resistance program. First of all, there was the question of the constitutionality of any kind of state aid to segregated private schools. This question was apparently resolved against the Massive Resisters when the U. S. Supreme Court in December of 1971 affirmed a lower court decision banning federal tax-exempt status for private schools set up to avoid public school desegregation. This was a severe blow to the hopes of the private schools, for without some form of state aid most of them could not long survive.

There was also a socio-economic problem involved which had the effect of heightening class tensions in the white community. This resulted from the fact that most of the private schools charged a monthly tuition fee of forty dollars or more. Obviously such a fee had the effect of excluding poor whites from enrolling and making the schools exclusively upper class. There was much grumbling among lower class whites about this inequity.

Of equal importance, the private schools faced serious personnel and physical plant problems, since new schools are expensive to build and teachers are quite reluctant to leave the security of the public schools for an uncertain future in private schools. In some instances, the plant difficulties were solved by leasing church properties. This, however, provoked the ire of moderate religionists and at the same time brought to the fore the issues of church-state separation and state aid to religion. Hoping to lure more teachers into the private schools, the states of Alabama, Arkansas, Georgia, Louisiana, and Virginia passed laws protecting teacher tenure in private institutions. These laws seem to have induced a number of southern teachers to make the switch from public to private schools.

Yet another deliberate tactic of the Massive Resisters when tokenism had become a reality was to have local white school boards make the reality of court-ordered desegregation unpleasant and irksome for black students. As revealed in 1970 by testimony before the Senate Select Committee on Equal Educational Opportunity, this was clearly a premeditated tactic that was tenaciously pushed. It involved such things as "internal segregation" of school facilities, pre-dawn bus rides for black students, hostility from white teachers, harassment by white students, large-scale expulsion of blacks for trivial reasons, and the defacing or removal from school property of pictures of such black luminaries as Booker T. Washington and George Washington Carver. The rationale behind this tactic was obvious. The segregationists hoped to make life so miserable for blacks in the unitary schools that they would get fed up and demand the return of their own schools where they at least had a genuine sense of identity. Some blacks did get fed up and made such demands (as CORE did, for example, in the 1970's), but most did not.

Perhaps the most widely publicized tactic of the South's counterrevolutionaries in the late sixties and early seventies was the ceaseless condemnation of school busing to achieve racial balance. This obsession with the alleged evils of busing was typified by this statement attributed to Governor John McKeithen of Louisiana: "I will not allow my children to be bused . . . to be treated like cattle." The issue was primarily an urban one. For by the late 1960's most of the small rural segregated schools in the South had been consolidated into large integrated community schools.

The anti-busing ploy did not really become a matter of great concern until desegregation plans drawn up by the Department of Health, Education and Welfare and approved by federal courts began to require, or at least to permit, busing of children to reduce racial imbalance within a given school system. The Massive Resisters rationalized their opposition to busing by citing such grounds as high cost, excessive time in transit, child fatigue, physical danger to the children, and the destruction of the neighborhood schools. It seems obvious, however, that these grounds were mere rationalizations, and that the white South's real cause for opposing busing was a social and ideological one. Put simply, the segregationists opposed busing because it had significantly reduced school segregation and for the first time brought thousands of poor black children the advantages of middle-class white schools. The segregationists conveniently forgot that they had never opposed busing of blacks to distant segregated schools before 1954 when the purpose of busing was to prevent, not further desegregation. They also ignored the fact that for years school authorities have been busing most white students in rural areas as well as students attending parochial and certain big city schools.

As a result of a series of court decisions requiring unitary school systems, Massive Resistance legislators could do little if anything to further their anti-busing program. Instead they had to depend on propaganda, inflammatory rhetoric, protest demonstrations by white parents, scare tactics, and political pressure directed against Congress and the President. Of the charismatic demagogues who took up the busing issue in the second decade of Massive Resistance, none got more political mileage out of it than George Wallace of Alabama.

The last Massive Resistance tactic to be discussed here was the pervasive use of southern courts and law enforcement agencies to harass blacks and keep token desegregation at an absolute minimum.[7] Instead of using their courts to facilitate the growing demands for social justice, large numbers of southern judges and court officials did everything in their power to frustrate the orderly implementation of Brown. In this tactic of obstructionism, the judges willingly cooperated with policemen who arrested integrationists, prosecutors who pressed flimsy charges against them, justices of the peace who summarily convicted them, and juries that were eager to convict "outside agitators" while acquitting klansmen and other segregationist troublemakers. This tactic led to such a perversion of the South's criminal justice system that it often seemed that the courthouse was the strategic center of Massive Resistance rather than the state house or governor's mansion where power politics is the accepted rule.

In the 1960's Alabama's Eugene ("Bull") Connor symbolized for much of the nation the South's legal-judicial authoritarianism. Elected police commissioner of Birmingham in 1937, Connor was reelected five times before losing office in 1962, when voters eliminated the city commission form of government. Connor, however, refused to give up his office, inasmuch as his term was not due to expire until 1965, but the Alabama Supreme Court ousted him in May, 1963. In the meantime he achieved world-wide notoriety during the Birmingham civil rights demonstrations of April, 1963. Within three weeks, Connor and his men arrested 400 demonstrators, including Martin Luther King, Jr. To help in controlling the demonstrators, Connor made extensive use of police dogs and fire hoses. He defended his use of the dogs by saying, "That's what we trained these dogs for—to enforce the law." In his later years Connor mellowed somewhat, and he died at the age of 75 in March, 1973, after suffering a stroke.

While law enforcement officals, especially those who belonged to the Klan or the Councils, were in a position to frustrate the goals of desegregationists, state and local judges were even more strategically placed to stymie the egalitarian revolution. Traditionally local court judges in the South, many of whom are mayors, have had but a rudimentary knowledge of the law and often have been little more than political hacks. Given that tradition, a large amount of "rigging" of southern justice against blacks was inevitable. This rigging, at its worst in Alabama and Mississippi, took several forms. It involved browbeating of civil rights defendants and their witnesses, admission of almost anything as evidence, the use of loosely drawn "breach of peace" statutes to convict peaceful demonstrators, holding court in odd places like gasoline stations, refusal to keep records of minor court litigation, and tacit encouragement to the police to ignore rights of litigants who happened to be black or who were linked to the civil rights movement. To be sure, some of the more outrageous convictions were later reversed in state or federal appellate courts. Reversal, however, always takes time and money, and in the meantime irreparable damage may have been done.

The rigging of southern legal and judicial institutions against integrationists seems, in retrospect, to have been among the most effective backlash tactics devised by the South's counterrevolution. It intimidated militant blacks and their white sympathizers and, by making a travesty of constitutional democracy, helped to keep even tokenism from the Deep South for almost a decade. When Massive Resistance was riding high, state legislators and governors got most of the credit for whatever victories the South won. It now appears that the region's judges and law enforcement officials were equally responsible for the movement's early successes and for the prolongation of the politics of conflict.

A tabular summary of the major kinds of anti-desegregation programs adopted by southern and border-state legislatures in the first decade after Brown can be found in Table A. One can also get some idea of the effectiveness of these programs in helping the South evade desegregation by studying the data contained in Table B (segregation-desegregation status for 1964–65) and Table C (college desegregation, 1964–65). Unfortunately, no statistics are available concerning the number of egalitarians victimized by southern "underlaw" in the ten-year period following Brown.

VII. PRESSURES FOR CONFORMITY

THE LEGISLATIVE, executive, and judicial programs that formed the core of Massive Resistance were designed not only to counter the initiatives of egalitarians in Washington and other parts of the nation. They were also clearly designed to control those liberals and moderates *within* the South who might be tempted, for whatever reason, to hop on the Brown revolution's bandwagon. Their purpose, in other words, was as much to enforce ideological conformity at home as to cripple the "subversion" of outside agitators.

The Massive Resisters tried to enforce conformity to the southern way of life by various means. Among these were character assassination of liberals, ad hominem argumentation, economic pressure on non-conformists, intimidation of educators and journalists, legal harassment of civil rights organizations, censorship of library and public school books, and the silent condonement, if not encouragement of physical violence. These pressures for conformity were most intense and effective in the late 1950's. It was not until the middle of the next decade that southern egalitarians began to speak out in significant numbers in support of desegregation.

One widely reported episode of the Massive Resistance era typifies rather well the extreme pressures for conformity that were everywhere in the counterrevolutionary South after 1954. The episode involved Alabama's "Big Jim" Folsom, who had never been more than a traditional segregationist, and who had once said, "I have sailed the seven seas of mankind and met the seven races of man, and there ain't no difference in any of them."

Folsom's troubles began when Harlem's Adam Clayton Powell was quoted as saying he had drunk Scotch with Folsom at the Alabama Governor's Mansion in the mid-1950's, at which time they had agreed the South's racial problems would eventually work themselves out. When word of this biracial "summit diplomacy" leaked out in Alabama, all hell broke loose. Indeed, the Powell matter became the chief issue when Folsom ran for governor in 1962. Although Folsom's answer to the charges was typically humorous, it was revelatory of the pressures he was feeling: "They say I sent my chauffeur out to pick up Adam Clayton Powell at the airport. Well, I did send my chauffeur out there. Would y'all have liked it if I had gone out there *myself*? And they say I drank Scotch with Adam Clayton Powell in the Governor's Mansion. Shucks, y'all know Big Jim don't drink fancy stuff like that. I drink hard likker like you folks." But the segregationists were not amused, and Folsom went down to defeat for making waves.

Of course, the Massive Resisters were never able to forge a monolithic consensus for their racist policies among the South's whites, let alone among blacks. The politics of conflict kept intruding. Yet for more than a decade, the Southwide pressures for conformity to the counterrevolutionary line were insidiously at work and dangerous to resist. By deceiving outsiders into thinking that southerners were solidly behind their leaders, this coerced conformity made it possible for the South's politicians to deal from positions of strength when negotiating with federal authorities. In this way it also helped prolong the life of the anti-Brown backlash.

The price that the South ultimately paid for turning the ideology of Massive Resistance into a rigid orthodoxy was considerable. It included the exile of many of the region's best minds, abridgement of vital press and speech freedoms, curtailment of the right of protest and free association, emasculation of religion and higher education, further estrangement from the mainstream of American life, alienation of many formerly docile blacks, and the rekindling of those postbellum fires of hate and racial bigotry that had been smoldering, and now and then surfacing, in the South since Appomattox. To outsiders, the price seemed exorbitant in light of the paucity of benefits gained, but the segregationists saw things from a different perspective. In terms of their perspective, no price could be too high if it saved Jim Crow.

Throughout its up-and-down career, Massive Resistance was bedeviled by the fundamental problem of reconciling its rigid ideology with the kind of tactical pragmatism that was necessary if headway were to be made against the egalitarian revolutionaries. Doubtless this problem has plagued all counterrevolutions of the past as well as many revolutions. But in the case of the Massive Resisters, the practical difficulties were compounded by their rejection of a basic democratic principle—i.e., the principle of peaceful, ongoing evolutionary change. Any ideology that rejects this principle makes it impossible for oppressed minorities to realize even their most limited objectives, and thus stimulates revolutionary demands for an overturn of the entire status quo. Only a handful of southern blacks went that far on the road of revolution, but in the late sixties blacks throughout the South were rethinking their options and strategies.

When none of the South's diversionary programs proved to be viable tactics for escaping Brown, the Massive Resisters were compelled to shift their *locus operandi* to the halls of Congress, federal court chambers, and, on occasion, to street and campus barricades. And while they occasionally scored victories in Congress, the courts, and on the streets, they eventually had to admit that there was no place to hide from the long reach of the Brown decision.

8.

Critical Confrontations

I. Non-violent Showdowns with the Courts

AFTER ITS CHRISTENING in 1956, the South's counterrevolution moved steadily from an incremental politics to an extremist, all-or-nothing strategy. Predictably this politics of conflict involved the Massive Resisters in a succession of critical, and sometimes violent, confrontations with federal authority, virtually all of which they lost. The first of these were non-violent showdowns with the state and federal courts. Following these came the violent encounters at Little Rock, New Orleans, Athens (Georgia), Ole Miss, and the University of Alabama. These in turn were paralleled, and followed, in the 1960's by bitter fights in Congress between the proponents and opponents of new civil rights legislation. In the six sections of this chapter, two of the three categories of showdowns—those with the courts and on the campuses—will be examined in detail. Chapter 9 will deal with the showdowns in Congress.

It is logical to commence this analysis with a discussion of judicial showdowns, for the federal judicary was undeniably the first federal agency to stand up to the Massive Resisters. Eventually the federal executive and legislative branches did their part in throwing back the South's counterrevolution. But their contributions came after the critical judicial decisions had been made, and were in a sense merely follow-up support of court orders. This was especially true of executive initiatives in the fifties and sixties.

Everybody now agrees that the Supreme Court's holdings in Brown I and Brown II were the catalytic sparks that precipitated the emerging egalitarian revolution. But having invalidated Jim Crow schools, the Supreme Court then left it up to the lower federal courts to supervise Brown's implementation at the local level and to decide to what other areas than education the Brown doctrine should be extended. Of course, state appellate courts also had a hand in overseeing the desegregation process, but by and large this task was the challenge and responsibility of the federal bench.

The judges most directly involved in segregation litigation after 1954 were those who served on the southern district courts and the Fourth and Fifth Circuit Courts, headquartered in Richmond and New Orleans respectively. In the peak years of Massive Resistance, there were fifty-eight judges assigned to the federal courts in the South—forty-eight serving on twenty-eight district courts and ten serving on two appeals courts. The majority of these judges were neither egalitarian revolutionaries nor anti-southern "outsiders." Rather they were native-born and native-trained southerners, who suddenly found themselves thrown into the vortex of the gravest domestic crisis the nation had known since the Civil War.

Except possibly for J. Waties Waring of South Carolina, the federal judges who were serving in the South when the Brown case began appear to have been at least traditional or nominal segregationists. Still, with a few exceptions at the district court level, these southern judges (especially those on the Fourth and Fifth Circuit Courts) resisted the extreme social and other pressures that sought to make them the last bastion of Jim Crow. Deliberately, and perhaps wisely, the Supreme Court had "passed the buck" to the lower federal courts. While the judges on those courts could hardly have been pleased with their new job of supervising the transition from dual to unitary schools, most of them carried out their responsibilities in this area with considerable skill and relative integrity.[1]

Initially, however, the situation was confused. So confused, in fact, that in their earliest exegeses of Brown, the lower federal courts seemed bent on limiting and restricting its total impact. Thus, in the summer of 1955 a three-judge federal court, composed of Judges John J. Parker, Armistead M. Dobie, and George Bell Timmerman, held further hearings in the Briggs case from Clarendon County, South Carolina, and chose to concentrate on what Brown I did not expressly say. The court's decision, announced by Judge Parker, assumed that the Constitution had an impact of negation only. Not surprisingly, the decision disappointed both black and white litigants.

It is true that in the Briggs case the three-judge court ordered the defendants to proceed toward desegregation. Yet it stopped short of requiring that this be accomplished in the 1955–56 school year. In a dictum much quoted by Massive Resisters, Judge Parker wrote:

> [*The Supreme Court*] *has not decided that the states must mix persons of different races in the schools or must deprive them of the right of choosing the schools they attend. What it has decided, and all that it has decided, is that a state may not deny to any person on account of race the right to attend any school that it maintains. . . . The Constitution, in other words, does not require integration. It merely forbids discrimination.*[2]

Parker's fine distinction (a question-begging one) between integration and non-discrimination or desegregation was a highly restrictive exegesis of Brown which was picked up and used by a number of federal courts as a valid precedent. Though the South's counterrevolutionaries clung to it as a "last straw" and eventually based the "freedom of choice" concept on it, the distinction was shot through with deficiencies. It ignored the whole question of the harm done by racial segregation. It implicitly accepted any kind of segregation not positively and presently mandated by statute. It overlooked the central constitutional issue of the legal *right* of

blacks to fully equal educational opportunities. And, in the final
analysis, it was logically inconsistent with Brown. But it was not
until the 1960's, in subsequent decisional law on the subject, that
the Supreme Court finally laid Judge Parker's Briggs dictum to
rest. In the meantime it had done substantial mischief.

In an amplification of Brown, the Fourth Circuit Court of
Appeals in July of 1955 invalidated segregation laws affecting
travel on city buses in Columbia, South Carolina. Two U. S. Supreme Court cases that antedated Brown provided the rationale
for this holding. In 1946 the Court in *Morgan* v. *Virginia* (328
U.S. 373) used the interstate-commerce concept to strike down a
Virginia statute requiring racial segregation on public buses crossing state lines. And in 1950 in *Henderson* v. *United States* (339
U.S. 816) it invalidated segregation of railroad dining-car facilities. In November of 1955 the Interstate Commerce Commission
struck another blow at transportation segregation by finally ter-
minating all racial segregation in trains and buses crossing state
lines as well as discrimination in rail and bus facilities such as
waiting rooms and restaurants. While these actions appeared to
have taken away every legal prop of the Jim Crow system of buses
and trains, city bus segregation continued to exist in many parts of
the South for quite some time. In Montgomery, Alabama, it took
a massive black boycott to end bus discrimination in that Deep
South city.

In the fall of 1955 state and federal courts in three southern
states invalidated constitutional or statutory provisions for public
school segregation, without, however, granting immediate relief to
black litigants. The supreme court of Florida, in a 5–2 ruling,
struck down the state's school segregation policy as a legal principle, declaring that compliance with the Brown holding "is our
inescapable duty." At about the same time, the supreme court of
Texas held that state schools there might proceed with desegregation without regard to state segregation statutes, since all school
laws and state constitutional provisions requiring racial segregation were now invalid. Associate Justice Few Brewster called
"utterly without merit" the argument that Texas segregation laws
were unaffected by Supreme Court decisions in the field of race.
Finally, in Memphis, Tennessee, Judge Marion S. Boyd, a

Tennessee-born and Tennessee-trained federal district judge, ruled that Tennessee's school segregation laws were all unconstitutional. He also approved a state-devised gradual desegregation program for the state's colleges. Though Judge Boyd insisted that the state make a good faith effort in the direction of school desegregation, he did not demand that the effort be a speedily consummated one. Like Judge Parker, Judge Boyd seemed bent on interpreting Brown in such a way as to give the defiant South the benefit of every doubt.

On November 7, 1955, the U. S. Supreme Court, pronouncing the single word "affirmed," applied its Brown holding to public recreation facilities. The judgment affirmed on that date was a decision of the Fourth Circuit Court outlawing segregation at Sandy Point Park, a state bathing beach on Chesapeake Bay, and at Fort Smallwood, a public beach operated by the city of Baltimore. At the same time, the Court vacated a decision of the Fifth Circuit Court at New Orleans which had sustained Atlanta's segregation policy on the Bobby Jones public golf course, and instructed the district court to follow the holding in the Maryland case. From the outset, one of the troublesome ambiguities in Brown had been the extent of its applicability, if any, to areas beyond the field of education. By the end of 1955 the Supreme Court had made it pretty clear that it was not likely to uphold any kind of state-coerced segregation of the races in public facilities that were tax-financed. But, of course, practice does not always immediately follow legal theory, since the two are often separated by a "politics gap." It would therefore require several more years of tedious litigation as well as remedial legislation by Congress before integration of the South's public parks, schools, colleges, beaches, hospitals, swimming pools, libraries, and golf courses became an accomplished fact. Integration of private facilities open to the public would prove to be an even more complicated problem.

Three more court opinions were announced in the summer of 1956 which foreshadowed the eventual collapse of total Massive Resistance in Virginia and Texas. On July 12, 1956, Judge John Paul, a federal district judge in Virginia, held that black plaintiffs were entitled to admission to the Charlottesville public schools on a non-racial basis, effective at the start of the new school year. In a sharp statement from the bench, Judge Paul took note of the evasive tactics of the Massive Resisters when he said, "I would close my eyes to . . . obvious facts if I did not realize that the State has been, for some months, pursuing a deliberate and well-conceived . . . 'policy of delay' in these cases."[3] That was hardly news to anybody in Virginia, but its articulation by a federal judge was not without significance.

Less than a month later U. S. District Judge Albert V. Bryan issued an injunction restraining Arlington County (Virginia) from continuing to segregate its schools on a racial basis. The order was to take effect on "January 31, 1957, in respect to elementary schools and at the beginning of the 1957–58 school year for junior and senior high schools."

A little earlier, on June 28, the U. S. Fifth Circuit Court held that the Mansfield, Texas, school board could not delay desegregation merely because of adverse public opinion in the community. The court's order stated that the defendants were to be "forever restrained from refusing admission . . . to any of the plaintiffs shown to be qualified in all respects."

In a case with somewhat broader ramifications, the U. S. Eighth Circuit Court held on October 25, 1956, that members of the Hoxie, Arkansas, school board and other school administrators had a federal right to be free from "direct and deliberate interference."[4] The Hoxie decision sustained a district judge's order enjoining leaders of the Capital Citizens' Council from obstructing in any way the desegregation of the local schools. Interest in the Hoxie case was heightened when U. S. Attorney General Herbert Brownell chose this occasion for his first post-Brown intervention on behalf of desegregation. Even more important, the outcome of the case made available to harassed school officials the injunctive protection of the federal judiciary. Judge Robert L. Taylor quickly made use of the Hoxie precedent in his handling of the well known counterrevolutionary agitator, John Kasper, who had been harassing the Clinton, Tennessee, school board. Generally speaking, however, neither southern school boards nor southern judges took advantage of the Hoxie precedent to facilitate the transition to unitary schools.

The year 1957 saw both an increase in southern resistance to

Brown and an increase in anti-segregation court decisions. On the last day of 1956, the U. S. Fourth Circuit Court unanimously affirmed lower court orders requiring the authorities of Charlottesville and Arlington County to desegregate their schools. And it was less than two weeks later that Judge Hoffman shocked Virginia's Massive Resisters by calling the state's pupil placement law "unconstitutional on its face." While it is true that the Fourth Circuit Court had earlier validated North Carolina's pupil placement law, Judge Hoffman was careful to distinguish the two statutes by noting that the Carolina law, unlike Virginia's, did not provide either for the automatic closing of all integrated schools or for the cut-off of state and local funds to such schools. It was, of course, the Hoffman opinion that forced Virginia to adopt a local option plan for handling school desegregation.

In February Judge Hoffman again shocked Virginia's segregationist zealots by ordering the cities of Norfolk and Newport News to desegregate their schools "as of August 15, 1957." Taking direct aim at the counterrevolutionary programs of the Byrd-dominated state government, Hoffman declared that

> *by reason of the obvious lack of attempt to promulgate any plan looking forward to desegregation gradually or otherwise, there remains nothing for this court to do other than to restrain and enjoin the school board ... from refusing solely on account of race or color to admit to or enroll or educate in, any school under their operation, ... any child otherwise qualified for admission to and enrollment and education in such a school.*

The Fourth Circuit Court subsequently upheld Judge Hoffman's order. It was also about this time that U. S. District Judge Henry Brooks issued final desegregation orders to school boards in three western Kentucky counties. Two of these had had serious racial disturbances in the previous autumn.

On July 16, 1957, Virginia's Massive Resistance was further eroded when a special three-judge federal court upheld the NAACP in most of its objections to the forced answering of 100 "interrogatories" drawn up by attorneys for the state. This litigation directly stemmed from the so-called "NAACP laws" which

Virginia's general assembly had passed in 1956. Since the NAACP had by 1957 filed more lawsuits in Virginia than in any other southern state, it is hardly suprising that Virginia's Massive Resisters were in the vanguard of anti-NAACP legislating.

Likewise in July the federal judiciary in Delaware made a contribution to the egalitarian revolution when U. S. District Judge Paul Leahy handed down what was apparently the first "all-state" desegregation order. Directed to Delaware's state board of education rather than to a specific school board, the order required the state board to submit a desegregation plan for all public school districts not yet integrated. In the words of the order, any decree that might be issued "by this court directed to the state board is, *a fortiori*, directed to any local board over which it, in turn, has authority."

Since the South's backlash reached its peak of obstructionism in the years 1956–58, it was natural that these were also the years when the federal district and circuit court judges were most involved in the segregation crisis. In early 1958 it was estimated that more than 150 court actions involving school segregation and related issues had been litigated in federal and state courts since 1954. And though judicial review of the nearly 200 segregation laws adopted in the first four years of Massive Resistance was a slow process, the courts had reviewed and invalidated around a dozen by February 1958.

In the summer of 1958 Florida was one of five southern states still maintaining total segregation of all public schools and state colleges. The others were Alabama, Georgia, Mississippi, and South Carolina. Florida, however, was shortly forced into the "token desegregation" camp by a federal court order, which had now become the principal—almost the only—instrument for effecting desegregation. In this instance U. S. District Judge Dozier A. DeVane, a staunch believer in states'-rights federalism, ordered the admission of all qualified black students to the graduate schools of the University of Florida. While DeVane limited his decision to a single institution, it was assumed that desegregation of the remainder of the state university system would soon follow. Seeing the approach of the inevitable, Governor Collins at this point decided that Florida would no longer litigate in behalf of

Massive Resistance. That made it possible for the University of Florida Law School to admit, in the fall of 1958, its first black student, who was not, however, Virgil Hawkins, the original litigant.

Certainly the most dramatic and far-reaching judicial intervention against Massive Resistance in 1958 was that by the U. S. Supreme Court in the continuing Little Rock crisis, which had started the previous year. On August 28, 1958, the Supreme Court convened in an unusual special session to dispose of a motion by the NAACP to vacate a stay order issued by the Eighth Circuit Court, the effect of which was to stall the desegregation process in the Arkansas capital.

After having heard arguments from both sides, Chief Justice Warren on September 12 announced the Court's per curiam decision. As expected, the Court denied the request of the Little Rock school board to stay an integration plan for the 1958–59 school year which it had voluntarily adopted. The Chief Justice further stated that "The expression of the views supporting our judgment will be prepared and announced in due course." Meanwhile the Court's decision was to be "effective immediately, and shall be communicated forthwith to the District Court for the Eastern District of Arkansas."

On September 29 the Supreme Court announced its supporting opinion, and to emphasize the importance of the occasion, all nine justices signed the opinion. It was a solemn warning to the state of Arkansas as to the folly of Massive Resistance and was certainly the most significant judicial pronouncement on the segregation issue since the two Brown opinions. After conceding that the Little Rock school board had acted in good faith, the Court traced recent disturbances directly to actions by state officials, "which reflect their own determination to resist this Court's decision in the Brown case." Then the Court warned:

> The constitutional rights of respondents are not to be sacrificed or yielded to the violence and actions of the Governor and Legislature. . . . Important as is the preservation of the public peace, this aim cannot be accomplished by laws or ordinances which deny rights created or protected by the Federal Constitution. . . . Thus law and order are not here to

*be preserved by depriving the Negro children of their consti-
tutional rights.*[5]

The Court's unanimous opinion in this case did not immediately destroy Massive Resistance nor did it signal the start of
wholesale integration of the Arkansas public schools. But it probably prevented a fatal set-back to the South's evolving program of
token desegregation.

Since much of the legislation passed by the South's counterrevolutionary legislators in the mid-1950's was aimed at the
NAACP, it is not surprising that much of the Massive Resistance
court litigation involved judicial review of the anti-NAACP laws.
Almost without exception, statutes passed by segregationist legislators to harass the NAACP were invalidated when reviewed by
the federal courts. Alabama had been one of the first southern
states to try to suppress the NAACP by demanding the names of
its members and then banning the organization when its leaders
refused to supply them. In 1956 an Alabama circuit court held the
NAACP in contempt and fixed the fine at $10,000, to be in-
creased to $100,000 if the names were not produced within five
days. In the meantime the organization was forbidden to operate
in Alabama. The NAACP appealed, and on June 30, 1958, the
U. S. Supreme Court unanimously held that the fine levied against
the NAACP and the demand for disclosure of members' names violated the "liberty" assured by the due process clause of the fourteenth amendment.[6] In the words of Justice Harlan, who spoke
for the Court, ". . . it is immaterial whether the beliefs sought to
be advanced by association pertain to political, economic, religious or cultural matters, and state action which may have the
effect of curtailing the freedom to associate is subject to the closest scrutiny." The Alabama supreme court, however, refused to
reverse its earlier decision sustaining the injunction against the
NAACP, and it required three more U. S. Supreme Court decisions (the last in 1964) before the Alabama judges complied.

Prince Edward County, Virginia, one of the original Brown
litigants, made the headlines again in 1959. Litigation against
segregation in the County had really begun on May 23, 1951,
when a class suit was filed on behalf of certain black children.
Despite that initiative, the County's schools were still solidly seg-

regated as the 1950's drew to a close. Finally, on May 5, 1959, the Fourth Circuit Court ordered Prince Edward County to admit all qualified black students to its white high school at the start of the 1959–60 school year.

As had been predicted, Prince Edward County authorities moved to shut down their public schools rather than implement the Circuit Court's desegregation order. In physical terms, this meant that around twenty elementary and secondary schools serving the two races were closed and their students locked out. With the start of the 1959–60 school year, most of the 1,500 displaced white students were taken care of in makeshift "private" schools run by a foundation which segregationists had recently set up. Both state and county authorities promptly rushed to the aid of the new schools by offering several kinds of public assistance. In 1960 the Virginia legislature approved a tuition grant program to enable parents to send their children to private segregated schools. At about the same time, the Prince Edward County Supervisors authorized supplementary tuition grants as well as property tax credits up to twenty-five per cent for gifts made to local private schools. The County offered black parents a chance to set up private black schools, similarly subsidized, but they rejected the offer. As a result, a majority of the County's approximately 1,700 black students suddenly found themselves deprived of further educational opportunities.

Incredibly, the Prince Edward County public schools, with state connivance, remained closed for four years. Finally, in 1964, the U. S. Supreme Court instructed a lower federal court that it could both order the Board of Education to reopen the schools and direct the County Board of Supervisors to levy whatever school taxes might be necessary to operate them. Justice Black, writing for a nearly unanimous Court, held that the county had "denied petitioners the equal protection of the laws" by closing the public schools and at the same time subsidizing "private" white schools. He also warned the Massive Resisters that "The time for mere 'deliberate speed' has run out."[7] However, not until 1969 did a special three-judge federal court rule that Virginia's evasive tuition grant program "indisputably" contributed to segregated schooling and was thus unconstitutional. Yet, even after that finding, the judges denied an NAACP request that the court require all monies expended under Virginia's tuition grant program to be returned forthwith to the public treasury.

The reopening of the Prince Edward County schools in 1964 was important symbolically and also in a very practical sense for the students directly involved. It did not, however, immediately bring about unitary school systems in Virginia. Obstructionist southern school boards kept right on running their dual school operations, secure in the knowledge that unitary education could not be forced on the South except by a long and costly series of new desegregation suits. Moreover they were quite certain that a majority of their white patrons—perhaps an overwhelming majority—still preferred dual to unitary schools. Indeed, it was not until after 1967, when Title VI of the 1964 Civil Rights Act forbidding federal aid to segregated school systems was finally implemented, that the pace of desegregation in the South significantly accelerated.

In planning their programs of "legal" evasion of Brown, the South's counterrevolutionaries relied as much on cleverly drafted pupil placement laws as on private schools and tuition grant programs. And here as elsewhere, it was the courts, not the executive or legislative branches, that rendered the placement-law gambit an ineffectual means of evading Brown. The purpose of such laws was to hide race as a factor in pupil assignments and to stress such "objective" factors as school capacity, pupil preparation, dangers to public order, social and psychological relationships, health standards, and choice and interest of pupils and parents. The problem for the courts was to determine whether the placement laws really contained objective factors that were being impartially administered or whether they were simply ruses to prevent any and all desegregation. Initially, the courts had some trouble in deciding how objective and fair the pupil placement laws were, but eventually they saw through them as little more than clever tactical evasions.

In 1958 a federal district court held that Alabama's 1955 pupil placement law was not unconstitutional on its face but recognized the possibility that it might be unconstitutionally applied. On appeal, the U. S. Supreme Court affirmed the district court's judgment.

Virginia's 1956 pupil placement law listed eight factors that might be considered in pupil placement. One of these factors was operational efficiency. Since the legislature's 1956 general appropriations act defined school efficiency as a system in which white and black students were segregated, a federal district court took judicial notice of the interrelation of these items and declared the state's pupil placement act unconstitutional on its face.

Even though the courts found some of the Massive Resisters' pupil placement laws not to be unconstitutional per se, as in the case of Alabama's and North Carolina's, in later years they usually found them to be unconstitutional in their administration. This meant that placement laws, while perhaps an obstacle to massive integration, could not prevent some degree of token desegregation. Yet the South was right in assuming that tokenism could be kept minimal for a long time, since the federal courts' task in examining hundreds of cases of this sort necessarily took a great deal of time and involved prolonged hearings. Professor Peltason has argued that in handling placement-law litigation, "The Supreme Court itself has retreated. By affirming pupil-placement laws, the Court sanctioned token integration."[8] The charge is doubtless valid for the period of the late 1950's but not for subsequent years.

Long after Massive Resistance began its precipitate decline, the Supreme Court kept hammering away at the remaining vestiges of the Jim Crow system. Thus it set aside sit-in convictions based on breach of peace statutes.[9] It reversed sit-in convictions based on criminal trespass statutes.[10] It ordered the desegregation of hospital facilities.[11] And, at the end of the sixties, it held that a neglected portion of the federal code—42 U.S.C. 1982—forbade all racial discrimination, private as well as public, in either the sale or rental of property.[12]

By all odds, the most significant confrontation between Massive Resisters and the judiciary in the 1960's took place in Mississippi in 1969. It seemed to most observers to be the final showdown between the courts and the tail-end of the South's counterrevolution, now in headlong retreat. The 1969 confrontation had been preceded by one in Virginia the previous year when the Supreme Court ruled that "freedom of choice" plans could be regarded as constitutionally valid only when they offered a "real promise of aiding a desegregation program" and where no alternative means for realizing that objective was "readily available."[13]

The 1969 Mississippi case took on added importance when Attorney General Mitchell came out in favor of postponing the transition from dual to unitary schools in the South. Before that, in August, the U. S. Court of Appeals at New Orleans had granted thirty-three Mississippi school districts an indefinite stay of a lower court integration order, provided they showed some progress toward disestablishment of their dual systems in the coming school year. When the NAACP appealed that decision to the Supreme Court, the Attorney General intervened on the side of the southern school districts, maintaining that it was "simply unreal to talk of instant desegregation" of the South's dual systems.

As expected, the Supreme Court vacated the order of the Fifth Circuit Court of Appeals and directed that court to order immediate operation of "unitary school systems within which no person is to be effectively excluded from any school because of race or color."[14] The Court's *per curiam* opinion stated that

> *The question presented is one of paramount importance, involving as it does the denial of fundamental rights to many thousands of school children, who are presently attending Mississippi schools under segregated conditions contrary to the applicable decisions of this Court. Against this background the Court of Appeals should have denied all motions for additional time because continued operation of segregated schools under a standard of allowing "all deliberate speed" for desegregation is no longer constitutionally permissible. Under explicit holdings of this Court the obligation of every school district is to terminate dual school systems at once and to operate now and hereafter only unitary schools.*

Thus at long last, the Supreme Court, fed up with the South's defiance of its desegregation holdings, junked the "all deliberate speed" formula of Brown II and replaced it with a much more coercive formula ("unitary schools now") of the sort that the NAACP had pressed hard for back in 1955. As happened in the aftermath of Brown, there was a good deal of loose talk after this decision suggesting that segregated schools would very shortly be a thing of the past. The talk, though, was based more on hope than on hard facts.

For all its bold rhetoric, the Alexander case formula, which amounted to a demand to integrate now and litigate later, did not as quickly or as completely replace the old Brown II standard as egalitarians hoped it would. Enormous difficulties still stood in the way of full desegregation, both in the South and the North. Some of the federal district judges in the South remained hostile to what they felt was "instant integration," and the Nixon Administration had in effect switched sides in the segregation controversy, without, of course, endorsing a return to the discredited Jim Crow system. As segregated schools continued to thrive into the 1970's, one found it hard to disagree with Professor Archibald Cox of Harvard that "there are limits even to the power of the Supreme Court of the United States to command assent."[15]

Nevertheless the Alexander case did demonstrate quite clearly that the federal judiciary, in the 1960's as in the 1950's, was on the cutting-edge of the egalitarian revolution. By this time, the courts had received a good deal of assistance from Congress and the executive branch—especially the Department of Health, Education and Welfare—but the courts were still the chief targets of the South's counterrevolutionaries. And though they were not alone responsible for the decline of the South's backlash, their contribution to that result was a major one.

II. The Little Rock Showdown

THE SCENARIO of Massive Resistance included not only peaceful showdowns with the courts but also street and campus confrontations, where the unvarnished bigotry of white racists was most apparent and repulsive. These violent encounters were the natural corollary of the ideological bipolarity that had become the chief source of rigidity paralyzing the South in the post-Brown years. As the embittered South lost its perspective for nuance and flexibility, every confrontation with the egalitarian revolution was interpreted by the demagogues as a question of survival. For them, survival was indeed the issue.

Again it must be stressed, however, that the South's ideologi-

cal bipolarity coexisted with political multipolarity, which is to say
that the region's political systems did not constitute a monolith—
if indeed they ever had—but rather involved independent political
centers which tended to act less and less cohesively in the face of
federal coercion. The border states, for example, had agreed to go
along with something approaching total integration. The states of
the upper South had adjusted to token desegregation. Only the
Deep South at the dawn of the 1960's remained implacably committed to a policy of total Massive Resistance. Not surprisingly,
therefore, it was in the Deep South that the violent showdowns with
the federal executive branch took place.

The first of the really serious federal-state showdowns testing
the mettle of Massive Resistance occurred in a most unlikely place
—the charming, progressive city of Little Rock. The ironies implicit in that showdown were many. Before the crisis broke, Arkansas had begun the transition to desegregation without fanfare
or violence. The city's school board and school superintendent
were at most traditional segregationists and generally open-
minded. One of the city's papers, the *Arkansas Gazette,* was noted
for its liberal editorial policy. The business community, which
included a goodly number of Jews, was forward-looking. In the
early part of 1957 two strong segregationists had been decisively
defeated when they tried to unseat moderate incumbents of the
Little Rock Board of Education. And Governor Orval E. Faubus,
who would soon be viewed as a kind of counterrevolutionary
Houdini, had up to that point been thought of as one of the more
moderate southern governors, if not indeed a liberal populist.

The Little Rock showdown appears to have been the result
of the coming together of a number of "negative" things: a break-
down in community leadership creating a political vacuum; an
ineffectual police chief who was strongly opposed to integration;
an ineffectual U. S. district attorney; the absence of a resident U. S.
district judge; the incumbency of a lame-duck mayor and city
council, recently repudiated by the voters; inadequate desegregation planning by school officials; and a most untimely visit to
Little Rock, on the eve of the crisis, by Governor Marvin Griffin
of Georgia.

Soon after the announcement of Brown I, Little Rock school

officials let it be known that planning for desegregation would begin at once. The "Phase Program" that finally evolved from their planning envisaged token desegregation, beginning in September 1957, at Central High School, whose pupils were drawn chiefly from the city's lower and middle classes. The basic intent of the Phase Program was to provide a minimum amount of desegregation spaced over a maximum period of time.[16]

In the summer of 1957, the school authorities examined around sixty applicants and selected nine carefully screened black students to attend formerly all-white Central High. The local Massive Resisters, led by the Capital Citizens' Council, launched their all-out campaign against desegregation in August with newspaper ads, mass meetings, rumor-mongering, and ceaseless pamphleteering. Their campaign reached its climax on the night of August 22 when Governor Griffin and Roy V. Harris, then executive director of the States' Rights Council of Georgia, spoke to a huge anti-integration rally. Griffin told the crowd that if the federal government tried to force his state "to integrate the races, I will be compelled to tell them to get their blackeyed peas and soup pots out of Georgia." Harris, speaking ominously of a "second Reconstruction," urged Arkansas to support Griffin's program of nationally advertising the South's case for segregation. He also assured his listeners that Georgia would use the highway patrol and "every white man" in the state to prevent the implementation of Brown.

Observers are now generally agreed that the August rally was the catalytic event that virtually overnight converted Faubus from a pragmatic segregationist into a charismatic demagogue. He apparently was following the changing temper of his people, and near the end of August he said it was clear that "the sentiment within the past three weeks has changed." He also conceded that it was Governor Griffin's electrifying oratory that triggered the increase in anti-integration sentiment in the Little Rock area.

In August the newly formed Mothers League of Central High initiated court action to halt the projected integration of Central High, and Faubus testified in support of their petition. The Arkansas Chancery Court thereupon issued an injunction prohibiting the school board from proceeding with its desegregation plans. At that point, however, Judge Ronald Davies, then the visiting judge on the Arkansas federal bench, countered the chancery court's move by issuing a new injunction voiding the one issued by the state court and directing the school board to go ahead with its planned desegregation. The injunction issued by Judge Davies also warned Faubus and other state officials not to interfere in any way with the desegregation of Central High, which a federal court had first approved on August 15, 1956.

Governor Faubus, now fully committed to a total Massive Resistance policy, saw that there was no turning back. In the evening of September 1, he conferred with Superintendent of Schools Virgil T. Blossom, who tried to persuade the Governor to issue a strong law-and-order statement. Faubus, however, refused to do so, and hinted that he might be forced to block the desegregation of Central High.

On Monday, September 2, Governor Faubus proceeded from interposition to nullification by calling out units of the Arkansas National Guard and sending them to Central High to prevent its desegregation. In a television address explaining his action, Faubus said he was forced to mobilize the Guard in order to "restore the peace and good order of this community." At about the same time, the school board asked the nine black children who were scheduled to integrate Central High the next morning to stay at home until the courts had clarified the legal issues.

Again Judge Davies acted promptly and ordered the board to go ahead with its Central High desegregation program. And on September 4 the nine black students put in an appearance at Central High, now surrounded by white militants, but the National Guard blocked their admission. The next day the school board, caught in the middle of the state-federal showdown, petitioned Judge Davies for a temporary delay in implementing desegregation. The judge, however, rejected the board's petition.

Shortly after that, Judge Davies requested the U. S. Attorney General to file a petition for a preliminary injunction against Faubus and certain officers of the Guard. The petition was filed, and on September 20 Judge Davies granted the injunction, which enjoined Faubus, the National Guard commander, and their agents "from obstructing or preventing by use of the National Guard or otherwise attendance of Negro students at Little Rock High

School." Faubus thereupon removed the Guard, though not without taking a swipe at Judge Davies, newsmen, and integrationists.

Finally, on Monday, September 23, Central High was desegregated with the help of city police and a few state troopers. But by noon, the counterrevolutionary mobs outside were so large and menacing that authorities removed the blacks from the school. Mayor Mann in the meantime had been making desperate pleas to the Eisenhower Administration for some kind of assistance, so far without result. Equally unavailing had been a personal conference between Faubus and the President.

After it became clear that the state of Arkansas had no intention of enforcing Judge Davies's order, President Eisenhower on September 25 reluctantly sent several companies of the United States Army to Little Rock to assure the peaceful desegregation of Central High. The President in effect put the city of Little Rock under martial law, and after the appearance of units of the 101st Airborne Division at Central High, the mobs dispersed and the black students enrolled.[17] The Regular Army troops remained at the school until late November, at which time they were replaced by a contingent of the Arkansas National Guard which had been federalized for duty at Central High.

The dramatic crisis at Little Rock did not really end in 1957. The black students at Central High were harassed for several months, and in July of 1958 Orval Faubus, now a hero to Massive Resisters, won election to a third term by a big majority. Also in the summer of 1958 the Little Rock school board sought and received a thirty-month stay against integration with the argument that "conditions of chaos, bedlam, and turmoil" made such a retreat necessary. After a U. S. Court of Appeals reversed the stay, the Supreme Court finally ended the Little Rock litigation by upholding the Appeals Court order in *Cooper* v. *Aaron*.

If Mr. Eisenhower's dispatch of troops to Central High did not immediately solve the Little Rock crisis, it settled at least a few things. It effected the token desegregation of Central High. It demonstrated once again that the federal Constitution, as interpreted by the Supreme Court, is the supreme law of the land. It almost certainly averted serious violence. It irrevocably committed the federal executive branch to the implementation of Brown. And it dealt a near-fatal blow to the hopes of the extreme Massive Resisters, who, having lost "the battle of the courthouse," had now resolved to test the possibilities of "confrontation politics."

As for the *meaning* of the Little Rock crisis, most analysts of the situation would probably agree that the following are among the more important conclusions to be drawn from that tragic, and perhaps unnecessary, experience:

1. A federal form of government, by its very nature, breeds jurisdictional controversies between the central and regional authorities, which regional demagogues will not hesitate to exploit to their own advantage.

2. The complex American federal system and the ambiguities embedded in the federal Constitution place an enormous interpretive burden on our courts.

3. The federal judiciary, however vital to constitutionalism, is not an effective problem-solving agency unless fully backed up by the executive branch with its vast array of coercive instruments.

4. In the American polity, state usurpation of federal prerogatives is even more common (and dangerous) than federal usurpation of state prerogatives.

5. In any crisis where community "influentials" remain silent, tensions are likely to escalate until extremists take over. And when a mob takes over—even a small mob—moderates desert the streets.

6. While patience is a necessary virtue in law enforcement, once the law is openly flouted, especially by organized groups, it must be vigorously enforced.

7. Beyond a certain point, the greater the delay in the implementation of an unpopular public policy, the more costly and painful the job will finally be, particularly for those directly involved.

8. By postponing their intervention, President Eisenhower and the Justice Department probably accelerated and exacerbated the ultimate showdown.

9. Little Rock was not merely a constitutional crisis pitting revolutionaries against counterrevolutionaries, it was also a crisis of values and leadership.

10. The American tradition of governmental decentralization, notably in the field of public education, has fostered the growth of elitist regional power-structures that have gained a strangle-hold on major areas of public policy.

11. The gravest crises of American politics have generally resulted from a dialectical confrontation of federal pragmatism with regional Catonic moralism.

12. Little Rock proved anew that revolutionary initiatives and counterrevolutionary backlash move continually during times of rapid change in circles of reciprocal influence.

13. Contrary to popular folklore, "outside agitators" at Little Rock were more numerous among the Massive Resisters than among the desegregationists.

14. Few southern politicians are more quixotic and unpredictable than "neo-Populists" such as Faubus and Wallace.

15. Federal-state relations in the U.S. constitute a delicately balanced process that is basically a symbiotic association, dependent for its proper functioning on mutual good will and the states' deference to the doctrine of national supremacy. In the absence of an "unseen hand" to keep the federal mechanism perfectly balanced, the system is usually in a state of disequilibrium and thus in need of the federal judiciary's corrective intervention in the role of "master equilibrator."

16. The dramatic showdown at Little Rock seems to have been the axial point of the South's counterrevolution, the moment of truth when the Holy Writ of Interposition became incarnated as flesh and blood in the person of Governor Faubus. Everything prior to that revelatory event was *preparatio evangelica*. Nothing in the defiant South would afterwards be the same.

Faubus was, indeed, a protean, charismatic spokesman for reaction for a brief moment. Yet within a matter of weeks, it was reasonably clear that there was not going to be a thousand-year reign of the saints of Massive Resistance, however grandiose the hopes and dreams of the counterrevolutionary zealots.

III. The New Orleans Showdown

THE NEXT CRITICAL ENCOUNTER between the egalitarian revolution and the South's backlash occurred at New Orleans in 1960. In this instance the federal executive was not as directly involved as it had been at Little Rock. Still, the possibility of its intervening to enforce federal orders always loomed in the background of the controversy. This possibility appears to have had some effect on the strategic planning of the more rational Massive Resisters.

The factors involved in the New Orleans showdown were, in many respects, similar to those that precipitated the Little Rock crisis. The New Orleans school board failed to provide imaginative leadership; the board selected lower class schools for the first desegregation; city officials did not actively involve themselves in desegregation planning; the community's influentials allowed the mobs to seize the initiative by default; the expected moral suasion of the Catholic Church never emerged; and the greater New Orleans Citizens' Council unscrupulously manipulated white feelings until a consensus of white opinion against the projected desegregation was crystallized. Back in the mid-1950's the state legislature, led by Senator William Rainach and Representative John Garrett (both from Bible-belt Claiborne Parish) had planted the seeds of the 1960 violence by passing with minimal opposition a massive array of "anti-desegregation" laws. And, most important, the state's official reaction to Brown steadily hardened after Rainach forced all other politicians into an extreme pro-segregation stance by branding many of them "soft" on the race issue.

U. S. District Judge J. Skelly Wright set the stage for the New Orleans showdown when he ordered the school board on May 16, 1960, to implement in the fall his personally devised desegregation plan, which began with the first grade.[18] In mid-August Governor Jimmie Davis, noted guitarist and author of "You Are My Sunshine," announced that he was taking over administration of the New Orleans schools under recent state legislative authorization. At the same time he announced that he was ready to go to jail rather than consent to even token integration. The NAACP then petitioned a three-judge federal court in New Orleans to forbid state interference with school desegregation.

On August 26 the three-judge federal court declared a new "segregation package" of state laws unconstitutional, ordered Governor Davis to keep his hands off New Orleans schools, and directed the school board to proceed with integration. The board then requested additional time. A few days later Judge Wright, "impressed with the sincerity and good faith of the board," extended the integration deadline to Monday, November 14.

The delay that Judge Wright granted the board, which seems unwise in retrospect, was all the Massive Resisters needed to reactivate their counterrevolutionary forces. It was a godsend to them, for in early September it appeared that a majority of New Orleans citizens were prepared to go along with token integration. Two groups of moderate white parents came to the fore at this time— Save Our Schools and the Committee for Public Education—and they received the endorsement of leading civic organizations as well as sections of the press. Six days before first-grade integration was to commence, there was a school board election which became extremely heated. It was won by a moderate quite handily. In fact, his 55,000 votes exceeded the combined total of a trio of segregationist candidates who promised to close the city schools rather than accept any degree of integration.

The Massive Resisters, though defeated in New Orleans, were riding high in Baton Rouge, eighty-five miles to the north. Governor Davis, under heavy pressure from the extremists, decided to throw the entire force of the state government into the battle, and between November 4, 1960, and the end of February 1961, he called the legislature into special session a total of five times. Since Louisiana law specified that special sessions of the legislature should be limited to the subject matter specified by the governor's call, there was no danger that the legislators would stray from the subject of segregation.

The first emergency session opened on November 4, and the zealots in charge of the legislature promptly guided a package of twenty-nine bills to the House Judiciary Committee, Section B, where favorable consideration was assured. Within four days, all twenty-nine bills were steered through both houses with minimal opposition. The clear purpose of the new measures was to remove control of the New Orleans schools from the school board to an eight-man legislative committee. One bill in the package also required state law enforcement officers to arrest any federal marshal or judge who might seek to block the committee's operation of segregated schools.

On November 10 Judge Wright firmly reasserted the power of the federal judiciary. He restrained the new legislative committee from interfering in any way with the orderly desegregation of the New Orleans schools and thus in effect invalidated the recently enacted "segregation package." After that, the school board proceeded with its first-grade integration plans.

But Governor Davis and the Massive Resisters were in no mood to surrender to a mere federal judge. On November 11 the governor announced a call for a second special session of the legislature to meet for thirty days, beginning on the Tuesday after the planned integration of New Orleans schools. Then on Sunday evening, November 13, Davis went on television to explain the actions recently taken by the state government. He denied that he wished to close the public schools, since that, he said, would be a "scorched earth" policy of self-penalty. But he did express the view that segregated schools should and could be maintained in Louisiana, since the Brown opinion in his view was itself unconstitutional. Then, revealing his commitment to states'-rights federalism, he told his people:

> *I know that you sense the grave danger to all state power that lies in entrusting the formation of national social policies to a judicial body appointed for life. I believe the Supreme Court, in attempting to prohibit the state of Louisiana from using its power to operate schools, has clearly usurped the amendatory power that is constitutionally vested in the states and their citizens. . . . Louisiana is entitled to use every legal means to resist this usurpation of its power.*

On Saturday, November 12, the State Education Superintendent, Shelby Jackson, proclaimed the following Monday (desegregation day) a school holiday. All of the state's sixty-four parish school boards complied with the holiday proclamation save the boards in Orleans and Rapides (Alexandria) parishes, which voted to open their schools as usual on Monday. For this and other actions Jackson was directed by Judge Wright to show cause on November 18 why he should not be held in contempt of court. Through the remainder of the crisis, a contempt citation hung over Jackson's head, thus minimizing his effectiveness as a Davis strategist.

Judge Wright issued his restraining order against Jackson and the school holiday at 10 A.M. on Sunday. As Wright was announcing his order, the legislature was reconvening to complete its first special session after a brief recess. In rapid fire order it replaced the special committee with the entire legislature as the supervisor of the New Orleans schools and appointed an assistant sergeant-at-arms to go to New Orleans with a "legislative police force" to prevent desegregation there. It also fired the New Orleans superintendent of schools, Dr. James F. Redmond, for refusing to divulge the names of the black students who had been approved under the desegregation program. Apparently the legislators believed that by replacing the committee with the entire legislature (140 members), they had made it impossible for Judge Wright to issue further restraining orders, as there was no legal precedent for enjoining an entire legislative body.

But Judge Wright was not to be deterred by the lack of precedent. And after taking notes during the evening in front of his television set (the special session was televised), he enjoined the entire Louisiana legislature and its agents from seeking to enforce the laws they had just passed or from taking "any other action interfering with or circumventing the orders of this court." Significantly, the restraining orders this time were requested by the Orleans Parish School Board, which in the previous summer had asked the governor to "interpose state sovereignty to prevent integration." Equally significant, Judge Wright became the first judge in American history to impose a restraining order upon an entire state legislature.

After Judge Wright issued his orders, the New Orleans principals made plans to open their schools as usual on Monday morning, without, however, divulging the names of the schools that had been picked for desegregation. Then, as planned, four black girls proceeded on Monday to formerly all-white McDonough No. 19 and Frantz Elementary, thereby bringing the first public school desegregation to the Deep South. Both schools were in the ninth ward, a most unlikely place to begin such a revolution in human behavior.

As soon as the desegregation was announced, white parents began a boycott of the schools. Every white child was taken out of McDonough No. 19 and all but two were withdrawn from Frantz Elementary. On the following day, the politicians, sensing a chance to advance their own interests, got into the act. Governor Davis urged the people to "keep a cool head." Rainach demanded a scorched-earth policy and urged whites to "empty the class-rooms where they are integrated." Leander Perez, livid with racist indignation, asked for demonstrations against the NAACP, the Communists, the "Zionist Jews," Judge Wright, and the "weasel, snake-head mayor" of New Orleans. Then, stooping to the lowest kind of racism, he told the segregationists: "Don't wait for your daughter to be raped by these Congolese. Don't wait until the burr-heads are forced into your schools. Do something about it now!"

As happened in every Massive Resistance showdown, after the politicians spoke, the teenagers and the zealots acted. The day after the demagogues spoke their mind, a mob of two or three thousand white extremists demonstrated at the New Orleans Civic Center, swept through the state supreme court building, converged on city hall, and then headed for the federal courts and the board of education building. After that the mob roamed at will through the business district, hurling stones and bottles at passing blacks. In the evening black teenagers took to the streets to seek revenge for the stoning of their people, and the resulting disorder led to 250 arrests, mostly of blacks.

Though legislative interposition had failed to halt the march of token desegregation, street disturbances and the white boycott grew more intense and menacing in the succeeding weeks. A crowd of jeering housewives gathered daily at McDonough No. 19 and especially at Frantz, and their faces, congealed with hate, became famous to television viewers around the world. The mob was even more interested in harassing whites who broke the boycott than in harassing blacks, but the women, mostly from lowerclass backgrounds, did both. And since the state government had in effect legalized playing hooky from schools, the "vacationing" white students roamed the streets for days, singing "Glory, Glory, Segregation" to the tune of "The Battle Hymn of the Republic."

The state's counterrevolutionary legislators returned to the fray the day after desegregation came to New Orleans. The first twelve-day special session expired on the 15th, the same day that the second session was scheduled to open. The legislators were still in a defiant mood, and the first act of their new session was a concurrent resolution commending the white parents who had taken their children from the desegregated schools and promising them the support of the legislature in their "brave fight." It was widely believed that the legislature would also institute impeachment proceedings against Judge Wright and initiate criminal action against the school board, but neither of these far-out ideas ever became a reality. The legislature did, however, declare all acts of the "now defunct New Orleans School Board" illegal and warned banks and business firms not to do business with the board. In addition, the enraged legislators ordered the funds of the Orleans Parish school board to be transferred to the legislature and set up a tuition-grant program for children attending private, non-sectarian schools. They also again fired Superintendent Redmond for keeping secret the names of the white schools that were to be integrated. Any legislator who dared challenge the new "nullification" package of laws was immediately branded a traitor to the southern way of life. There was, therefore, little opposition to the last-ditch program of defiance by Governor Davis and the legislative zealots.

The federal judiciary reentered the picture on November 30, when a three-judge court called the legislature's attempt to nullify a judgment of the Supreme Court "a preposterous perversion of Article V of the Constitution." The court's decision meant, in effect, the death of the mythic doctrine of interposition. And with its collapse, the rest of the pro-segregation package enacted in the previous month fell by the wayside.[19] Subsequently the U. S. Supreme Court upheld the lower court's decision, stating in the process that interposition is "without substance" and has never been a legitimate legal doctrine.[20]

Even after the federal courts had flatly rejected interposition as a limitation on federal power, Governor Davis and his counter-revolutionary followers continued to resist. The White Citizens' Councils were now directing the boycott at Frantz and Mc-Donough schools, and it was virtually 100 per cent effective. Pressed for money to continue his costly anti-integration crusade, Davis called a third special session of the legislature, which convened on December 17. Several additional pro-segregation measures were passed at this session, but the legislature rejected Davis's proposal for a one-cent increase in the sales tax to finance the expanding private-school grants program. Segments of the business community were also now opposing Davis's bitter-end defiance, chiefly because Mardi Gras had been put in jeopardy. On December 14, 105 business and professional men of New Orleans signed a three-quarter page ad in the *Times-Picayune* which appealed for an end to street demonstrations and for support of the school board.

The fourth and fifth special sessions of the legislature were held in January and February 1961, as John F. Kennedy was taking over in Washington. The Massive Resisters were still in charge and were still going through the motions of defying the Supreme Court. Among the last bills approved by the fifth special session were an informer bill and one providing for a school closure referendum. After signing the bills, Governor Davis held a press conference and announced that there was a good chance all the schools in the state would be closed. He refused, however, to go into details about his announcement.

Desegregation of the New Orleans schools continued to be extremely "tokenistic" throughout 1961, and opposition from hard-core segregationist zealots showed no signs of lessening. In 1962, however, a series of events brought about the total defeat of Massive Resistance in Louisiana. On March 27, 1962, Roman Catholic Archbishop Joseph Francis Rummel announced that henceforth all Catholic schools in the archdiocese would be desegregated. This was quite significant, since the New Orleans Archdiocese embraced eleven parishes with more than 75,000 parochial school children. The Archbishop's decision was confirmed the next month when Leander Perez and two other Catholic Massive Resisters were excommunicated for their opposition to desegregation.

The "last straw," quite fittingly, came from Judge Wright. On April 3, 1962, Judge Wright, in one of the last decisions he handed down as a district judge, upheld 102 blacks petitioning for desegregation and in the process invalidated Louisiana's pupil placement law. Specifically he ordered integration of the first six grades in all parish schools on a first-come basis. Judge Wright's decision on April 3 did not, of course, mean the collapse of all resistance to Brown in Louisiana, but it did signal an acceleration of token desegregation.[21]

The lessons of New Orleans were largely the same ones that should have been learned—but were not—from the Little Rock experience. A few of these seem sufficiently important to bear reiteration.

1. When community elites shirk their responsibility of directing social change, they invariably create a power vacuum that extremists rush to fill.

2. Experiments in social change, such as school desegregation was, are much more difficult to bring off peacefully in lower-class than in upper-class areas.

3. When the politicians in a crisis opt for demagoguery instead of conflict resolution, the street mobs take that to be an official blessing for whatever extra-legal actions they may commit.

4. In the post-Brown era, the myth of interposition-nullification never was—and never had been—a viable doctrine on which to base opposition to the federal government.

5. New Orleans demonstrated, as did Little Rock, that the specter which haunted America in the 1950's and 1960's was not a leftist revolution—as the South's charismatic demagogues constantly alleged—but the backlash of counterrevolutionary white racism. That is but another way of saying that what imperiled southern democracy after 1954 was not a red hammer and sickle—despite all the hysterical nonsense about

Communism—but the flag (and ethos) of the late Confederacy.

IV. THE UNIVERSITY OF GEORGIA SHOWDOWN

THE THIRD of the critical post-Brown confrontations between egalitarians and Massive Resisters came hard on the heels of the New Orleans crisis. It took place in early 1961 at Athens, Georgia, the site of the University of Georgia. Like the showdowns at Little Rock and New Orleans, this one was precipitated by desegregation orders handed down by a federal judge. But unlike the two earlier showdowns, the Georgia crisis involved desegregation at the university level rather than the elementary and secondary levels.

The confrontation at Athens went back to June 1959, when two blacks, Hamilton E. Holmes and Charlayne Hunter, both honor graduates of segregated high schools, applied for admission to the University of Georgia. Authorities there put off processing their applications for a year. After they finally interviewed the black applicants, they rejected their applications, allegedly for technical rather than racial reasons. With straight faces the university's top officials maintained that though the institution had been totally segregated for 175 years, it was not actually following a segregation policy.

In February of 1960 Governor Vandiver encouraged his state's Massive Resisters by promising, "We are going to resist again and again and again. . . . We will exhaust every legal means and remedy available to us." But on January 6, 1961, U. S. District Judge William A. Bootle finally ordered the university to admit Miss Hunter and Mr. Holmes to the 1961 winter quarter. This was accomplished on January 9, 1961. Two days later, however, counterrevolutionary extremists, including prominent klansmen, touched off a wild campus riot after a Georgia-Georgia Tech basketball game. For hours the rioters rampaged around campus, shouting obscenities, smashing property, hurling bricks at police and firemen, and trying to gain entry to Miss Hunter's dormitory room. At the height of the trouble, university officials suspended the black students and drove them to Atlanta. Somewhat later riot charges were filed against two white students and nine non-students.

Governor Vandiver, who belatedly sent a few state troopers to help the Athens police put down the riot, promptly invoked a new law prohibiting the payment of state funds to integrated schools or colleges. Judge Bootle responded by invalidating the law and by ordering the university to readmit Miss Hunter and Mr. Holmes by 8 A.M. on the following Monday. That was done without further riots or demonstrations, although for some time desegregation in Georgia remained minimal.

The chief result of the confrontation at Athens was the abandonment by state authorities of total Massive Resistance. Governor Vandiver, undergoing a "conversion" to expediency, called a special legislative session, which adopted the substance of the Sibley Committee's recommendations. These recommendations, coming from the study committee which the 1960 legislature had created, advocated repeal of most of the Massive Resistance legislation previously passed and adoption of a "local option" bill such as North Carolina and Virginia had earlier approved. In the fall of 1961 total segregation at the public school level in Georgia collapsed when the Atlanta schools—along with those in Dallas, Memphis, Tampa, and Galveston—desegregated without incident. By this time, total Massive Resistance had been defeated in all but three southern states: Mississippi, Alabama, and South Carolina. And their day of reckoning was not far away.

V. THE OLE MISS SHOWDOWN

AFTER LITTLE ROCK, New Orleans, and Athens, it was obvious that time was running out for the South's counterrevolutionaries, and they knew it. But they were determined to make a last-ditch stand for reaction in the Deep South states of Mississippi and Alabama, and it was in those states that the Kennedy Administration first became a direct participant in the politics of conflict spawned by Brown.

The 1962 showdown at Ole Miss came about as a result of the coalescence of four things: the determination of a young black man, James Howard Meredith, to enter the University of Mississippi; Governor Ross Barnett's fanatical opposition to the slightest integration in his state; a series of complex federal court rulings culminating in an order to Ole Miss to desegregate its facilities; and the decision made by President Kennedy and his top advisers that the charismatic demagogue Ross Barnett must not succeed where Faubus, Byrd, Davis, and Vandiver had failed.

James Meredith was an unlikely hero, but hero he became because of the obtuse intransigence of Mississippi's counterrevolutionary leaders. A native of Mississippi, he served nine years in the U. S. Air Force, and early in 1961 applied for admission to Ole Miss. The university, as expected, refused to admit him. He then took his case to court. And after a nightmare of litigation, the Fifth Circuit Court on June 25, 1962, held that Ole Miss had denied him admission "solely because he was a Negro" and ordered U. S. District Judge Mize "to restrain university officials from denying his enrollment." The university's claims that Meredith was unqualified were dismissed as "frivolous." Early in September the U. S. Supreme Court confirmed the Circuit Court order.

At this point, Governor Barnett, invoking the discredited mythology of states'-rights federalism, issued an extraordinary interposition proclamation. In it he announced that all interference by federal officials with Mississippi affairs was illegal, and he therefore ordered the arrest of any representatives of the federal government who were found to be "in violation of this Executive Order . . . [or] the laws of the state of Mississippi." Barnett's proclamation, one of the quainter relics of the Massive Resistance era, was almost a parody of states'-rights federalism, filled as it was with references to state sovereignty, tenth amendment reserved powers, illegal judicial decrees, and federal "usurpation."[22] In addition to trying to rehabilitate interposition, Barnett proposed that every state official be ready "to go to jail, if necessary, to keep faith with the people." As though that were not proof enough of his *bona fides* as a Massive Resister, he also had the University's Board of Trustees appoint him "special registrar" of Ole Miss.

With the help of state and local police, Governor Barnett and Lieutenant Governor Johnson three times blocked Meredith's enrollment at Ole Miss. For his nullification actions, Barnett was found guilty of contempt by the U. S. Court of Appeals and ordered to pay a fine of $10,000 a day unless he should promptly purge himself of the contempt.

After vainly trying to negotiate with Barnett, President Kennedy on September 29 addressed a proclamation to the officials and people of Mississippi, directing them to stop all illegal resistance to federal authority. On Sunday afternoon, September 30, the federal government flew Meredith to Oxford from Memphis and had him driven to the Old Miss campus in a state police car, preceded by a large force of U. S. Marshals.

As the word spread that "the nigger" was on campus, counterrevolutionary zealots converged on Oxford from all over the state. Many arrived from Jackson, where Ole Miss had played a football game the day before, and all day they filled the campus with chants and cheers, such as "Where's the nigger? Get a rope!" The members of the school band returned from Jackson in their traditional Confederate uniforms, and the Confederate battle flag —the fighting colors of the Old Miss Rebels—seemed to be everywhere. Crowds of students walked along Rebel and Confederate Drives wearing tiny caricatures of Colonel Rebel, the school's mythical mascot, while adult agitators flocked to the campus in droves, itching for a riot.

The riot erupted more or less spontaneously around 7 P.M. when throngs of angry whites moved to the Lyceum Building, where the federal marshals were headquartered. Screaming "Two, four, six, eight, we don't wanna integrate!" the rioters attacked the "federal enemy" with rocks, bottles, and other missiles in a battle that reached its peak of violence around midnight. During the fighting, some 375 marshals and rioters were injured and two men were killed, one of whom was a French journalist.[23] As the sun rose on the great gray oaks of the rolling Ole Miss campus, the scene was more reminiscent of a battlefield than of a grove in academe. It was as though all the pent-up frustrations experienced by white Mississippians since 1954 had suddenly erupted and cascaded over the campus like a jet of water under pressure. As the clean-up began, one thing was clear—the Bloody Sunday insurrection was the nearest thing to all-out warfare the post-Brown era had seen.

What kept the Ole Miss riot from being an even bloodier tragedy was the massive, if belated intervention of federal troops. President Kennedy, hoping he could avoid the use of troops, sent more than 400 U. S. Marshals to the Oxford campus of Ole Miss, where on Sunday afternoon they took over the administration building as their command post. Still hopeful, the President at 10 P.M. on Sunday told the nation over television that the court's orders were being carried out at Ole Miss, and at the same time reminded the students that "the honor of your university and the state are in the balance." But the riot had already started, and things went from bad to worse. So around midnight the President bowed to the inevitable and ordered Regular Army units concentrated at Memphis to proceed to the Ole Miss campus, along with several units of the Mississippi National Guard he had earlier federalized. By daybreak federal troops both occupied and surrounded the campus, and it was their show of force that finally drove off the remnants of the 2,500 rioters.

Within a few days the Kennedy Administration had committed more than 30,000 troops to the Oxford area, but withdrawal of the bulk of these began soon after the pacification. By the end of October only five hundred soldiers were left, and most of those departed in the next few weeks. The last of the federal troops were withdrawn in July 1963.

Protected by federal marshals and troops, Meredith registered for classes on Monday morning. Though ostracized and constantly harassed while a student at Ole Miss, he was graduated on August 18, 1963, with a bachelor's degree in political science. After graduation he moved to New York, got a law degree from Columbia, and became active in politics and the civil rights movement. In the 1960's, while leading a civil rights march through

Mississippi, he was shot from ambush and wounded, but not seriously. In the early 1970's he returned to Mississippi to live, and promptly became a leading figure in black politics there.[24]

The Ole Miss showdown confirmed once more that in any confrontation between state and federal authorities, the former are bound to lose, despite their minatory rhetoric, since no state has the resources to withstand military intervention by the federal government. It also confirmed what should have been learned at Little Rock, namely, that when forced to intervene in a domestic crisis, the President should intervene expeditiously and with sufficient strength. Initially, President Kennedy relied perhaps on too few federal marshals, but after the riot started, he reacted with "federal overkill."

Counterrevolutionaries are rarely contrite about their abortive efforts to restore a discredited social system—no matter how costly those efforts may have been—and that was certainly true of the Mississippi Massive Resisters after the Ole Miss showdown. Governor Barnett continued angry and defiant, and declared, "We will never surrender." In a broadcast address to his people on Monday night, October 1, Barnett blamed the riot on Washington, saying, "the federal government has been the aggressor from the outset." Most white Mississippians apparently believed that, and it was no surprise when a Mississippi grand jury subsequently charged Chief Marshal McShane with willfully "inciting a riot." It was also no surprise when the most pro-segregation of the candidates—Lieutenant Governor Paul Johnson—won the 1963 gubernatorial election.

VI. THE UNIVERSITY OF ALABAMA SHOWDOWN

THE FIFTH AND LAST of the campus showdowns between Massive Resisters and the federal government occurred in Alabama a few months after the Ole Miss crisis. It was, in many respects, a re-run of the Ole Miss scenario, with the federal government—and the egalitarian revolution—once again emerging as the victor. But there was, of course, a different cast of characters.

By this time Governor Wallace resembled the legendary Roman hero Horatius in his grim determination to defend what was left of Massive Resistance in the Deep South aganst the federal "Etruscans." But unlike his Roman counterpart, Wallace was not defending a bridge but the schools and colleges of Alabama, and to assure their continued segregation he promised personally to "stand in the schoolhouse door."

Wallace's moment of truth, long postponed, finally arrived in 1963, when a federal court ordered the University of Alabama to admit three black students in June—two to the main campus at Tuscaloosa and one to the University Center at Huntsville. The university had been desegregated for three days in February 1956 by a young black woman, Autherine Lucy. But after Miss Lucy's expulsion following a campus riot, the university returned to its segregated ways.[25]

The court had ordered the Tuscaloosa campus to be desegregated on June 11. Anticipating trouble and trying to ward it off, President Kennedy, at 11:30 A.M. on that day, issued an executive proclamation ordering the Alabama Governor and all other state officials to "cease and desist" from obstructing the court-ordered desegregation at the university. In the meantime the Department of Justice had earlier dispatched to Tuscaloosa a team of high-level officials, headed by Deputy Attorney General Nicholas De B. Katzenbach, and 2,000 Regular Army troops were on stand-by alert seventy miles away.

As expected, Governor Wallace ignored the President's proclamation and went to Tuscaloosa shortly before noon on June 11. Redeeming his resistance pledge, he greeted the two black students, accompanied by Katzenbach and two other Justice Department officials, from behind a specially constructed podium at the main door of Foster Auditorium. After Wallace stopped the students from entering, Katzenbach read the President's "cease-and-desist" order to him. The governor then responded with a "proclamation" of his own, condemning "this unwelcome, unwanted, and unwarranted intrusion upon the campus of the University of Alabama."

Rebuffed by Wallace, Katzenbach retreated to his car and escorted the two blacks to their dormitories. Soon after that, the Alabama National Guard, some of it already in Tuscaloosa, was federalized. At 5:36 P.M. one hundred of the federalized guardsmen escorted the black students on their second trip to the auditorium. General Henry C. Graham of Birmingham, commander of the Guard units, told the governor, "It is my sad duty to ask you to step aside, on order of the President of the United States." And Wallace, having made his point to the delight of all Massive Resisters, graciously left the campus. His entire act had, of course, been a charade, but it had redeemed the pledge he had made to his followers, and his timely withdrawal had averted the possibility of violence. Two days later, the University Center at Huntsville was desegregated without incident.

Within two hours after Governor Wallace capitulated, President Kennedy spoke to the nation by radio and television and became the first President in American history to state unequivocally that segregation is morally wrong. Describing the escalating civil rights movement as a genuine revolution that was basically moral in nature, he said that "The time has come for this nation to fulfill its promises." He also reminded his white listeners that it was their task and obligation "to make that revolution . . . peaceful and constructive for all."

There was still some life in the South's political counterrevolution, but total Massive Resistance was dead everywhere by the end of 1963. It collapsed in South Carolina shortly before it did in Alabama. On January 28, 1963, previously all-white Clemson College admitted a black student, Harvey B. Gantt, with a lot of publicity but no violence, and in September public-school desegregation came to South Carolina without trouble. Tuscaloosa was, in fact, the last campus showdown in the Massive Resistance era.

If campus confrontations ceased after Tuscaloosa, off-campus troubles did not. In 1963, in fact, there were more than 10,000 racial demonstrations, such as sit-ins and pray-ins, and approximately 5,000 blacks were arrested for participating in them. And on June 12, the day after President Kennedy appealed for an end to the "fires of frustration and discord," Medgar Evers, Mississippi field secretary of the NAACP, was shot from ambush in his own driveway, presumably by a segregationist extremist. The slain black leader was buried in Arlington National Cemetery and became one of the most venerated martyrs of the egalitarian revolution.

August 28, 1963, was a high point in the egalitarian revolution—and a low point in the South's backlash. For it was on that day that the "March on Washington," involving more than 200,000 blacks and whites, reached its climax with the moving address by Dr. Martin Luther King, Jr., on the steps of the Lincoln Memorial. "I have a dream," Dr. King said on that occasion, "that one day this nation will rise up and live out the true meaning of its creed." Though the March seriously taxed Washington's public service facilities, it was entirely peaceful and set new records for crowd size and media coverage.

In the latter half of 1963 two tragic events occurred that shook the nation and the world and exacerbated racial tensions in the South. On the morning of September 15 a dynamite bomb, presumably thrown by counterrevolutionary Negrophobes, blasted a black Baptist church in Birmingham. Four girls, ranging in age from ten to fourteen, were killed in their Sunday school rooms, and their bodies mutilated. Other worshipers were injured by flying debris, and additional casualties resulted from the rioting that followed the bombing. Dr. King wired Governor Wallace that "The blood of four little children . . . is on your hands." The Governor indignantly disclaimed all responsibility for the Birmingham violence.

About two months later, on November 22, President Kennedy was assassinated in Dallas. While racism was apparently not a factor in that tragedy, many observers suggested that the general spirit of violence spawned by the South's counterrevolution may well have contributed, indirectly, to shaping the assassin's warped mentality. In any event, few, if any, Massive Resisters mourned President Kennedy's departure from the White House.

As the presidential election year of 1964 neared, there was a real question whether the mounting signs of racial extremism and violence in the South were a fortuitous set of aberrations, as most southerners held, or the manifestation of a conscious policy of political repression and murder. Of course, no state or local government official publicly condoned violence. Yet there now seems little doubt that the region's counterrevolutionary zealots, spearheaded by the Klan, did indeed seek to make murder a calculated instrument of the Massive Resistance movement. The deaths of Medgar Evers and the little girls at Birmingham, as well as the earlier slayings of black and white civil-rights activists, graphically dramatized that fact.

In the succession of violent confrontations that stretched from Little Rock to Birmingham, the Massive Resisters, making the most of the dialectic of counterrevolution, were seeking nothing less than to shoot down the American Dream. Most Americans outside the South professed to be surprised and appalled by that effort, as were most foreigners. But to the extent that violence is as southern as fried chicken and hominy grits, they should have expected something of the sort. Be that as it may, it is clear that the Massive Resisters, like counterrevolutionaries everywhere, regarded history as a storehouse to be looted rather than a record to be learned. And saddest of all, what they looted was not the nobler universal aspects of the southern heritage but the mean and meretricious ones.

9.

Congress and Massive Resistance

I. First Initiatives

THE FEDERAL COURTS and Presidents Eisenhower and Kennedy led the forces that brought token desegregation to the South. It remained, however, for Congress and its chief enforcement agent, the Department of Health, Education and Welfare, to give the coup de grace to the South's counterrevolution by transforming tokenism into something approaching massive compliance with Brown.

Congress's intervention in the segregation struggle was reluctant and belated, coming as it did in 1957, three years after the announcement of Brown I. Congressional intervention in the year of Little Rock took the form of the Civil Rights Act of 1957, which, though of minimal practical importance, amounted to legitimation of the egalitarian revolution by the national legislature.[1] The final version of the act was a watered-down revision of the Eisenhower Administration's 1956 proposal for civil rights legislation. The act, however, was not sufficiently watered down for Strom Thurmond who, as has been stated, personally filibustered the measure for a Senate record of over twenty-four hours.

The 1957 act contained a total of five titles. Title I authorized the creation of an executive Commission on Civil Rights, to be composed of six presidential appointees, which was empowered to investigate allegations relating to suffrage abridgement. Title II authorized the President to appoint one additional Assistant Attorney General in the Department of Justice. Title III extended the jurisdiction of federal district courts to include civil action resulting from suits seeking equity relief against civil rights deprivation. Title IV empowered the U. S. Attorney General to seek court injunctions to stop interference with *voting* rights, but not educational or other civil rights. Title V established criminal penalties for persons convicted of violating the act, and for the first time fixed the qualifications of federal jurors.

Other than in what it symbolized, the most significant aspect of the 1957 act was the authorization of the new Civil Rights Commission. John Hannah, the president of Michigan State University, was appointed chairman, and the Commission made its first report to the President in September 1959. Subsequent special acts extended the Commission's life, and in the following years a number of highly detailed investigative reports were produced that significantly influenced the course of future legislation in the civil rights field. Indeed, to this very day the reports of the Civil Rights Commission are the best single source of authoritative data on the course of the egalitarian revolution after 1957. That is why they are the indispensable point of departure for any serious study of Massive Resistance.

To the dismay of civil rights militants, Congress passed no additional civil rights measures in the 1950's nor did it bother to put more teeth into the 1957 act. Not surprisingly, therefore, no blacks were registered through the act's civil remedies. In the 1960's, however, Congress became more active in the civil rights field as Massive Resistance persisted, and some of its enactments were of crucial importance in assuring the decline and fall of the South's backlash.

The Civil Rights Act of 1960, like its predecessor, was a

modest effort to extend the concept of equality of opportunity. Also based on administration suggestions, its passage through the last Eisenhower Congress was facilitated by the close collaboration between Senate Majority Leader Lyndon Johnson and Minority Leader Everett Dirksen. The most important part of the act was Title VI, which authorized judges to appoint referees to assist blacks in registering and voting. Title II was also important, since it provided criminal penalties for bombings and bomb threats, and for mob action designed to obstruct court orders, whether racial incidents were involved or not. Additional provisions authorized the setting up of special schools for military dependents where local facilities were unavailable and made mandatory the preservation of state records of federal elections for a minimum of twenty-two months.

As welcome as they were to the proponents of the egalitarian revolution, neither the Civil Rights Act of 1957 nor that of 1960 significantly handicapped the backlash activities of the Massive Resisters. For another year or two it would be the federal courts and President Kennedy, along with the rapidly expanding civil rights movement, that would keep the South's counterrevolution from reaching its goals.

II. THE CIVIL RIGHTS ACT OF 1964

THE CIVIL RIGHTS ACT of 1964, the most comprehensive civil rights measure ever approved by Congress, was very much an idea whose time had come. Many regard it as a memorial to President Kennedy, who had asked for such a law in the previous summer, a few months before his death. It was also quite clearly a product of the new stage in the egalitarian revolution, which involved more direct action, civil disobedience, and occasional resort to violence, and of the new stage in the South's counterrevolution, characterized by mass arrests, intimidation, bombings, and premeditated murder. Yet despite the strong pressures for its enactment, it was not finally passed until the Senate for the first time in its history voted to end a civil rights filibuster which southern die-hards had mounted.

The provisions of the 1964 act were embodied in eleven Titles. Title I proscribed a number of southern practices, such as strict literacy tests, that had been used to prevent blacks from registering and voting. Title II, the most controversial part of the act, in effect revived the repudiated Civil Rights Act of 1875 by guaranteeing blacks equal access to public accommodations such as hotels, motels, restaurants, and places of amusement. Title III empowered the Attorney General to file suits for the desegregation of public facilities other than public schools. Title IV required the U. S. Office of Education to render technical assistance to school boards preparing desegregation plans, and authorized the Attorney General in certain circumstances to file suits to force the desegregation of racially separate public schools. Title V extended the life of the Civil Rights Commission for four years and increased its powers. Title VI provided that federal funds could be cut off from federally supported programs that were found to be discriminatorily administered. Title VII established a five-man Equal Employment Opportunity Commission and banned job discrimination on account of race, color, religion, sex, or national origin. Title VIII obligated the Census Bureau to gather voting statistics by race. Title IX authorized the Justice Department to intervene in pending civil rights cases. Title X created the Community Relations Service. Title XI, labeled "Miscellaneous," provided that nothing in the act was intended to limit existing powers of the Attorney General or other federal agencies or to prevent their intervening in any civil rights action or proceeding.

While earlier civil rights legislation had only minimally affected the South's counterrevolution, the Civil Rights Act of 1964 was a near-fatal blow to the hopes and aspirations of the Massive Resisters. In a relatively short time it brought about an increase in black voter registrations, helped expedite southern school desegregation, opened almost all public accommodations in the South to blacks, led to an increase in black employment in government, and diminished, if it did not destroy, long-established hiring discrimination in southern industry.

As anticipated, a number of angry segregationists promptly

filed lawsuits challenging the constitutionality of the 1964 act, chiefly on the ground that the measure gave the federal government powers that went far beyond those permitted by the Constitution. The first part of the Act to be challenged was Title II, the "public accommodations" provision, which predictably was bitterly opposed by southern hotel owners and restaurateurs, whose chief spokesman was Lester Maddox. The Supreme Court, however, made short shrift of the segregationists' arguments. And in December 1964, less than six months after the act's adoption, it sustained Title II as a valid exercise of the commerce power. While the Court's opinion was unanimous, there was some disagreement among the justices as to the basis of their holding.[2]

At a critical point in the segregation struggle, the Supreme Court had once again entered the picture by legitimating federal legislative controls that reached into areas of private discrimination previously thought to be outside the reach of federal power. In so doing, the Court further weakened the formerly sacrosanct distinction between state and private action as, following Congress, it seemed to expand the limits of "state responsibility," and broaden the definition of interstate commerce.

In the latter half of 1964 the Massive Resisters had a moment of hope when the Republicans nominated Barry Goldwater, who had voted against the Civil Rights Act of 1964, to be their presidential candidate in the fall election. But after Lyndon Johnson trounced the Arizona Senator in November, they virtually despaired of ever having another friend in the White House. All in all, 1964 was not a good year for the South's counterrevolutionaries.

III. THE VOTING RIGHTS ACT OF 1965

IN THE MID-1960's equal opportunity at the ballot box became as great a concern of the egalitarian revolutionaries as equal opportunity in the schoolhouse. That concern was dramatized and strengthened by the 1963 reports of the Commission on Civil Rights, which revealed that at least one hundred "hard-core counties" in the Deep South had almost completely disfranchised voting-age black adults there.

The Voting Rights Act of 1965 was a direct result of the pressures exerted by civil rights activists for a more effective law to end the disfranchisement of blacks and other minorities. It was also to some extent a response to the massive Selma-to-Montgomery march and the violent deaths of Mrs. Viola Liuzzo and the Reverend James Reeb. This is not to suggest that Congress would not have passed the law except for the pressures generated by the Selma crisis, but there is no denying that those pressures were a factor—and a big one—in congressional deliberations. The civil rights cause was likewise helped by the timely intervention of President Johnson, who, shortly after Reeb's murder, went in person before Congress to request action on a new Voting Rights Bill in the name of the "long-suffering men and women" who had "peaceably protested their rights as Americans."

The 1965 act, which was signed into law on August 6, differed from previous civil rights legislation in one important respect —namely, in that it provided for direct federal action, not just individual lawsuits, to assure blacks the right to register and vote when qualified. For this reason, the South's counterrevolutionaries mounted an all-out effort to defeat the bill before it could become law. Their failure to do so was another sign of the declining fortunes of the Massive Resistance movement.

President Johnson, keenly aware of both the practical and the symbolic significance of the act, went over to Capitol Hill to sign it. The formal signing took place in the President's Room off the Senate chamber, where on August 6, 1861, Abraham Lincoln had signed a bill freeing slaves who had been pressed into service by the Confederacy. After the signing, the Justice Department moved swiftly to implement the act. The next day a suit was filed attacking the Mississippi poll tax, which sometimes prevented blacks from voting. Three days after that similar suits were filed against the Alabama, Texas, and Virginia poll taxes. On August 7 the Justice Department suspended literacy tests and related voter qualification devices in the seven states covered by the act. Those states were Alabama, Alaska, Georgia, Louisiana, Mississippi, South Carolina, and Virginia. Also affected by the Department's action were twenty-seven North Carolina counties and Apache County, Arizona. On August 9 Attorney General Katzenbach named the first group of counties and parishes in the states of Alabama, Louisiana, and Mississippi where federal examiners would be appointed to expedite black voter applications. Before the end of August President Johnson was able to report to the nation that 27,385 blacks had already been registered by federal registrars, thus demonstrating the value of the new act.

Possibly the most important provision of the Voting Rights Act of 1965 was that which authorized the Civil Service Commission to appoint federal officials as voting "examiners" with the power to register qualified adults to vote in all elections after state or local officials had refused to register them. The examiners were also empowered to protect the right of such persons to vote by patrolling polling places on election day.

Also important was a provision of the act suspending literacy tests and similar voter qualifications rules when the Attorney General and the Director of the Census concluded that a state or political subdivision thereof came within the scope of the act's automatic triggering formula. In addition, the Act stipulated that an inability to read or write English was not to be a bar to voting if a person had successfully completed the sixth grade, or its equivalent, in a school under the American flag that conducted classes in a language other than English. The purpose of this provision was to enfranchise those Spanish-speaking Puerto Ricans in New York and other cities who were kept from voting because of laws requiring literacy in English as a prerequisite for the franchise.

Taking aim at one of the South's favorite disfranchisement devices, the act directed the Attorney General to institute "forthwith" in the appropriate federal district courts suits challenging the validity of the poll tax as a voting prerequisite, since such a prerequisite appeared to violate both the fourteenth and fifteenth amendments. (The twenty-fourth amendment, ratified in 1964, had invalidated the poll tax as a prerequisite for voting in *federal* elections.)

Of particular significance was the fact that the act provided ample enforcement machinery at the federal level to assure the speedy end of illegal disfranchisement of blacks, and at the same time stipulated heavy penalties for persons convicted of violating the act. As a sop to the South, the sponsors of the act included a provision setting forth methods by which political subdivisions might free themselves from the appointment of federal examiners. There was, however, no provision for reinstating suspended voting qualification tests.

The South's counterrevolutionaries responded to the 1965 act with the only weapon left to them—massive litigation in the form of numerous suits and counter suits intended to block or weaken the implementation of the act. The Supreme Court, however, continued to be unsympathetic to the South's position. And in 1966 Chief Justice Warren, writing for a near-unanimous Court, rejected South Carolina's challenge to the act and concluded that the parts of the Voting Rights Act under review were constitutional as "a valid means for carrying out the commands of the Fifteenth Amendment."[3] A short time later, the Court upheld that part of the act which in effect abrogated New York's English literacy requirement. In this instance the Court reversed the decision of a three-judge lower federal court which had invalidated that portion of the act relating to literacy requirements as an invasion of the states' reserved powers as set forth in the tenth amendment.[4] Also in 1966 the Supreme Court completed the destruction of the poll tax by ruling in a Virginia case that such taxes introduced "wealth or payment of a fee as a measure of a voter's qualifications" and thus constituted "an invidious discrimination" in violation of the fourteenth amendment's equal protection clause.[5]

The Voting Rights Act was yet another grave setback to what was left of the South's backlash, and its impact on the black vote in the southern states was immediate and far-reaching. Before the decade of the sixties had come to a close, black voter registrations in the eleven states of the Old Confederacy increased by more than 100 percent. This, of course, was the genesis of the black political power movement that became important in the late 1960's.

IV. OTHER CONGRESSIONAL ACTIONS

IN 1966, AS MASSIVE RESISTANCE receded into history, the egalitarian revolution took off in a number of new (and often unsettling) directions. It was the year of revolutionary slogans such as "black power," "deghettoization," "freedom now," and "burn, baby, burn." And as the concerns of the civil rights movement spilled over into the problems of housing, urban slums, jobs, and law enforcement, there was an increase in northern violence and a "white backlash" against black militance, most notably in the white ethnic centers of the North. Much of the urban violence was a delayed fall-out from the Watts riots of August 1965—perhaps the worst in this country in the twentieth century.

Even before a 1966 Gallup Poll indicated that 52 per cent of whites believed that the Johnson Administration was pushing racial integration too fast, Congress was beginning to reflect what appeared to be a general "slow-down" mood in the nation. The most dramatic evidence of the change in congressional attitudes toward the egalitarian revolution was the rejection of a major administration civil rights bill, which President Johnson first announced in his State of the Union Message to Congress on January 12. The House passed the bill in August, but it died in the Senate. The Senate's defeat of the bill took the form of two negative votes on cloture petitions whose purpose was to shut off a southern filibuster. After the second cloture vote, Senator Eastland of Mississippi boasted, "The civil rights advocates who hope to force an interracial society have been completely routed." Referring to the Civil Rights measures passed since 1957, he added that it would not be long before "We can start the fight to repeal those vicious measures."

The 90th Congress, meeting in its first session in 1967, was even more conservative on civil rights than the 89th Congress had been. This growing conservatism resulted from several factors.

There were more Republicans in the new Congress. Members were becoming increasingly alarmed by the steadily rising militancy of the civil rights movement, characterized by H. Rap Brown's statement, "We are at war, and we are behind enemy lines, so you better get yourselves some guns." Many congressmen resented (and feared) the merging of the civil rights movement with the anti-Vietnam campaign which occurred in 1967. Both in and out of Congress, there was a splintering of the egalitarian revolution's leadership, with many militant leaders now disdaining legislation in favor of direct action. All this, of course, made it impossible to present a unified front for a specific legislative program as had been done in previous years with positive results.

Though President Johnson sent another package of civil rights proposals to the Hill in 1967, Congress took final action on only one of them. That was a bill to extend the life of the Civil Rights Commission for an additional five years. It was the least controversial of the President's proposals. Yet even this bill was amended in the Senate to include a rather strict limitation on the Commission's future expenditures. Not surprisingly, Senators Eastland, Thurmond, McClellan, and Ervin—all southerners— voted against sending the bill to the floor from the Senate Judiciary Committee, but the Senate finally passed it late in the year by a voice vote.

In 1968, a presidential election year, Congress became somewhat more liberal and approved two measures that had long been advocated by civil libertarians. The first was a bill to reform federal jury selection procedures, which in the past had often been discriminatory against racial and other minority groups. The bill provided for the random picking of jurors from voter lists, and it forbade discrimination in their selection on racial, religious, sexual, or economic grounds. The bill's passage through Congress was facilitated by the fact that its sponsors played down the measure's civil rights aspects. Its main purpose was to make sure that future federal juries would be made up of men and women representing "a fair cross-section of the community."

More important from the civil rights point of view was the Civil Rights Act of 1968, which was chiefly but not exclusively concerned with expanding the concept of "open housing." The heart of the act was Title VIII, a sort of omnibus provision that was in effect a federal fair housing law and the first such law passed by Congress in the twentieth century. Title VIII prohibited racial and religious discrimination in the sale and rental of housing, with the ban to be imposed in three time stages, culminating in December 1969. Exempted from the act's reach were dwellings of four units or less sold without the services of a broker, as well as private clubs housing their own members on a non-commercial basis. Enforcement of the act's provisions was made a joint responsibility of the Justice Department and the Department of Housing and Urban Development.

Title I incorporated a number of new anti-riot measures which conservatives strongly supported. The most controversial of these, variously known as "Thurmond's Rider" and the "Rap Brown Law," was a provision that defined a riot as a public disturbance involving "an act or acts of violence" by anyone in "assemblages of three or more persons," and made anyone who crossed a state line to participate in an assemblage that turned violent subject to five years in federal prison and a fine of ten thousand dollars. In sponsoring Title I, Thurmond and other spokesmen for Massive Resistance obviously hoped to discourage large-scale civil rights demonstrations and to chill the exercise of first amendment rights by egalitarian revolutionaries. The first use of the "Rap Brown Law" was the much argued prosecution of the Chicago Seven in the wake of the riots at the 1968 Democratic National Convention.

The 1968 act, like its predecessors, would never have made it through Congress except for the ceaseless pressure of egalitarians working through the politics of protest and conflict. Most persuasive in this regard were the riots that engulfed black slums in more than a hundred cities after the assassination of Dr. Martin Luther King, Jr., in the spring of 1968. It is hardly too much to say that the 1968 open housing law was a memorial to Dr. King as the Civil Rights Act of 1964 was a memorial to President Kennedy. It is both ironic and tragic to reflect that it takes a political assassination or a series of bloody riots to convince Congress of where its duty to the people lies.

Though Congress entered the segregation crisis with the

greatest reluctance, there can be no denying the fact that once it began to legislate against discrimination, any hope the Massive Resisters may still have held of rolling back Brown simply became unrealistic. Congress, of course, never adopted all the proposals suggested by the egalitarian revolutionaries, but it passed enough to make the black man's hopes something more than hollow dreams. As long as the President, the courts, and the bureaucratic agencies "liberally" interpreted congressional enactments, the egalitarian or black revolution was bound to keep rolling along.

10.
Abatement of Massive Resistance

I. REASONS FOR DECLINE OF THE MOVEMENT

Most scholars who have probed the history of the South's counterrevolution in depth have assigned it a life span of about ten years, extending from the fall of 1954 to the summer of 1964. Seen in these temporal terms, Massive Resistance may be said to have begun as a white backlash to the Supreme Court's Brown decision and to have survived as a viable political movement until the passage by Congress of the Civil Rights Act of 1964. President Johnson, aware of the historic importance of the latter event, signed the 1964 act on July 2 in a public ceremony that was carried to the nation by television from the East Room of the White House. In his remarks on that occasion, the President once again denounced all forms of racial discrimination, declaring "It cannot continue." It must not continue, he said, for "Our Constitution, the foundation of our republic forbids it. The principles of our freedom forbid it. Morality forbids it. And the law I will sign tonight forbids it." At the time it appeared that most Americans agreed with their President.

The enactment of the Civil Rights Act of 1964 did not, of

course, instantly destroy Massive Resistance as an active force in southern politics. The movement had been declining more or less steadily since the early 1960's, and vestiges of it would survive into the 1970's. But, both practically and symbolically, the 1964 act did signal the end of Massive Resistance as a respectable ideology and as an effective counterrevolutionary obstacle to the implementation of Brown in the South. In their hearts, the majority of Massive Resisters doubtless continued to believe in the myths of their movement, but after 1964 they were rebels without a legal or moral cause, ideological pariahs in search of a viable creed. Their drums, if not silent, were muted, their rhetoric diminished, and over all the campuses and statehouses of Dixie, there brooded a strange and sullen stillness.

Since the decline and fall of Massive Resistance, students of southern politics—as well as the counterrevolutionaries themselves—have come forth with a plethora of reasons for the movement's eclipse. Obviously a number of factors were at work eroding from the start the tactical effectiveness of the southern backlash. For the purposes of this analysis, it is assumed that ten reasons, more or less interrelated, were ultimately responsible for the near-total collapse of Massive Resistance in the mid-1960's.

1. Almost everybody now agrees that one of the principal reasons for the movement's decline was the continued firmness of most federal courts in disposing of segregation cases in the decade after Brown. Of course, individual district judges sometimes equivocated, and on occasion evinced fierce hostility toward the doctrine enunciated in Brown. But the U. S. Supreme Court and the federal circuit courts, with only an occasional show of ambivalence, stuck tenaciously to the logic of the Brown holding and invalidated virtually every southern ruse designed to avoid compliance with court-ordered desegregation. Had the federal judiciary not stood firm in support of the Brown decisions, the whole history of Massive Resistance might have been quite different.

2. The post-Little Rock commitment of the federal executive branch to Brown's enforcement was certainly a critical defeat for the South's counterrevolution at a time when

the true believers were riding the wave of euphoric optimism. As it turned out, Eisenhower was less enthusiastic about enforcing Brown than Kennedy and Johnson, but once Faubus threw down the interposition gauntlet, he acted with vigor and decisiveness.

3. Congress's belated legitimation of the egalitarian revolution through a series of increasingly "liberal" civil rights acts appears now to have been the straw that broke the "southern camel's back." As long as Congress was neutral, or at least not actively opposed to Massive Resistance, the segregationists still had rational grounds for believing in victory. However, once Congress joined the courts and the executive branch in espousing the cause of equality, all hope of victory for the South disappeared.

4. Another, less tangible, factor contributing to the demise of Massive Resistance was a new national consensus that emerged from many sources in the early 1960's. This was a widespread feeling or belief that the federal government should do more to advance the cause of equal opportunity for black Americans than it had done and, at the same time, deal more decisively with the southern backlash. While this consensus, for a number of reasons, dissipated in the late 1960's, its emergence in the Kennedy years proved to be a serious jolt to the strategy and hopes of the segregationists.

5. The unscientific and extra-constitutional nature of the South's counterrevolutionary ideology proved to be a fatal flaw when the ideology was tested (and found wanting) in showdowns with the federal courts and other federal agencies. Whatever utility the ideology may have had in homogenizing southern opinion was more than counterbalanced by the failure of its component myths to survive the scrutiny of judges, administrators, and social scientists.

6. The political extremism and tactical bungling of the South's charismatic demagogues likewise contributed to the demise of Massive Resistance. This is hardly a startling conclusion, for counterrevolutionary politics is invariably reactionary politics. And though reactionary politicians may on occasion be imaginative and tactically creative—as Faubus,

Barnett, and Wallace, for example, sometimes were—they more frequently turn out to be their own worst enemies. Determined to make the impossible possible, they merely succeed in making the possible (some form of rational compromise) impossible.

7. The emergence in the mid-1950's of a new and younger breed of black leaders, of whom the most influential was Dr. Martin Luther King, Jr., helped greatly to solidify the black community against the old order of things and also led to an intensification of the legal and political pressures on the resisting southern establishments. To say this, however, is not to disparage the efforts of such earlier black leaders as Walter White, Adam Clayton Powell, Jr., and Thurgood Marshall, without whose pioneering work the implementation of Brown would have been even more difficult than it was.

8. The creation of a biracial civil rights movement in the late fifties as a sort of vanguard of the egalitarian revolution served as a vital catalyst for mobilizing both white and black liberals against the Massive Resisters at a time when organization and dynamic leadership were most important. The pressure politics generated by "the movement" played a major role in persuading Congress to legislate against discrimination in all its forms.

9. The growing disenchantment of southern moderates after 1960 with the counterrevolution's extremist leadership gradually produced more open dissent in the South, which helped indirectly to soften the intransigence of die-hard legislators, governors, and bureaucrats. This disenchantment in the white community, which became fairly widespread, was most conspicuous in the South's churches, colleges, universities, nationally oriented businesses, and urban newspapers.

10. The loose, undisciplined structure of the Massive Resistance movement proved in the long run to be a fatal defect. The resisting states were never united under a single regional government as was the case after 1861, and the pro-segregation consensus that outsiders found so stultifying in the 1950's was more coercively contrived than spontaneous. Indeed, all the historical evidence suggests that throughout its

brief life-span Massive Resistance was always more of a collusive hope than a conspiratorial plot against the future.

In reflecting today on the decline and fall of Massive Resistance, the conscientious scholar must avoid the temptation to see the South's counterrevolution in strict deterministic terms. Certainly many of the events that made up the movement did seem to move in an inexorable, almost predestined way, as though obeying the implacable dynamics of great impersonal forces. But throughout the movement's history the accidental and the aberrant had a place, as witness the fortuitous arrival of Governor Griffin in Little Rock in August 1957, and the assassination of President Kennedy, which was shortly followed by the "unfreezing" of the bill that became the Civil Rights Act of 1964. One must, in other words, temper the deterministic models of social science (more common in the study of revolution than of counterrevolution) with a few voluntaristic leaps of faith and a reaffirmation of the realm of free will. The crucial play of the unique, the personal, and the arbitrary will always intrude to defy the best made models of political scientists and philosophers of history.

If it is true, as most scholars now believe, that revolutions are made not by insurgents but by incumbents, the South's segregationists must bear the responsibility not only for the rise and fall of their own movement but also for the creation of the black or egalitarian revolution. This would seem to be a perfectly logical (if to them unpleasant) conclusion, for they were the incumbents in 1954 who had it within their power either to facilitate the process of peaceful change or to stand firm against any and all innovations. That they opted for the latter over the former is both the tragedy and the scandal of post-1954 southern leadership.

II. Forces Advancing the Egalitarian Revolution

IN ADDITION to the ten major factors that brought about the decline and fall of Massive Resistance, a number of secondary and tertiary forces have been, and still are, at work assuring the continuation of the egalitarian revolution and preventing a full-scale rebirth of the southern backlash. Some of these forces are regional in scope, while others are national and international.

Perhaps at the top of such forces one should list the mechanization and modernization of southern agriculture. For these phenomena, which have been operative since the late 1930's, have affected southern race relations in a variety of ways. They have, for example, reduced the number of black laborers needed in cotton and tobacco cultivation by around 70 per cent. They have considerably increased the productivity of those blacks remaining on southern farms and thus have advanced their material well-being. They have disrupted the old paternalism that used to characterize southern agriculture, thereby driving thousands of blacks from depressed rural areas to developing urban centers. And, not least in importance, they have sparked a move toward crop diversification throughout the South, which has dethroned "King Cotton" and brought about more profitable economic ventures such as cattle-ranching and chicken-raising. Statistics clearly show that crop diversification has led to an increase in the gross income of both white and black farmers, and, at least indirectly, has led to a diminution of racial tensions.

Two other socio-economic trends, urbanization and industrialization, have had a discernible impact on the black man's status in America. While it is by no means clear that racial tolerance is a universal concomitant of progress along the road of technological-industrial-urban modernization, available evidence does seem to indicate that progress increases along that road. Specifically, urbanization and industrialization seem to enhance the position of blacks in the following ways:

1. They increase the overall economic opportunities open to blacks, thereby making them more secure, independent, and assertive.

2. They expand black educational and cultural opportunities for the reason that the South's urban schools, by any standards of excellence, are superior to all but a few of its rural schools.

3. By bringing more blacks together in a smaller place, they advance black cohesion and solidarity and encourage the development of more militant black leadership.

4. To a significant degree, they are responsible for politicizing blacks and for the first time making them activists in the political process. While blacks still suffer a certain amount of suffrage deprivation in the backwater rural areas of the South, this no longer occurs anywhere in the urban areas.

5. The big integrated urban factory, which brings blacks into daily contact with white workers, seems to produce over time some liberalization of the racial attitudes of lower-class whites. Of course, it is a well-known fact that familiarity may breed contempt as well as understanding, but increasingly it seems to be breeding tolerance—if not true friendship— rather than intolerance.

The decline of white racism and the concomitant increase in equal opportunity for blacks has nowhere been more marked than in the textile field. As late as 1960, less than three per cent of the textile industry's one million workers were blacks, and most of these held only menial unskilled jobs. As the South gradually acquired around 90 per cent of American textile production, southern mills and mill towns remained rigidly segregated in virtually every respect.

By the end of the 1960's, however, egalitarianism was on the march and segregation was in retreat with a speed that would have been unthinkable a few years earlier. Indeed, in 1970 it was estimated that the textile industry was moving faster in pushing minority employment than any other major segment of U. S. industry. The Bureau of Labor Statistics reported in 1970 that the number of blacks employed by the textile industry in that year was approximately 14.3 per cent of the textile work force, as compared with an average of about 10.1 per cent in all manufacturing firms. In southern textile mills, the percentage of black employment had risen to 20 per cent of the total.

There were many reasons for this rather sudden about-face in textile race relations. Among the more important ones were the

1964 Civil Rights Act, the leverage of federal contracts that forbid discrimination, and the ubiquitous pressures of the egalitarian revolution. And though one cannot prove that such measures as the 1964 Civil Rights Act changed many white southern hearts, it is a fact that they changed (and are changing) the overt behavior and hiring practices of a lot of formerly all-white southern textile firms. At work also, of course, were the changing nature of the South's economy and an awakening of "social conscience" in the industry as a whole.

Among demographic forces advancing the egalitarian revolution one of the most significant has been the growing migration of southern blacks to northern urban centers. This migration, much of which ended up in the North's already crowded ghettos, affected the counterrevolutionary South in two ways. It reduced the number of blacks in the once heavily black areas of the Deep South, thus diminishing socio-economic tensions and potential conflict points. And it increased the non-southern camp of the egalitarian revolution, which in turn intensified the pressures on southern governments still defying federal authority.

During the 1960's, the states that made up the Confederacy experienced a total loss of out-migrating blacks of 1,473,000. The losses ranged from 4,000 blacks leaving Texas to 279,000 leaving Mississippi, 30.4 per cent of the state's 1960 black population. In terms of age, the blacks most likely to migrate were those between 10 and 24 years old. With the advent of the 1970's, it seemed that the massive black out-migration was continuing by car, truck, bus, plane, and trains, the more popular of which were dubbed "chicken bone specials."

It is also a fact, as southerners like to point out, that in the decade of the sixties more people moved into the South than out of it for the first time since the 1870's. This fact, however, does not quite mean what it seems to mean. For the 1960's surplus of immigrants over emigrants resulted from the fact that 1,340,000 newcomers—many of them retirees—swelled the population of Florida. The other ten states of the Old South actually experienced a combined loss of 660,000 people through out-migration during the decade. If blacks continue to leave the South as whites move in, by the end of the 1970's three-fourths or more of the nation's black population will be living outside the South. This will almost certainly mean an increase of racial troubles in the North and a decrease of such troubles in the South.

A little noted force of progress in race relations has been the attitudinal changes among many southerners that have followed desegregation of schools, colleges, and military units. Several studies made by the U. S. Commission on Civil Rights confirmed that where school desegregation has been realized in the South, it usually works better than expected. Thus, of southern students and educators (white and black) who were interviewed, almost all stated that the process of desegregation had gone better than they thought it would. Seven out of ten black high school students who were questioned believed they were getting a better education than formerly in their segregated schools. Approximately nine out of ten white students interviewed saw no difference in their own learning progress since the advent of desegregation. Both white and black students appeared satisfied with teacher desegregation, feeling that the teachers were generally teaching without observable racial bias. In 1970 a Gallup Poll revealed that a large proportion of parents, in both the North and South, were willing to send their children to desegregated schools, although many objected to the technique of busing to achieve racial balance.

The attitude changes resulting from military desegregation seemed even more striking. Most informed observers agreed that within a few years after Brown, the armed forces had become the most fully integrated institutions in our society. To be sure, there was a revival of racial troubles in the military in the sixties and seventies at bases in Germany and Vietnam and on certain of the Navy's big ships. Still, all things considered, it appears that military desegregation has been far more successful than most people thought it would be.

No survey of pro-integration forces should neglect the fine work done by the U. S. Commission on Civil Rights. Since the late 1950's, the Commission has scrupulously monitored civil rights activity inside the federal government and throughout the nation, and in the process has achieved a kind of gadfly or conscience status. Some of its data-packed reports have made headlines, such as the one published in the early 1970's that analyzed the civil rights compliance of forty federal executive departments and agencies. Most of the time, however, it carries on its research behind the scenes.

Temporary by statute and small by federal standards, the Commission has frequently criticized high officials for "footdragging" on desegregation, and has thereby incurred the ire of several Presidents and attorneys general, as well as the enduring hatred of Massive Resisters everywhere. Despite its staff and budgetary deficiencies, the Commission merits credit for at least four major accomplishments. Through its research reports, it provided the first hard data about the scope of racial discrimination in the nation. Its hearings and reports played a major role in building up the pro-Brown consensus of the 1960's. Its findings helped to prod Congress into legislating against discrimination. And by means of overt and covert pressures, its members have kept the spotlight on officials who embraced the doctrine of "benign neglect" of civil rights. Understandably, civil libertarians were dismayed when the Nixon Administration, in late 1972, forced the resignation of the Reverend Theodore M. Hesburgh from the Commission after fifteen years of service. As much as anyone, Father Hesburgh had become the voice of racial justice within the federal government.

One of the most encouraging events in recent years from the point of view of racial amity has been the precipitate decline of those segregationist pressure groups that were such a potent force in southern politics in the early post-Brown years. Most of them have simply vanished, leaving scarcely a trace behind, and those that remain are relatively inactive today. The Councils, which were never strong outside the Deep South, seem mainly concerned now with the establishment of segregated private schools where unitary public schools have become a reality.

During the heyday of Massive Resistance, none of the South's major counterrevolutionary groups was more feared than the Klan, and today none is more impotent. The Klan is not, of course, wholly dead, since the concept of "klanism" seems indestructible, yet the organization is certainly dormant and in some places non-existent. Early in 1970 the former Grand Dragon of the North Carolina Klan, James Robertson Jones, was released from federal prison in Danbury, Connecticut, and immediately started talking about reviving the Klan. He did not, however, receive much support in the Tar Heel state, and it seems unlikely that he will make a comeback as a segregationist demagogue.

In the Deep South, Robert Shelton, the Klan's national spokesman, has been trying to rebuild his shattered organization with its headquarters in Tuscaloosa, but apparently without a great deal of success. He also was released from prison a short time before Jones, and he spent much of the early seventies raising money at testimonial dinners held in his honor.

One could plausibly argue that during some periods of its history the Klan has been an authentic voice of the South's poor whites, a kind of underground populism for those whites who felt alienated from politics as well as organized religion. But such an argument has little merit today. The South's poor whites are no longer quite so poor, religion is not quite so reactionary, and both the Democrats and Republicans, not to speak of the Wallaceites, have shown an increasing interest in the problems of poor people of both races. Furthermore the Klan's record of violence in the 1954–1964 decade destroyed whatever respectability it once had with all but the most extreme segregationists. That violence, indeed, was one of the chief reasons why the whole federal establishment—or nearly all of it—joined forces with the egalitarian revolution by the early 1960's. In the future the Klan is less likely to resemble Hitler's Gestapo than the Masons and Shriners.[1]

As the Klan goes into eclipse, there is a company of "Young Turks" emerging in the South dedicated to forgetting the past and exploring the future. Believing that the South has had too much history and that its people have been stultified by tradition, the "new breed" southerners are seeking novel institutional structures through which to implement their new programs. Perhaps the most influential of these is the L.Q.C. Lamar Society, organized in 1969 and named for the nineteenth-century Mississippian who was a Reconstruction era Senator and later an associate justice of the United States Supreme Court. The Society's basic goals are to sponsor studies of various kinds, encourage regional planning, and propose policy alternatives to public officials. While critics charge that the Society is more reflective of a mood than equipped with a viable program, its leaders, notably H. Brandt Ayres, editor and publisher of the Anniston (Alabama) *Star*, suggest that it may one day evolve into a kind of "distant early warning apparatus" with the expertise for handling crisis situations. Quite obviously the group has not as yet evolved that far. But even if the Lamar Society never becomes a militant liberal force, it at least will have made a small contribution to the cause of common sense in race relations—and in the Deep South where the contribution was most needed.

A minor but symbolically important progressive trend is the "Blackening" of southern sports. Basketball, especially at Florida State and the University of North Carolina, seems to have led the way, but southern football powers are now beating the bushes— South and North—for promising black recruits. Tennessee broke the Southeastern Conference's color bar by signing defensive back Lester McLain in 1966. By 1972 the press was able to report that blacks made up 10 per cent of that Conference's football players and were a significant minority at other formerly all-white southern colleges. At least three southern football powers—Tennessee, Georgia Tech, and Mississippi State—even had black quarterbacks in 1972. The rush to "Blacken" the southern gridiron appears to have started in 1970 when Southern California—with a number of Alabama and other southern black players—roundly defeated the lily-white forces of Paul (Bear) Bryant's Crimson Tide of Alabama. The Alabama coach was later quoted as saying, "That was the best thing that ever happened to the South." In any event, it started a trend that seems to be permanent.

One international force has helped to push forward the egalitarian revolution—the decline of colonialism and the rise of the Third World. This phenomenon, symbolized by the rising power in the United Nations of colored Asians and Africans, has been a big morale-booster to American blacks and a source of heightened racial pride. Unfortunately, the United States government has not always cooperated with the developing nations. And, indeed, while Presidents and Congresses from 1957 on were making significant inputs to the egalitarian revolution at home, they were quite often following a foreign policy of global counterrevolution. Civil libertarians were quick to point out this anomaly, and by the 1970's our counterrevolutionary posture abroad had been somewhat diminished.

Another regional force of progress was the good example set

by a few southern cities in handling racial problems, most notably Atlanta. Though scarcely a black paradise, Atlanta has had little racial strife since World War I days; and even in the heyday of Massive Resistance it was relatively enlightened in racial matters. It has never had much influence in state affairs until recently because of an obsolete pattern of legislative districting that favored rural areas, but for some time now, its political and business leadership has been constructive and forward-looking. Its most influential leaders in the Massive Resistance years were veteran Mayor William B. Hartsfield and Ralph McGill, editor of the *Atlanta Constitution*, both of whom were liberal on racial issues and opposed to Massive Resistance. Blacks constitute about 51 per cent of the city's population, and a number of strong black leaders have come from the black community, particularly from Atlanta University. School desegregation came a little late to Atlanta, but when it came there was no violence or disruptions of any kind. And in a recent election, the city's voters elected a black vice-mayor.[2]

Two additional national forces have recently played a most important role in furthering the cause of equal opportunity throughout the nation. They are the "discovery" of the black man by the mass communications media and the proliferation of black history courses in schools and universities. For the first time the news magazines, television networks, and movies are dramatizing the accomplishments and problems of black Americans with relative integrity while at the same time unmasking the insidious nature of white racism. And in virtually every school and college in America today there is at least one course in black history or black culture. Of course, this heightened racial sensitivity can lead to a censorship of books and films dealing with the negative side of the black experience, but it surely was a necessary, and long overdue corrective to the previous crude stereotypes that passed for black characterizations. In the long run, these educational efforts by the media and academic institutions may well turn out to be the most effective therapy against racism yet devised. But it is equally true that before the long run becomes the present, thousands of additional blacks will needlessly have suffered from the virus of white racism.

The last of the forces of progress to be described here is at the present time one of the most controversial and consequential. That is the rapidly increasing politicization of southern blacks, which has already resulted in a significant rise in black political power in each of the eleven states of the Old South. The scope of this development is underscored by two related phenomena—the expansion of the South's black electorate and the increase in the number of black elected officials.

In this century, the "repoliticization" of southern blacks began with the Supreme Court decision of 1944 invalidating the white primary (*Smith* v. *Allwright*). It did not, however, become a major force in southern politics until the passage of the Voting Rights Act of 1965. At the start of the 1940's, only about 250,-000 southern blacks were registered to vote. Three years after the Supreme Court killed the white primary, the number of black registrants had more than doubled.[3] By 1952, around 20 per cent of voting-age blacks had registered as voters in the South. By 1966, the comparable figure was 46 per cent. And, at the end of the sixties, it was about 66 per cent. (See Table D for 1970 voter registration data.)

The 1972 presidential primary victories of George Wallace reinforced the northern stereotype of the South as a political monolith dominated by "rednecks" and racism. Such a view ignores the rise of black political power which, despite the Wallace victories, continued unabated after the election. By way of contrast, the number of elected black officials in the eleven southern states was only seventy-two as late as 1965, whereas the figure had grown by the end of 1972 to 1,158. Included in this total were three dozen mayors, hundreds of aldermen, city councillors, county commissioners, and school board members, as well as numerous justices of the peace and state legislators. Moreover, in 1972 Andrew Young (Georgia) and Barbara C. Jordan (Texas) became the first blacks elected to Congress from their states in this century. Ironically, Arkansas, where Governor Faubus once carried Massive Resistance to the point of nullification, now leads the South in the number of elected blacks with a total of 180.

Several of the South's elected blacks have gained national prominence. Chief among these are Julian Bond (state legislator from an Atlanta district), Charles Evers (Mayor of Fayette, Mississippi), and the Mayor of Tuskegee, Alabama, who is married to a daughter of a former member of the White Citizens' Council. Also well-known nationally is James Meredith, who returned to the Ole Miss campus at Oxford in the spring of 1972 (his first visit there since 1963) to lecture to an enthusiastic audience on Mississippi's political history. In the process he also launched his candidacy as a Republican for the Senate seat of the arch-segregationist, James O. Eastland.[4]

Of course, black political power is no panacea, and it alone will not destroy white racism nor usher in a new day of racial amity. Yet the evidence to date indicates that it has already had a significant impact on southern politics and society. It has made white politicians more responsible and responsive to the aspirations of blacks. It has moderated the racial bias of white officeholders. It has helped elect white moderates, such as Georgia's Governor James Earl Carter, Jr., to key offices. It has almost everywhere resulted in better public services for black neighborhoods. It has opened the door to greater economic and social opportunity for blacks. And, in a not so obvious way, it is liberating southern whites from the racial hang-ups and stereotypes that have so long interfered with their pursuit of rationality in politics and other areas of southern life. As Representative Andrew Young recently remarked, "We've got to realize that there are no black problems—the problems that black people face would be here if everybody were the same color."

III. The New Status Quo: Tokenism

MOST OF THE WESTERN WORLD'S counterrevolutions have ended in one of three ways—by an apocalyptic defeat, a clear-cut victory, or by gradual abatement without a definitive resolution of basic conflicts. As was demonstrated in the preceding sections of this chapter, the political counterrevolution that Massive Resistance became ended, not with an apocalyptic bang of total victory or total defeat, but with a whimper of gradual abatement.

Total Massive Resistance was dead everywhere by the mid-1960's, and a new status quo in the South's race relations was taking shape. The label most frequently applied to the new order of things was "tokenism," which, though pejorative, was roughly accurate. Practically speaking, tokenism meant that while many, if not most, southern school districts were still maintaining dual school systems, they had been forced by the courts to admit at least a few "token" blacks to their formerly all-white schools if the districts were biracial. Token blacks were also to be found in most of the region's colleges, state governments, and public service agencies. In Marxist terminology, the emergent status quo of tokenism was a violence-bred "synthesis," dialectically derived from the Massive Resisters' "thesis" (segregation) and the egalitarians' "antithesis" (integration). And like all syntheses that emerge from the politics of conflict, tokenism was an ongoing process that quickly engendered a new group of opposition forces (gravediggers) which showed every intention of continuing the dialectic of struggle until yet another synthesis would crystallize.

In the late 1960's, as the full effects of the Civil Rights Acts of 1964 and 1965 began to be felt, tokenism in the South began evolving into a more substantial kind of egalitarianism. Thus in 1965–66—the first school year in which Title VI of the 1964 Act was effective—the percentage of black students attending biracial schools in the southern and border-state region increased to 15.9 per cent. Moreover, starting in January 1965, the Office of Education initiated negotiations with individual school districts to encourage them to prepare appropriate voluntary desegregation plans. On April 29, 1965, the Office issued its first set of uniform, generally applicable standards implementing Title VI in the area of school desegregation, which came to be referred to as "guidelines." Though the guidelines later became highly controversial, they were a vital catalyst in advancing school desegregation in the 1960's. No less important was the fact that the 1964 Civil Rights Act for the first time gave the Department of Justice statutory authority to bring suits to compel school districts to desegregate. By the spring of 1967, the Department was a participant in more than 100 cases involving school desegregation. It should be pointed out, however, that the expansion of tokenism in the sixties was a good deal less significant in such sensitive areas as housing, employment, religion, journalism, recreation, and the upper echelons of government, though even in these areas there was at least some progress toward more equal opportunity for blacks.

With the South's new status quo slowly evolving from tokenism to greater egalitarianism, many white southerners found themselves for the first time involved in biracial groups whose values and goals were in sharp contrast to those of the all-white groups that had previously claimed their total loyalty. While this "affiliative cross pressure" has doubtless created emotional problems for such whites, especially for those unable to tolerate ambiguity or dissonance, its effect on southern society has probably been to reduce social tensions and racial conflict. Experience seems to suggest that cross-pressured individuals tend to serve as bridges between social and other groups as they seek to defuse the tensions and conflict arising from their special situation.

Besides being a "cross-pressure laboratory," the contemporary South also provides a classic example of the phenomenon that social scientists call cultural lag. This is quite evident in the way that cultural (and social) change in the South still lags behind the material and technological changes that recently have revolutionized southern industry and agriculture. And this remains true despite the fact that the Jim Crow system which spawned so many of the South's social and cultural patterns has legally been dead since the mid-1960's. Scholars have detected a similar lag in virtually all changing societies, so perhaps the only remarkable thing about all this is that the South has not experienced even more maladjustments and violence as the various parts of its cultural complex resist changing at the same tempo. In any case, the most intractable (and tragic) problem created by this lag is a legacy of bitterness, suppressed rage, and mythic thinking that is likely to poison southern politics for some time to come. But changing societies do eventually alter the myths, values, politics, and ideologies that make up their superstructure, and there is no reason to assume that the South will be an exception to this rule.

It is not possible today to say with certainty what form the

South's emergent social order will finally take when counterrevolution has fully abated. Pessimists, including most black militants, predict that the situation will steadily deteriorate until the South (and the nation) will be composed of two entirely separate societies with little in common save a mutual detestation. Optimists, on the other hand, forecast an ongoing, if spotty liberalization of southern racial values and, in time, the emergence of a cohesive biracial society. It seems rather more likely that the ultimate resolution of the racial conflict that gripped the South in the post-Brown years will turn out to be less clear-cut and definitive than the visions of either contemporary pessimists or optimists suggest. For some reason, history seems to prefer ambivalence to lucidity.

At the end of the first post-Brown decade, the situation in the South could perhaps best be described as a non-violent "concord of discords," to use a phrase popularized by William Penn during the fight for religious toleration. Admittedly this is not an ideal situation from any point of view, but it is certainly better than continued warfare between egalitarians and segregationists. Those analysts inclined toward Social Darwinism would even go so far as to argue that the violence engendered by the South's counterrevolution was not so much a sign of the region's disintegration as the necessary price of social progress. To the degree that such arguments are valid, one would be justified in concluding (and hoping) that the decline of Massive Resistance was both the death-rattle of a discredited past and the birth pangs of a brighter future.

II.

An Interpretive Explanation

U P TO THIS POINT, our analysis has focused on the *precipitants* of the egalitarian revolution and its southern "antithesis"— the Brown decisions and the Southern Manifesto in particular—and on the ways in which these things led, dialectically as it were, to a succession of crises and showdowns over the implementation of Brown. The aim of this final chapter is to propose an explanation of the South's racist backlash by examining its *preconditions,* which is to say those circumstances that made it possible for the precipitants to engender a political counterrevolution along with the conflict and violence that entailed. Obviously this is a much more formidable task than the simple description of the stages through which Massive Resistance progressed, and it is one which must be approached with caution and scholarly humility.

The present study has been premised on the assumption that a number of forces were at work in southern culture and character which, by a complex process of interaction and "preconditioning," produced the Massive Resistance counterrevolution. Those factors deemed to be most decisive, causally speaking, have been labeled political, economic, psycho-cultural, and religious. Each of these will be discussed and evaluated in separate sections of this chapter.

Southerners and the South have always fascinated scholars, journalists, and foreign visitors—so much so, in fact, that over the years an incredibly large body of interpretive studies has been accumulated varying in quality from the highly perceptive to the grossly distorted. The first such studies go back to the late eighteenth century, by which time it was assumed that the southern way of life, if not wholly unique, was more than a little distinctive. Typical of the South's interpreters of that day was Thomas Jefferson, who concluded that southerners act, think, and feel as they do because of the rural, small-town, and pastoral environment in which most of them spend their lives. Reluctantly accepting slavery as a "necessary evil," Jefferson also held the view that southerners, despite their racist practices, tend to be superior in virtue and civility to northerners, who have been corrupted by big cities, industry, and waves of immigration. Though not blatantly racist, Jefferson's rather smug interpretation amounted to a kind of "Anglo-Saxon, agrarian supremacy" doctrine.

In the first half of the nineteenth century, a sort of Neo-Jeffersonian interpretation of the South was popularized, which might be called the old plantation thesis. Among the chief proponents of this theory were southern ideologues like Virginia's George Fitzhugh, who made up what Professor Hartz has called "The Reactionary Enlightenment."[1] Unlike Jefferson's gentle pastoralism, Fitzhugh's explanatory (or rationalizing) thesis was unblushingly racist. It assumed that southerners of his day were virtuous, honorable, gracious, noble, and high-minded because of the pervasive influence of the big plantations, which required slaves for their effective operation. The thesis further postulated that southerners constituted a happy family where compassion and true community reigned, while northerners were being increasingly corrupted by too much materialism, individualism, and competitiveness. Writing in the antique idiom of Aristotelian organicism and teleology, Fitzhugh held it to be "an historical fact that this family association [of the South], this patriarchal government for purposes of defense against enemies from without, gradually merges into larger associations of men under a common government or ruler."[2] Quite clearly Fitzhugh's cameo of southern plantation life was idealized and thus unreal. He nonetheless was on the mark in stressing the ugly aspects of modern industrialism and in perceiving that northern labor was in the process of losing its social character, even though his clear perception of the mote in the Yankees' eye scarcely justified his glamorization of slavery.

Other southern interpreters who shared some, though by no means all of Fitzhugh's premises were Albert Bledsoe, Chancellor Harper, Edmund Ruffin, and Calhoun. In the long run, their ideas were destined to have little influence outside the South. And even in the South, they were steadily eroded by the advance of ideas that were more materialistic and national in nature. As Professor Hartz has perceptively written, the political thought of the Reactionary Enlightenment

> *symbolizes not the weakness of the American liberal idea but its strength, its vitality, and its utter dominion over the American mind. The strange agonies the Southerners endured trying to break out of the grip of Locke and the way the nation greeted their effort, stand as a permanent testimony to the power of that idea. It is not every day in Western history that a "great conservative reaction" dies without impact on the mind of a nation.[3]*

On the eve of the Civil War, a very unusual southerner published an interpretation of the southern way of life which was almost diametrically opposed to that earlier offered by Fitzhugh and his school. The theorist was Hinton Rowan Helper, who, because of his social and economic views, became anathema to most white southerners. Helper agreed with Fitzhugh that an understanding of the slavery system was absolutely essential for a proper appreciation of the nature of southern character and culture. He did not, however, accept Fitzhugh's romanticized conception of slavery as a benign institution, and, in fact, reached an opposite conclusion. Helper believed that slavery was not only uneconomic, but, more important, exerted an extremely deleterious influence on southern character. Instead of elevating the tone of southern society, as alleged by its apologists, he believed it debauched both master and slave and held back the industrialization of the South's economy, which would be the eventual transformer of southern behavior. Arguing both for an end to slavery and for a start toward economic development, Helper told his compatriots, "Your rivers and smaller streams, now wasting their waters in idleness, will then turn the wheels of multitudinous mills. Your bays and harbors, now unknown to commerce, will then swarm with ships from every enlightened quarter of the globe."[4] There were other interpreters of the period who, like Helper, linked slavery with the most characteristic (and negative) features of the southern way of life, though most of these were not southerners.[5]

In the latter part of the nineteenth century and the first decades of the twentieth, the most popular explanation of the South's racism and other peculiar behavioral patterns was the so-called "Black Reconstruction Thesis." According to this hypothesis, which southern historians strongly supported, the most criticized aspects of southern character could be adequately accounted for as a natural (and therefore rational) reaction to the anti-white "misbehavior" of the Reconstruction scalawags and carpetbaggers.[6] The South, it was argued, adopted white supremacy as a doctrine and segregation as a public policy only after the corruption, immorality, and political extremism of the Black Reconstruction governments left it no honorable alternative. From the South's perspective, this theory had the virtue of ascribing all the negative features of southern character to a single scapegoat— "outside agitators."

In the 1920's the distinguished historian Professor Ulrich B. Phillips sought to define the essence of southern character and culture by a thesis that almost amounted to "racial determinism." It was his view that the chief constant in the southern way of life has been "a common resolve indomitably maintained" that the South "shall be and remain a white man's country." This resolve might be "expressed with the frenzy of a demagogue or maintained with a patrician's quietude," but it was in all times and places "the cardinal test of a Southerner and the central theme of southern history." The chief difficulty with the Phillipsian thesis, which obviously has much in its favor, is that it does not adequately explain *why* race consciousness got such a stranglehold on southern character. In other words, it is more of a description of certain obvious realities in southern life than an explanation of their origin.

In 1930 twelve southerners in Nashville, led by the poet John Crowe Ransom, issued the famous manifesto, *I'll Take My Stand*, that was both a normative and interpretive statement about southern character. Espousing a neo-Jeffersonian thesis, the manifesto asserted that agrarianism had always been (and should always be) the essence of the southern heritage and the test of southern loyalty. But it should be an agrarianism unrelated to "the high-caste Brahmins of the Old South," as Ransom wrote in *The Fugitive*.

The Nashville group called for anti-industrial measures and for a return to "the agrarian way of life." Rhapsodizing about this, Ransom wrote: "There are a good many faults to be found with the old South, but hardly the fault of being intemperately addicted to work and to gross material prosperity."[7] The doctrine popularized by *I'll Take My Stand* appealed to the romantic instincts of white southerners, but did nothing to halt the "bulldozer revolution," as Vann Woodward has called the South's burgeoning industrialization. More to the point, it failed to explain why southern character, with its racist components, changed hardly at all as the region ceased to be overwhelmingly agrarian and became semi-industrialized.

During the Depression, one of the most popular analytical tools used to explain southern (and national) behavior was Marxist social theory. According to this mono-causal theory, white supremacy is an integral part of the total structure of the South's quasi-feudal society, having been produced by the ongoing struggle between the region's exploitative classes and its hapless masses. This being the case, racism can be extirpated only by a revolutionary transformation of the South's social, economic, and political institutions, followed by a dictatorship of the proletariat in every southern state.[8]

In the 1940's, the concept of caste was a popular tool for explaining southern racism. Best known from John Dollard's

Caste and Class in a Southern Town (New Haven, Conn., 1937), the psycho-social caste hypothesis assumed a biracial rather than a unitary society in the South, and ascribed white racism there to the black man's unique caste position in a stratified system whose caste patterns benefit whites sexually, economically, psychologically, politically, and educationally. This hypothesis seems today unduly static and pessimistic and overlooks the fact that the blacks' status in the South has never been based on religious prescription—a key factor in traditional caste patterning.

Probably the best known interpretation of southern "uniqueness" is that offered in W. J. Cash's *The Mind of the South*. While Cash's work is considered something of a classic today, scholars have increasingly been critical of its deficiencies. The style, once widely praised for its lucidity, seems quaint, even archaic, by today's standards. In reaching for macro-generalizations, the author usually ends up sacrificing verifiability for universality. Basically Cash proposes a "mentalistic" interpretation of the South's distinctive behavior in race and other fields by postulating a monolithic "mind" persisting through all the winds of change. Cash summarizes the negative aspects of the "southern mind" in a famous paragraph on the last page of his book:

> *Violence, intolerance, aversion and suspicion toward new ideas, an incapacity for analysis, an inclination to act from feeling rather than from thought, an exaggerated individualism and a too narrow concept of social responsibility, attachment to fictions and false values, above all too great attachment to racial values and a tendency to justify cruelty and injustice in the name of those values, sentimentality and a lack of realism—these have been its characteristic vices in the past. And, despite changes for the better, they remain its characteristic vices today.*[9]

Of recent interpretations of southern behavior, none are superior to the explanations suggested by C. Vann Woodward, an old-fashioned, literary historian and native southerner. Rejecting Cash's emphasis on the unity and continuity of the southern "mind," Woodward prefers to stress the evidence of disunity, dissent, and irony in the southern experience. He also stresses, quite correctly, the degree to which Calvin had conditioned southern morals and Locke southern politics. But of all Woodward's interpretive ideas, his best known is the suggestion that the South's unique behavioral traits can be accounted for in terms of a regional tradition of poverty, failure, and obsessive guilt coexisting with a national experience dominated by abundance, success, and innocence. This has meant that the South has been both more aware of the tragic burden of the past than the North and less able to shake off its influence.[10]

Somewhat less well known are the explanatory hypotheses put forward in the Massive Resistance years by the Mississippi journalist, Hodding Carter. Echoing the frontier hypothesis discussed by Cash and others, Carter maintains that southern society and behavior have remained inexorably tied to the frontier right up to the present. He argues that even in those southerners who live behind the white-pillared facades of big mansions there has always lurked more of the frontiersman than most would care to admit. Carter also regrets the fact that the great European movements to this country virtually bypassed the South, thus leaving too long unchallenged the region's social, racial, and religious values. Operating in a semi-closed society, the South's political and economic leaders were able with impunity to neglect its vast endowments as they betrayed its true mission.[11]

This brief survey by no means exhausts the enormous literature devoted to explaining southern behavior. But it does at least suggest the variety and general nature of those contributions to the literature that are regarded as most insightful.[12]

I. POLITICAL AND GOVERNMENTAL FACTORS

TODAY MOST STUDENTS of Massive Resistance would concede that the crisis in human relations which exploded in the South in the wake of Brown was to some degree caused by political and governmental factors. They argue that such factors were more decisive than has been thought, and indeed were the most important single cause of the South's counterrevolution. It should, of course, be understood that this interpretation focuses on proximate rather than ultimate causes, in full awareness that no single cause acts independently of the other causes in a given field.

In 1903 in *The Souls of Black Folk*, W. E. B. Du Bois predicted that the main issue of the twentieth century would be "the problem of color—the relation of the darker to the lighter men in Asia and Africa, in America, and in the islands of the sea." That prediction, with all its tragic implications, is now in the process of coming true all over the world. Though Du Bois seemed to think that economics was more responsible for this problem than politics, the facts seem to support the causal primacy of the latter—at least as far as the American South is concerned.

At the start of this inquiry into the relationship between southern politics and southern racism, it is important to stress the fact that the racism inherent in the Massive Resistance movement seems to have been linked to a particular stage of political evolution in the southern states. In the 1950's the South's political systems were really in an era of transition from oligarchy to representative democracy. As usually happens in such transitions, there was a "legitimacy vacuum," in which old political moorings were breaking loose, entrenched myths and values were being uprooted, and traditional structures and behavioral patterns were being steadily eroded. It is true, of course, that the southern states have long had constitutions that were formally democratic in structure and, with some exceptions, in content. But all too frequently these have been paper facades behind which segregationist oligarchies were able to set up junta-type regimes, which were more or less responsive to the white majority but rarely if ever to blacks. When the Supreme Court shocked the South with its Brown decision, none of the states of the Old Confederacy had fully mature democratic institutions. Some were almost pure agrarian oligarchies. Others were groping toward a greater degree of representative democracy. And at least two, Alabama and Mississippi, had built so many authoritarian structures into their systems that they were democratic only in the most formal sense.

The first and most obvious feature of southern oligarchicalism was a modified one-party system, which meant in practice a virtual dictatorship of the most conservative wing of the Democratic party. While it is true that Democratic "factionalism" in certain states produced a kind of two- or three-party system, the fact remains that in the Massive Resistance era the South as a whole was a solid bastion of Democratic hegemony—save in presidential elections.[13]

Now from the perspective of the southern black, one-party government has generally meant that black citizens, when they were not disfranchised, really had but two choices—to vote for racist Democrats who were certain to win, or to vote for Republicans who were sometimes a little less racist but who had no chance of winning. Equally important, one-party government meant that the Massive Resisters were able to go almost unchallenged within the South as they shamelessly used the tactic of "nigger-baiting" to push their own careers and the fortunes of the Democratic party. A multi-party system is certainly no guarantee of fraternal egalitarianism. Yet it does seem logical to expect that the cruder forms of racism will flourish less often where there is genuine political competition than where there is little or none.

A second characteristic feature of southern oligarchicalism is the strong executive leadership that has long been the rule in most parts of the South. Of course, a strong executive need not automatically lead to authoritarianism nor to public policies based on race prejudice, and indeed at the national level, the nation has fared better under strong than under weak executives. Nonetheless if strong executives happen also to be unscrupulous, second-rate leaders—as all too many southern governors were in the post-Brown years—their capacity for mischief (both through acts of omission and commission) is greatly enhanced merely because of the vast power resources they command. Moreover, since southern legislatures have traditionally only met biennially in short sessions, the governor in most states has almost by necessity become the chief policy-maker and pace-setter. And if he is a racist, he contaminates his state's entire political system with his biases.

A third trait of southern politics facilitating, if not creating Massive Resistance racism was the widespread legislative malapportionment which, until recently, gave political control to rural and small-town legislators, among whom white supremacy has long been a basic value. Generally more fanatical on the segregation question than their urban counterparts, these back-country zealots competed throughout the post-Brown era with the gubernatorial Resisters to see who could best "keep the nigger in his place." To be sure, Massive Resistance might have developed even if southern legislatures had been perfectly proportioned according to the Supreme Court's "one man-one vote" formula. But it is at least conceivable that if the southern legislatures had been controlled by urban instead of rural politicians, the state governments of the region might have been a little less intransigent and a little more willing to accept token integration when the courts required it.

An interesting variation of "malrepresentation" was Georgia's unique county unit system of election and legislative apportionment, which, until the courts invalidated it, was a most effective way of deflating the popular vote of the state's big counties while inflating the impact of the rural vote. Professor Key was not exaggerating when he wrote that the county unit system, which black leaders strongly opposed, was "the most important institution affecting Georgia politics."[14]

Yet another feature of the southern political scene that helped to make Massive Resistance possible was the inherent social conservatism of the region's traditional leaders. Southern politics have for decades been dominated by a three-pronged "Power Elite," composed of lawyers, small businessmen, and farmer-legislators, for whom conservatism in race and other matters has always been a way of life. This conservatism doubtless developed from a number of sources—tradition, custom, socio-economic conditions, religion, psychological predispositions, and institutional structures. But whatever its origins, it canonized the "know-nothing" philosophy of the white supremacists and in effect outlawed the liberalism of all reformers, whether southern or non-southern. So pervasive, indeed, was this stultifying conservatism during the Massive Resistance era that one wonders, in retrospect, how any racial progress at all was made. Conservatism, which is not inherently racist, remains a massive cliché in most parts of the South, along with the political theory of Calhoun and Jefferson Davis. But as the egalitarian revolution continues its advance, the more primitive aspects of Dixie conservatism will gradually recede into the background.

A political factor that was both cause and effect of white racism in the years before and after Brown was that bizarre network of suffrage deprivation tools—some of which were quite legal for a time—which generations of southern politicians contrived after the 1890's. These included the white primary, the grandfather clause in voting laws, the poll tax, unfairly administered literacy tests, and racist registration procedures. In recent years, of course, all of these devices have been outlawed by judicial or legislative action. But as late as the mid-1960's, the last three were still being effectively used in many parts of the South to disfranchise black adults. And it is now clear that white racism in the South did not significantly decline until these suffrage deprivation tools were totally abolished.

Increasingly students of southern politics are coming to feel that the Populist movement, whose legacy still haunts the South, must bear some of the blame for the tenacity with which white supremacy hangs on there. As is now well known, the Populism that developed in the South and Midwest in the late nineteenth century was a strange mixture of frontlash and backlash politics— an amalgam of revolutionary economic policies and counterrevolutionary social ideas. And though it seemed for a time that the movement would succeed in uniting poor whites and blacks against the entrenched Bourbons, that dream vanished when Populist leaders like Georgia's Tom Watson turned into rabid racists and set the South on a segregationist course for years to come.

The history of southern Populism is well documented. For the purposes of this explanatory analysis, all that is required is a brief summary of the conclusions one might draw from the Populist experience respecting the relationship between southern politics and southern racism. (In many ways, this relationship is the most interesting and significant aspect of Populism):[15]

1. The defeat of Populism in the 1890's exposed the almost total lack of class consciousness among the poor people of the South. For a short time, some of the more radical Populist leaders sought to elevate the "class struggle" above

the color struggle. But after the Bourbon oligarchs bitterly assailed such tactics, they quickly ceased their flirtation with Marx.

2. Populism's ill-fated involvement with the race problem dramatized the fact that race has always been a central concern of southern politicians, whether of the right or the left. And even when the black man is not a decisive factor as a voter, as he was as late as the elections of 1892, he frequently has been the dominant *issue*.

3. The Populist revolt revealed the maze of tensions that have long separated urban-industrial from rural-agricultural interests in the South. This capitol-capital cleavage, especially prominent in Georgia and Louisiana, has probably inhibited race progress, since any kind of socio-economic or political split invariably complicates the black man's fight for freedom.

4. In the political field, the collapse of Populism, coming soon after the demise of southern Republicanism, meant that the creation of a viable two-party system in the South was to be indefinitely postponed. This development was a serious blow to the hopes of blacks and white liberals, a blow from which they are still suffering. It was symbolized by a chant that white southerners used to take pride in: "I'm a Democrat, because my daddy was a Democrat, and I'm g'wine to vote agin the Nigger!"[16]

5. The Populist experience underscored the degree to which the crusading of southern demagogues is fused with a "harsh Catonian moralism"—to steal a phrase from Max Lerner—which distorts their angle of vision and permits them to be liberal and illiberal at the same time. Like the archetypal Populist, Tom Watson, the South's current demagogues readily perceive the evils of alcohol, government corruption, high taxes, and plutocratic exploitation. But they see little or nothing wrong with white supremacy, anti-Semitism, or other forms of racism. What is worse, they seem totally unaware of the irony involved in celebrating the will of the masses of the people on one hand while upholding racist elitism on the other. In all times and places, Populists have been more

guilty of this anomaly than thoroughgoing conservatives who abstain from wooing the masses.

6. The fairly rapid transformation of Populism from a kind of bargain-basement socialism into right-wing, backlash politics illustrated in a graphic way the fragility of what passes for liberalism in the South. Far too many of the South's populistic, "liberal" demagogues, like Tom Watson and Huey Long, have been out-and-out political opportunists, who will "fuse" with blacks when that is expedient and vilify them when vilification is in style. To be sure, not all southern liberals have been as shamelessly opportunistic as Watson and Long were, but when the chips are down—as they were after 1954—most of the breed are likely to opt for compromise or prudential silence.

7. The Populist experiment, though a failure, saddled the South with a "conspiracy consciousness" that left the region's whites addicted to a simplistic conspiracy theory of history. In brief, that theory—elaborated in a thousand books and stump-speeches—reduced the South's problems to the perfidy of a handful of enemies: black people, liberals, outside agitators, northern bankers, and Jewish moneylenders. Easily the most poisonous ingredient of Populism, this racist conspiracy theory has contaminated southern politics ever since and provided the philosophical ambience within which Massive Resistance was able to flourish.

8. Populism's rise to prominence in the heyday of Henry Grady's New South movement demonstrated the fatuity of the dream of a racially harmonious South automatically evolving from free enterprise and industrialism. The "New South," far from solving the racial and other problems that perplexed the contemporary Populist movement, actually perpetuated the South's conservative, racist society and unwittingly set the stage for the twentieth century's politics of conflict. Equally important, Populism and the New South were not only coevals, they also were opposite sides of the same coin. The coin was the myth of the southern way of life, with Populism being the rural side and the New South the urban side. Both muddied the waters of southern politics

without laying the race question to rest. And to this day there is a strange ambivalence about southern politics which results, in part, from the South's failure to integrate two incompatible things—the "old plantation" dreams of the Populists and the urban-industrial fantasies of the New South prophets.

9. Populist firebrands like Tom Watson were among the first politicians to demonstrate how gullible the southern voter can be when appeals for his vote are embellished with racist rhetoric and stereotypical slogans. They were therefore among the creators of that tradition of rural demagoguery which has done so much to make southern voting behavior irrational and to keep black people from achieving first-class citizenship. It is true that in recent years southerners, both white and black, have shown evidence of becoming more sophisticated voters. Yet it is worth noting that every single Massive Resistance leader of any consequence was, in effect, a "neo-Populist." Certainly the common people of the South and elsewhere, since they are always the majority, have a right to expect that their public officials will be responsive to their collective needs and aspirations. But the kind of neo-Populistic politics that has dominated the South for almost a century now is a far cry from true participatory democracy, if, indeed, it is not outright authoritarianism.

In its heyday, which coincided with the maturation of Jim Crow, Populism not only failed to reconcile blacks and whites but actually helped to make racism a social and political dogma. This being so, there seems little likelihood that latter-day Populism, as promoted by George Wallace and Lester Maddox, will make much of a contribution to the solution of the South's racial problems. Undiluted Populism is no more desirable than arrogant elitism. Until southern politics ceases to be neo-Populistic and becomes truly democratic and progressive, the political process will be more of an enemy to the black man than a friend.

A final aspect of southern politics which helped, indirectly, to create the type of climate congenial to the growth of racism is something one rarely encounters in studies of the South. It is the phenomenon of *machismo*, a concept almost exclusively associated with Latin American politics. Reduced to its essence, *machismo* refers to a political tradition which seeks, consciously and unconsciously, to combine sexism and political action. It may be manifest in a variety of ways—personality traits, dress styles, sports preferences, mythic emblems, and totemic slogans. The chief premise of this tradition is the belief that political success is a function of the degree to which politicians are *machos*—i.e., strong and virile males who aggressively assert their masculinity on every possible occasion and in every possible way.

Notwithstanding the fact that scholars almost never include *machismo* among the determinants of southern character, it is one of the oldest of the South's political traditions—far older than Populism—and as such played a seminal role in the Massive Resistance story. If all segregationist leaders after 1954 showed at least a subconscious awareness of the importance of the *machismo* image—and, of course, in terms of electoral success the image was always more important than the reality—it was the Klan that carried the tradition almost to the point of caricature. Quite revealing in this regard was the Southwide popularity of the Klan's recruiting slogan—"Don't be half a man, join the Klan!" It is perhaps not too much to say that the whole history of the Klan, with its obsession with fraternity-style rituals and violent action, has been little more than a sustained attempt to live up to its public image of assertive masculinity.

The klansmen, of course, are not the only southerners who play "*machismo* politics." They are simply the most blatant about it. The fact of the matter is that no segregationist politician would ever knowingly violate the unwritten rules of the *macho* cult. Originally, a southern *macho* was a white "he-man" who had the guts to stand up to the perfidious Yankees. In the Massive Resistance era it meant an aggressive white male who was not afraid to indulge in "nigger-baiting" and who would make absolutely no concessions to integrationists.

One need have only a slight knowledge of the South to be able to spot the overt manifestions of political *machismo*. It stands out in the preference southern voters have for tall men over short men. It comes out in the big Texas hats and boots worn by county sheriffs and other politicians. It is visible in the southerner's love

for contact sports and in the hobbies preferred by politicians—
hunting, fishing, cock-fighting, and collegiate and professional
football. It is manifest in the politicians' addiction to wenching,
dirty stories, poker, and hard drinking, as well as in their aver-
sion to highbrow "culture." Not all southern politicians were
boxers as George Wallace was, and not all make a fad of physical
culture as Senator Thurmond does, but as a group they tend to put
the body above the mind and "masculine" traits above such "fem-
inine" traits as tenderness, compassion, and racial tolerance. And
finally it is obvious in the "virile" rhetoric of the region's demagogues, who anathematize their "weak" opponents with such
contemptuous epithets as "liberals," "parlor pinks," "effete weak-
lings," and "pussyfooters." Of course, none of these manifestations of *machismo* is restricted solely to the South. But it does
appear that they are more conspicuous and consequential there
than in any other place outside Latin America.

The key assumption of this analysis is that *machismo* politics
has helped to mold the South's well-known obsession with violence, and because of that, one is justified in saying that the "masculine mystique" surrounding and permeating the region's politics
has been one of the many political factors promoting white racism. The South's *machismo*-bred violence manifests itself in a
number of ways: assassination of liberal public figures (President
Kennedy and Dr. King), lynching of blacks, harassment of white
integrationists, murder of civil rights workers, Klan vigilantism,
homicide and rape statistics (among the highest in the nation),
and even in southern literature. In the Massive Resistance era, the
archetypal symbol of political *machismo* was James Gardner
Clark, Jr., Sheriff of Alabama's Dallas County, who confronted
the egalitarians with a cattle prod and billy club dangling at his
side and a defiant "NEVER" button pinned to his lapel.

The evidence is now overwhelming that because it serves
important functions within the South's cultural and political milieu,
violence (much of it against blacks) has been institutionalized in
southern *machismo* politics. This dual political tradition of *machismo* and violence is found in all parts of the South—in progressive and backward areas, in urban and rural areas, in agricultural
and industrial centers, and in Protestant and Catholic strongholds.

But historically speaking, both sides of the tradition have been most pronounced in the undeveloped sections of the Deep South. It is also a fact that *machismo* violence is likely to take more crude and primitive forms in the rural areas of the South than in the urban areas.

In addition to promoting violence against blacks and white liberals and governmental authoritarianism, *machismo* politics in the South has been responsible for the rise of a "cult of personality" there that bears many resemblances to the *caudillo* phenomenon of Latin America. In the South, of course, the "*macho*-bosses" are always white, and while they are not quite dictators in the Latin sense, they become extremely powerful sheriffs, mayors, senators, congressmen, governors, and legislative demagogues. And almost without exception they assert their masculinity at the expense of blacks.

Machismo in the South has also conduced to a near-universal belief that politics and government are the business of "white he-men"—a sphere of activity peculiarly appropriate to Caucasian males. To be sure, blacks and white females are increasingly becoming political activists, but both groups are still consigned, in most places, to the fringes of the political process. Until blacks and females become as numerous in government as they now are in elementary education, the *machismo* tradition in southern politics will persist.

If the phallic/power symbol of the North is the automobile, in the South it is the shotgun—the quintessential symbol of Dixie *machismo*. To prove that they are card-carrying members of the cult of virility, southern politicians must love guns as they love their wives; they must vigorously oppose all gun-control legislation; and they must let it be known that dominating Nature by hunting her prey is as natural to them as eating and drinking. The fact that the South's obsession with guns seems to conduce to a high violence and murder rate only intensifies the symbolic potency of the gun. This is so obvious that it now appears that the entire South is suffering from a regional schizophrenia in respect to guns. And it is richly ironic that both Governor George Wallace and Senator Stennis, strong "law and order" politicians who were critically wounded by gunmen in the early seventies, are reputed to be still staunch opponents of any substantial federal gun-control legislation.

One of the sadder aspects of racist *machismo* is the effort of certain black militants to set up a super-*macho* cult of their own that exceeds even that of the segregationists in the intensity of its "masculine mystique." The best illustration of this are the writings of Eldridge Cleaver. Somewhere in his *Soul on Ice*, Cleaver wrote that "The boxing ring is the ultimate focus of masculinity in America, the two-fisted testing ground of manhood, and the heavyweight champion, as a symbol, is the real Mr. America." The ironic thing about all this is that Cleaver seems less concerned to protest against the white man's masculinity cult than to express his anguish that black men have failed to live up to it!

In explaining the uglier aspects of white supremacy and Massive Resistance, one must be careful not to commit the fallacy of "political reductionism" by ascribing the rise of racism solely to political and governmental factors. Yet it is now beyond dispute that the South's peculiar politics was the prime mover behind the creation of the Jim Crow system, and that politics, though changing, remains the chief obstacle to the system's total dismemberment. As the argument of this section has shown, the aspects of southern politics that have most promoted racism are three—oligarchical political structures, the neo-Populist tradition of racist demagoguery, and (least understood) the insidious tradition of *machismo*.

II. Economic Factors

ONE CAN EASILY OVERSTATE the case for economic factors as the basic cause of southern racism, as Marxist and neo-Marxist analysts tend to do. Yet a careful scrutiny of the relevant data will show that a battery of economic structures and patterns can be more or less directly related to the general context in which Massive Resistance was born. These, of course, interact in circular fashion with the political factors just discussed, and it is often hard to tell where politics ends and economics begins— in the South as elsewhere. But in an analysis such as this, they ought to be distinguished.

In 1954 both the political and economic systems of the South were in a pre-modern, pre-industrial transitional stage. Southern politics, as we have said, were essentially oligarchical in the post-Brown era, while southern economics, in most states, were quasi-feudal agrarian. Southerners have lived traditionally under a subsistence rural economy with no major division of labor and little specialization of role and function. It is true that in the 1950's much of the South was moving from an agrarian-subsistence economic base toward the modern industrial model, but in the Massive Resistance era the old economic traditions were still the rule rather than the exception.

The exact degree of responsibility one should assign to specific economic patterns and structures in explaining a phenomenon such as racism can obviously not be determined with scientific exactitude. Yet certain generalizations can be made that will at least suggest future avenues of research. Certainly it is now clear that just as the emphasis on staple-crop agriculture and plantation farming in the Old South frustrated liberal social policies and froze the values of the slavery system into the southern ethos, so the stress on cotton and tobacco cultivation, big farm paternalism, and sharecropping in the New South hindered the move toward a pragmatic, utilitarian value system that would have mitigated some of the uglier features of white racism. As has been indicated, urban industrial capitalism is not in all respects the friend of racial minorities, but generally they fare better under that system than under a system of agrarian paternalism.

To the extent that class consciousness is a rational and useful tool of aspiring minorities, it seems plausible to conclude that the agrarian South, which has always repressed such consciousness, was a major force preventing poor whites and blacks from uniting in a common front against middle-class exploitation. It is well known that the South's economic oligarchs have long used "nigger scare talk" to put down class movements (early Populism, for example), keep unions on the defensive, and keep white "meddlers" in their place. Traditionally in the South if a poor white worker refused to work for $1.50 or so a day, there would always be somebody around to say, "OK then, the boss will find a nigger to take your place for a dollar a day." In recent years, unionization has made some progress in the South, but "nigger scare talk" is still apparently used in some places to keep the poor of both races apart and thus unable to pursue together their rational self-interest.

Moreover, as Dollard and others have pointed out, the South's paternalistic economic system, while not functionally divided in the modern industrial sense, has been rigidly stratified in one way—in the way in which black workers, until recently, were assigned caste-like "monopolies" of the most menial jobs.[17] In practice, this meant that blacks were excluded from textiles, white-collar jobs, positions requiring more than ordinary skill, and virtually all supervisory jobs, and were assigned to the lowest paid jobs in business and agriculture, most of which involved back-breaking manual labor and required little or no training. Blacks, in order to maintain at least a subsistence standard of living, had no choice but to take the jobs offered them—degrading though many of them were—and accommodate themselves to the white man's socio-economic world by learning and following elaborate rituals of deferential interpersonal behavior. It requires little imagination to perceive that workers consigned to a caste or quasi-caste status are not likely to have the time, energy, or motivation to make the effort that would be necessary to emancipate themselves from economic bondage. They thus perpetuate the white stereotype of blacks as "no 'count."

Another economic factor that has contributed to the perpetuation, if not the start of racism is the fact that the quasi-feudal South has throughout most of its history been a region with a surplus of human labor and a minimum of industrial job opportunities. As a result of this economic imbalance, black and white workers, blood-brothers in the class sense, became bitter enemies as they were forced to compete for the scarce jobs in agriculture and industry—or at least for those jobs that were not limited to one or the other race. The current flight of young blacks to the

North and the increasing tempo of industrialization should in time reduce the force of this "surplus labor" factor.

One final economic factor that is relevant to this discussion is the near-total absence of black capital in the South, without which blacks can never hope to be socially or economically autonomous. From colonial days, white entrepreneurs, all believers in white supremacy, have controlled virtually all the region's industry, business, commerce, and investment capital. True, in modern times there have always been a few southern "black capitalists"—mostly in insurance and banking—but all too often they have been Uncle Toms who exploited their own people in much the same way as white capitalists did. Until Black Power or something else produces a significant reservoir of "green power," the black man will continue to be relatively at the mercy of the white establishment with its tight control of the South's economic resources. Of course, increased money in the pockets and bank accounts of black people will not automatically guarantee the end of discrimination against them, but it ought to make it harder for whites to ignore the legitimate rights of blacks.

Perhaps the best argument against the use of "economic determinism" to explain southern racism is the fact that after "Tobacco Road was paved" in the fifties and sixties, white attitudes and racial behavioral patterns did not change all that much. The recent progress that the South has made in the field of race relations would appear to be more closely linked to legal, political, governmental, and educational changes than to innovations in the economic infrastructure. Economic changes have doubtless helped, but not decisively.

If the South's counterrevolution was a seismogram of a whole race and region in trauma—as this study suggests—it was a trauma induced by a good deal more than economic *Angst* and cool business scheming. The Marxist postulate of historical materialism, in whatever form expressed, will simply not do as an adequate explanation of the rise and fall of Massive Resistance. For the truth of the matter is that while economic considerations are usually close to the surface of all human events, they are rarely on top. It appears to have been that way throughout history, and so it was in the South in the decade after Brown.

III. PSYCHO-CULTURAL FACTORS

IF POLITICAL OLIGARCHICALISM, helped by economic backwardness, was the chief creator of the South's Jim Crow system and its Massive Resistance offshoot, it would appear that certain psycho-cultural dynamics were mainly responsible for the obsessive brutality of the region's racism. To examine that proposition, the analysis of this section will focus on some of the ways in which the clash of personality and culture may have exacerbated those southern racial problems which the politicians caused by institutionalizing segregation.

Central to this discussion is the assumption that many if not most of the uglier aspects of white supremacy were (and are) products of a perpetual tension between a strong strain of hedonism visible in southern character and a religion-saturated culture. This tension, which has both a constructive and destructive side, seems to have been partially behind a number of southern phenomena—exaggerated individualism, violence, literary creativity, revivalism, romanticism, and deep guilt obsession about sin, sex, and black people. Calvin dominates southern religion and culture like a colossus, but the gay god Bacchus is almost equally ubiquitous. Between them, the southerner seems destined to be forever torn and buffeted—a creature deceptively calm on the outside, but inwardly at perpetual war with himself. One may say therefore that disequilibrium is the normal state of the southern psyche, and equilibrium the exception.

The ubiquitous tension in the South between character and culture, which Cash and others have stressed, will be called here —for lack of a better tag—the "Calvin-Bacchus Syndrome." It is, of course, true that all cultures and all human beings have, since time immemorial, manifested some kind of dualism in their history. Yet whereas the "normal" or rational kind of dualism would seem to be that which searches for complementarity, as symbolized by the ancient Yin-Yang medallion, the dualism that cleaves the white southerner's character almost certainly is deeper, sharper, and more conflictful than that which obtains with the average American.

Specifically, it is hypothesized here that in the typical non-southern American's psyche, the cultural and hedonistic personality components are kept (most of the time) in a relatively fair balance by such forces as education, training, non-fundamentalist religion, and a generally more rational approach to the polarities of human existence. In southern character, on the other hand, it appears that the Calvinistic (cultural) and bacchanalian (psychological) elements are not effectively reconciled by the forces of harmony operative elsewhere. Instead these elements constantly confront each other in a posture of dialectical opposition where polarities are viewed as mutually exclusive instead of complementary. Thus, it is no exaggeration to say that the Calvin-Bacchus Syndrome, with its web of attraction and repulsion, guilt and hate, intimacy and exploitation, added a new and volatile dimension to the whole Massive Resistance experience. Or, to put the matter slightly differently, one may say that while this conflict model of dualism did not cause the South's counterrevolution, it helped to radicalize it and thereby delay the emergence of a true multiracial society.

Students of southern behavior have long been fascinated (and repulsed) by the many evidences of compulsiveness one finds in the southern way of life. When a southerner judges, for instance, he is inclined to judge with compulsive rigidity. When he "saves souls," he does so with compulsive assiduity. When he writes a novel, more likely than not, he will produce a compulsive, gothic probing of human depravity and violence. When he fights the devil, he does so with a compulsive fervor that only Savonarola could match. And when he lynches blacks, physically or symbolically, he goes about his task with a compulsive assurance of his own innocence and of the compelling need for such action. While this alleged compulsiveness in southern behavior has been described and explained in many ways, not enough emphasis has hitherto been placed on that struggle between the forces of Calvin and Bacchus which seem ever bent on destroying one another, but which only succeed in keeping the object of their affection—the white southerner's psyche—in a permanently *Angst*-ridden state.

Torn as they are between the stern imperatives of Calvin and the lures of Bacchus, thousands of southerners find themselves saddled with "free-floating" anxiety—like the prisoner in Kafka's *Trial*—and a host of nagging guilt feelings. Given their Calvinistic upbringing, most must feel, subconsciously at least, that their very humanity (with all its hedonistic components) is their sin, and thus their sin is irremediable. After that conclusion, it is but a short step to the quest for peace of mind through ritualized acts of expiation—revivalism, vigilantism, and, for the real zealots, lynching of blacks.

With its contrasting aspects of quiet serenity and primitive violence, the South, in Sorokin's terminology, is quite clearly a "contradictory behavioral culture." It is no less clear that southerners, like few other mortals, are afflicted with Hegel's "strife of opposites," and largely because of the perpetual psycho-cultural tug-of-war that most of them are trapped in. It seems highly likely that this unstable ambivalence would have produced far more revolutionary (and counterrevolutionary) events than it has except for three things—the South's long tradition of an organic society with fierce totems and taboos, the fact of barbarous criminal law codes, and the "sublimation" of the hedonistic personality component into such acceptable channels as politics, military careers, literary creation, contact sports, and revivalism.

The argument here is not that the hedonistic elements of southern character are either strictly instinctual in the Freudian sense or learned and instrumental, but rather that they are almost automatic psychological responses to the frustrations caused by the aridity and religious repressions of southern society. Since violence and hedonistic indulgence appear to be alternative responses to the severe deprivations of southern life, it may well be that if white southerners were less addicted to booze and sex than they seem to be, they would far more frequently take out their frustrations in violence against blacks.

To ascribe the rise of Massive Resistance solely or largely to the psychopathology of the segregationists would be to commit the error of the "solipsistic tendency." It is surely not wrong, however, to ascribe certain of the cruder manifestations of white supremacy racism to the cultural conditioning and psychological predispositions of those white southerners who created the post-Brown backlash.[18]

IV. EVANGELICAL RELIGIOUS FACTORS

SINCE ORTHODOX or evangelical Protestantism has been the chief shaper of the southern way of life, it is postulated here that religious factors were second only to politics in creating the chain of events that led to Massive Resistance. It is the aim of this section to explore that hypothesis by probing two questions. What are the known facts about the nature and influence of southern religion? And what elements of southern religion might conduce, directly or indirectly, to race prejudice and political movements based on race? In seeking to answer these questions, it will be important to avoid the fallacy of intended consequences, since religion—like all human institutions—has rational or intended functions but also social, psychological, and any number of adventitious side-effects. Indeed, it is no exaggeration to say that more often than not in history, it has been the *unintended* consequences of a thing that really matter.

The majority of social scientists who have studied and written about the South have not paid adequate attention to the overall impact of religion on the region.[19] However one measures it, that impact has been enormous. And its surface manifestations are obvious even to the most casual observer. One thinks, for example, of the profusion of churches in every town and hamlet, the proliferation of old and new sects, the Sunday blue laws, the crazy liquor regulations, the pervasive revivalism, the ubiquitous Bible salesmen, the biblical rhetoric of the region's lawyers, the endless gospel singing, and the intrusion of the clergy into almost every area of public and private life. And yet, a good deal of religion's impact on the South is variously disguised, and it is that fact that has tended to mislead even the experts.

Francis B. Simkins was surely on the right track when he wrote not long ago that "Faith in the Biblical heritage is a factor second only to White Supremacy as a means of conserving the ways of the South."[20] It is likewise true that the "Biblical heritage" that most of today's southerners grew up in was the heritage of evangelical, fundamentalist, Calvinist Protestantism. The pervasiveness of that heritage is so great that southerners, who proudly call their region the "Bible Belt," are literally immersed in the sights, sounds, and symbols of organized religion from the cradle to the grave. One might even say that there has long been in the South a de facto "fusion" of church and state, despite the first amendment and the Protestant principle of church-state separation. Southern politics, therefore, is more "theocratic" than most southerners would be willing to admit.

The overwhelming majority of southerners (white and black) are Protestants who identify themselves as Baptists, Methodists, or Presbyterians—the "Big Three" of the region's religious establishment. This means that the typical southerner was nurtured in a tradition that is fundamentalist in basic doctrine, evangelical (revivalist) in homiletics, puritanical in ethics, congregational in church governance, and Calvinist, Wesleyan, or Arminian in theology. The only southerners not a part of this religious tradition are the region's Jews, Catholics, high Episcopalians, Unitarians, and atheists—and even they have been rather strongly influenced by "fall-out" from the tradition.

In light of the foregoing facts, one would have to say that the concept of the "Solid South" makes more sense religiously than politically. Except for a few urban areas like Miami Beach where Jews predominate and New Orleans where Catholics are strong, religious homogeneity is such a basic fact of everyday life that there is simply no escaping its influence, be that influence good or bad. As the South became convulsed by change in the post-Brown era, the one thing that changed hardly at all was the hold of orthodox Protestantism upon every aspect of the southern way of life.

Though religion has been the chief shaper of the modern southern mentality and personality, the predominance of evengelical Protestantism is of relatively recent origin. Until the late colonial period, southerners tended to be irreligious, deistic, or nominal adherents of the Church of England.[21] But with the arrival in the South of Scotch-Irish Calvinists, Baptist and Methodist revivalists, and the camp meeting technique around the middle of the eighteenth century, the religious coloration of the South dramatically and rapidly changed.[22] In fact, it changed so fast that by the early nineteenth century, one could say that evangelical orthodoxy had the field pretty much to itself.

So much for the general nature and influence of southern religion. To come to grips with the second (and more specific) question posed above, three aspects of evangelical Protestantism will be examined to see in what ways, it any, they might conduce to racism. These are church organization, ethics, and theology.

In most of the South's evangelical churches there exists no authoritarian structure with mitered hierarchs who can dictate policy from above and force individual churches to implement it. There is normally a clergy-laity division, it is true, but the clerical leader—usually called preacher, minister, or pastor—must be content with the role of *primus inter pares*, and even that role is often put into question by aggressive deacons, elders, and presbyters. Some of the evangelical groups, notably the Southern Baptists (the region's largest denomination), have carried their radical congregationalism to the point of rejecting membership in the prestigious World Council of Churches, partly at least because of the Council's liberal stand on race. Two other organizational facts of some significance need to be noted. The first is that many if not most of the South's evangelical churches have been structurally separated from their non-southern brethren since the Civil War, and thus have tended to adopt a parochial view of social questions. The second is that the great majority of the evangelical churches are structurally divided on race lines, which means that there is a separate black wing in each of the major denominations. This structural division persists even though blacks can now attend white churches in most parts of the South. It is still relatively rare, however, for white churches to have blacks on their membership rosters.

It would be easy to talk about "organizational determinism" in trying to account for southern religion's conservatism on race, but the temptation must be resisted. The truth of the matter is that while congregational autonomy is indeed a basic principle, there actually is more denominational control of local church affairs than is generally supposed. Thus, when the state or regional head-quarters of a southern church deems the time ripe for an anti-vice, anti-liquor, or evangelism crusade, local churches and pastors "snap to" with the alacrity of a Spanish priest carrying out the policies of his bishop. In fact, in seventeenth-century New England, the catechistic definition of a Congregational church was "an aristocracy that spoke and a democracy that kept silent." That definition is almost as relevant today in much of the South as it was in colonial New England. Congregational democracy still prevails in theory (and mythology), but in practice a "power elite" of pastors and church officials usually runs things pretty much as it wishes. The folklore of southern Protestantism has long recognized the "hierarchic" reality behind the democratic myth, as witness the fact that during the Massive Resistance era Georgia Baptists referred to the Reverend Louie Newton, pastor of Atlanta's powerful Druid Hills Church, as "the Bishop of Druid Hills." All of this is to suggest that Michels' "Iron Law of Oligarchy" is as applicable to the evangelical churches of the South as to all other religious and secular organizations, whatever their rationalizing ideology may indicate to the contrary.

These facts inescapably lead to the conclusion that while the decentralized congregational polity of southern Protestantism did not cause racism or Massive Resistance, it enormously complicated the efforts to get rid of race prejudice and its off-shoots. For, as was shown, though congregational democracy has never been quite as real in the South as the theory would suggest, it has been sufficiently strong to make it all but impossible for a given denomination to achieve a consensus broad enough to launch a centralized attack on social problems such as segregation. Of course, if the social problem is a "noncontroversial" one such as booze or sexual promiscuity, congregationalism turns out to be no bar to effective joint action. As was also suggested above, the organizational isolation of southerners from the black and northern wings of the various churches has certainly inhibited liberalization of southern racial attitudes.

On the other hand, it needs to be stressed that although the Catholic Church (a small minority in the South) has one of the most centralized, authoritarian polities in all of Christendom, this fact appears to have had little influence in distinguishing Catholic from Protestant racial attitudes. For a long time the Pope and the Roman hierarchy have sharply denounced racism, but the message has still apparently not filtered down to some of the local parishes in the South. Most revealing in this regard is the fact that in early 1954 the Catholic Committee of the South was set up by the Church's southern bishops to discuss the moral problems of segregation and to seek ways of ending discrimination. But after Massive Resistance emerged, the Committee was dissolved, apparently because the Deep South bishops were frightened by the opposition of segregationist laymen like Leander Perez. Church centralism, then, is not a guarantee of social liberalism.

In the matter of ethics, it would be wrong to say that all the South's evangelical churches have committed themselves to a uniform body of moral principles. The various groups disagree on many ethical issues, and sometimes quite bitterly. It is nevertheless a fact that the great majority of southern evangelicals have reached a high degree of consensus on certain basic ethical principles, most of which appear to have a Puritan ancestry, if that phrase is broadly defined.

Certainly all evangelicals believe that God is the highest good and sin the greatest evil. Sin, being the transgression of God's laws, reveals itself as the great corrupting force of human life. It is also a fact that evangelicals have traditionally conceived of sin in individual rather than social terms.

The foundation of evangelical ethics is, of course, the Bible —literally interpreted. For it is in the Bible that God has revealed, through a series of injunctions and admonitions, the fundamental prescriptions and proscriptions applicable to human behavior. In seeking to realize a "sanctified personal life" in accord with biblical ethics, the true Christian must not be taken in by such other ethical standards as Catholic natural law or utilitarian relativism.

If the believer, knowing his life is not his own, would make his influence truly effective, he must constantly pursue the good and eschew all forms of evil. Pursuing the good means, above all, loving God, embracing the key virtues of sobriety, piety, honesty, and thrift, and living life always with moral fervor and a total dedication to work. The good works will not, of course, "justify" one before God—only faith can do that—but an emphasis on the practical rather than the contemplative virtues will testify to one's quest for divine grace and personal purity.

In the matter of sin, transgressions against God's laws take many forms, but the worst of these are individual carnal sins— i.e., sins of the flesh. Of carnal sins, those involving indulgence in drugs, alcohol, and extra-marital sex are the most reprehensible. That is so because they are explicitly condemned by the Bible, and because (secondarily) they do great harm to individual human beings, thereby weakening their testimonial "influence."

The ethical imperatives of God, as revealed in the Old and New Testaments, are *absolutely* valid for all times and places. For the devout evangelical, this means that his moral duty to God was finally fixed when the Bible was written, and he must never compromise right by succumbing to a little "social drinking" or dabbling, extra-maritally, in sex. The Bible's transcendent moral maxims require his unyielding obedience and they must take precedence over everything.

Since the biblical moral principles are absolutes and applicable to all human beings, it is altogether proper that they should be made doubly binding on individuals by being incorporated into every community's criminal law code. In that way, an act of disobedience involving any of them will be both immoral and criminal. This does not, of course, mean that the state should assume the entire responsibility for enforcing morals or that church and state should be fused. It simply recognizes that law and morals are intimately intertwined in every society, and both the state and religious agencies must therefore cooperate in the enforcement of morality. What is more, the enforcement of the moral law should be viewed as one of the primary obligations of a good government.[23]

While it is often assumed that a genuine Christian commitment precludes all kinds of racial prejudice, it is the argument of this analysis that the peculiar apartness of the South's moral code has been a major shaper of that racism which dominates the southern way of life. The shaping has taken a number of forms, direct and indirect.

The obsessive individualism of evangelical ethics has patently diminished the concern of southern Protestantism with today's moral and social conflicts—or at least with those that do not involve carnal immorality. Individual redemption and personal sanctification still rank higher than a social conscience, and this alignment of priorities is bound to mute the social reformism that might otherwise flourish in the evangelical churches. It was scarcely an accident that the South's evangelicals, almost to a man, opposed Walter Rauschenbusch's "social gospel movement." Their individualist bias made their opposition logical, if not inevitable.

Since individual conversion (or "salvation"), understood as an instantaneous act, is the necessary and sufficient purpose of their church, evangelicals feel they have discharged their responsibility to black people when they preach "the good news" to them and train black preachers and revivalists to found black churches to handle the follow-up work. In their view, not only is it unnecessary for politicians to abolish Jim Crow laws before black sinners can be "saved," it is not even necessary (or desirable) for blacks to "make their decision for Christ" in a white church. Indeed, evangelicals believe it is better for all concerned if blacks get the message in a black church (rigidly segregated) and make their profession of faith there.

Likewise the biblical literalism and inerrancy on which all evangelical moral principles are founded have indirectly served to prop up the segregation system. This follows from the fact that the Bible, while countenancing slavery, says nothing about the duty to integrate, and thus evangelicals long ago concluded that racial mores and folkways—or at least their reform—should be viewed as a matter for Caesar's realm rather than God's. The more extreme fundamentalists would go further and argue, as a resolution of the Arkansas Missionary Baptist Association recently did, that God was the first Segregator and that the Bible actually prescribes segregation by virtue of its account of the curse on Ham, the tower of Babel, and the separation of the continents. As though that were not proof enough of their point, they pose the rhetorical question, "If God wanted the races to integrate, why did He make them different?"

It would also appear that the legalistic bias of evangelical ethics has been a barrier to social reform. This is true for three reasons. It has muted the liberals' plea for the criminalization of racism, since evangelicals view racism either as not immoral or as a sin of the spirit instead of the flesh. Moreover, while neglecting most sins of the spirit, it has fully occupied the faithful with frenetic crusading in favor of criminalizing all the grave carnal sins—drugs, gambling, sex, and booze. Perhaps more important still, by ranking the individual's obedience to the "practical moral laws" above such spiritual imperatives as loving one's neighbor, this bias has almost certainly helped to diminish the evangelicals' concern with black people.

Finally, the other-worldly, anti-intellectual bent of evangelical ethics has produced a built-in bias against any social reforms, such as integration, which are prescribed by reason and social science instead of by Providence. It seems obvious that any ethical system that puts as heavy an emphasis on emotion, faith, and preparing oneself for the hereafter as does that of the evangelicals must be deficient in motivating its adherents to think deeply about, and to question "conventional wisdom"—be it white supremacy or whatever. It is a fact, and an ironic one, that the South's ascetic Protestants, by going overboard on the other-worldly, "anti-social" side of their ethics, have strayed far beyond their Reformation moorings. For Calvin clearly stated that the Church must be the social conscience of the land, and the sixteenth-century Anabaptists (indirect ancestors of the Baptists) firmly believed that every Christian is responsible for the tone and health of the society around him.

Despite their disclaimers, there can be no denying the fact that today's evangelicals, by making an extreme fetish of the church-state separation doctrine and by institutionalizing revivalism as a surrogate for social reform, have beat a great retreat from concern about the social order—except, or course, where the issue of carnal immorality is involved. And, irony of ironies, this suspension of ethical judgments on state affairs (particularly marked in the field of race and war policy) in the name of preserving church-state separation was occurring at the very moment the evangelicals were being transformed from isolated minority sects into the de facto Established Church of the South! Many factors were involved, but surely the evangelicals' ethical supernaturalism played a key role in the narrowing of southern Protestantism's social concerns to an almost paranoid obsession with carnality and the "work ethic"—and to a rationalizing defense of the white racist status quo.

Contrary to claims by the faithful, there is scant evidence to show that a formal or informal commitment to evangelical ethics significantly "purifies" white southerners. Indeed, the contrary seems to be the case. For, as has been noted, the South has had a long tradition of violence, and its homicide and rape rates continue to be among the nation's highest. Moreover, since much of this violence is committed by whites against blacks, it seems fair to conclude that if evangelical moral principles did not cause race bigotry, they have had precious little effect in extirpating this evil from the hearts and minds of white southerners. It is now generally agreed that the chief perpetrators of physical violence against blacks in the South are fundamentalist evangelicals, who also usually have a low socio-economic status. In this regard, America's greatest Protestant theologian once wrote:

> *If there were a drunken orgy somewhere, I would bet ten to one a church member was not in it. . . . But if there were a lynching I would bet ten to one a church member was in it. I don't find people belonging to churches giving a guarantee of emancipated race attitude or a high type of political morality. We can't assume that at all.*[24]

It is also interesting that in certain other parts of the world where the evangelical ethic is strong, white racism is a conspicuous phenomenon. One thinks especially of South Africa, Rhodesia, and parts of Great Britain. The degree of causality involved in this linkage, if any, must of course remain a matter of conjecture.[25]

It is not an easy task to show a linkage between theology and racism, but a few generalizations in that regard are in order here.

At the outset it is important to stress that because of its preoccupation with the subjective in religion, southern evangelicalism has never evinced much interest in, or talent for theological creativity. Indeed, one may say without much exaggeration that evangelical theology amounts to little more than an eclectic bowdlerization of the doctrines of Calvin, Arminius, and Wesley. What is more, the typical evangelical pastor constantly uses the professional theologian as a whipping-boy—especially those in the denominational seminaries who confront the problems of race with reason and the tools of science. Although there is denominational heterogeneity in evangelical theology, one is warranted in saying that there is an essential southern Protestant theology.

Among the aspects of that essential theology that might conduce to racism, one thinks at once of its epistemology. Simply put, evangelical epistemology holds that knowledge about God and religion is the highest form of truth, and that this truth, in form as well as content, is "timeless" and unvarying, though the techniques of its promotion may be altered from time to time. Man acquires that knowledge not through reason, science, or empirical research, but through emotional awareness and faith in the Bible as the authoritative and divinely inspired word of God. For the individual the most vital kind of knowledge is the "blessed assurance" that he is "saved," and this is most likely to be achieved through an intense emotional experience that will be facilitated by a revivalist setting.

From the perspective of this analysis, one may say that evangelical epistemology conduces to racism to the extent that it creates an atmosphere in which emotion is ranked above reason and in which science (social or natural) is disparaged as a relatively insignificant guide to life. Furthermore, by postulating that religious truth is the highest form of truth, the southern epistemology relegates such social truths as those embedded in the Brown decisions to a rather low place among the varieties and types of truth.

A second aspect of evangelical theology that unwittingly serves the cause of the white supremacists is its soteriological or "salvation" doctrine. Since knowing God and getting saved is the highest duty of an evangelical, it is only logical that his church's theology should postulate the salvation of sinners as the central theme of its teaching. Of course, southern evangelical churches do other things than convert the lost—they are big social centers, for example—but the salvation of individuals has become such an overriding concern with them that it often seems they do nothing else. The sense of urgency that surrounds this activity leaves little time for anything else. The evangelicals' salvation doctrine is simplistic in the extreme. Christ is the whole answer, which means that believing (and church-going) individuals are converted from condemned status before the Almighty to an eternal reward in heaven, through the merits of Christ's death. This is the essential core of evangelical theology, and it explains the southern obsession with evangelism and hortatory preaching.

Given the compulsive, obsessive, overriding nature of this salvation doctrine, it is wholly logical for evangelicals to view social reform as a secondary concern, if not impious, since it takes vital time away from the church's central mission. As long as the doctrine does not view racism as a barrier to "finding Christ," no urgency or guilt is felt about its persistence.

A third feature of evangelical theology that is relevant to this discussion is the doctrine of election. With the more fundamentalist of southern Protestants, this takes the form of a belief in "double predestination," which holds that God in His infinite wisdom has "elected" a few individuals to life everlasting, while condemning the great majority of men to eternal death in hell (reprobation). Practically speaking, this means that the more extreme versions of evangelical theology implicitly reject the brotherhood of man and the fatherhood of God as true doctrine, since unredeemed sinners are in effect sons of the devil. Given their cultural conditioning, it is hard for an evangelical not to believe that most blacks will wind up in the damned camp, with perhaps only a handful of "Uncle Toms" and "Aunt Janes" finding their way into the basically white camp of the "elect." Moreover, as has been shown, this belief in one of the several varieties of predestination has unquestionably conditioned white southerners to accept segregation as something foreordained by God himself, about which little if anything can or should be done. The evangelicals are not consistent predestinationists, however. In other areas of life, they seem to forget the sovereignty of God and become the most unfatalistic, free-will Arminians imaginable. But they are consistently fatalistic about the potential of blacks—man's free choice here can do nothing against God's predestined will.

A final aspect of evangelical theology that needs to be commented on is a peripheral, yet important one. That is southern Protestantism's visual and verbal symbolism of color. The evangelicals, of course, did not invent Christianity's symbolism—that goes back to the earliest days of the Church. But they have added new twists to the color tradition, and they refuse to change it despite the evidence that the tradition both breeds and reinforces racism.

Basically the color symbolism of the evangelicals involves a black-white dichotomy that permeates every aspect of the southern church's teachings. And, not surprisingly, the two colors are viewed primarily in moral rather than in aesthetic terms, with white symbolizing the good and pure, and black all kinds of evil. Christ, for example, is always depicted as lily white, and the famous "Head of Christ" by Warner Sallman (archetypically Caucasian) hangs in thousands of southern evangelical churches. In like fashion, pictures of the early church fathers and missionaries, which abound in Sunday school literature, depict their subjects as being pure Anglo-Saxons. A few of these may be shown with long hair, but there is not a swarthy, Mediterranean Semite among them!

Other examples of the color symbolism come to mind. The visual symbol of the holy spirit is the white dove, and the soul is spoken of as being white. The evangelicals' Christmas materials portray the Three Wise Men, including the "black king" Balthasar, as thoroughly "Aryan." The garments of the "elect" in heaven are said to be pure white, and at baptismal services females usually wear white. Even the evangelicals' church buildings are normally white, if not of red brick. Medieval Catholics had their Black Madonnas, and today's liberal Christians take it for granted that many of the early fathers of the Church were quite dark if not technically negroid. But the color symbolism of the evangelicals has succeeded in bleaching one and all until they have become almost albinic caricatures of the Anglo-Saxon "Aryan" type.

The verbal symbolism of color is no less pervasive among

evangelicals than the visual. This manifests itself in such phrases as "black as Satan," "pure as the driven snow," and "the outer darkness of hell." The perfect verbalization of the color dichotomy was achieved in an address by the nineteenth-century educator, Robert Bingham, who was a North Carolina evangelical. In that well-known address, Bingham said: "The load of the country in the South must continue to be pulled by a double horse team, so to speak, with the white horse 'in the lead' and the black horse on the 'off side,' to use the farmer's phrase."[26] It is well established today that thinking, to a significant degree, is chained to language. That being the case, it is hard to rebut the argument that the evangelicals' color symbolism—only the outlines of which have been sketched here—has played an overlooked role in perpetuating the dogmas and attitudes of white supremacy.

For some time now, winds of change have been blowing in the South's evangelical churches. But since the ethical, theological, and behavioral changes have so far been minimal, southern Protestantism continues to be extremely conservative, if not reactionary, on race and most other social issues. Most evangelical churches still do not have black members, and black pastors are all but unknown in the South's white churches. Thus, despite the small changes that have been made, it remains true that

> *The church is the most segregated major institution in American society. It has lagged behind the Supreme Court as the conscience of the nation on questions of race, and it has fallen far behind trade unions, factories, schools, department stores, athletic gatherings and most other major areas of human association as far as the achievement of integration in its own life is concerned.*[27]

People not familiar with the South have often expressed surprise at the prominent role played by fundamentalist preachers in the Massive Resistance counterrevolution. Thus, the Christian Civic League, one of Georgia's most intransigent segregationist groups, was headed by the Reverend E. G. ("Parson Jack") Johnston, pastor of the Independent Baptist Tabernacle of Columbus, Georgia. It was also a Georgia minister, the Reverend Montague Cook of Moultrie, who devoted his life to fighting the moderate race relations reports prepared by the Southern Baptist Christian Life Commission in the post-Brown years. According to Cook, "Racial fellowship is synonymous with integration," and is therefore bad. Moreover, it was a nationally known Southern Baptist leader, the Reverend Wallie Amos Criswell of the prestigious First Baptist Church of Dallas, Texas, who in 1956 so passionately defended segregation before the South Carolina legislature that his impromptu speech was nationally circulated by the White Citizens' Councils. In light of the Criswell speech, and similar evidence, one is hard put not to agree with the charge that southern Protestantism

> today appears more determined than ever to preserve the myth of "white supremacy." Of all the dark and tragic periods of church history (and there have been many) this is the church's saddest hour. Only in the spirit of naked hypocrisy can the church continue to sing: "Like a mighty army moves the church of God; brothers we are treading where the saints have trod. We are not divided, all one body we; one in hope and doctrine, one in charity."[28]

Liberal Protestantism outside the South has refused to see religion as a cop-out or as an anodyne imbuing the devout with an escapist sense of euphoria. And, indeed, in its more admirable manifestations, historical Christianity has been a goad to the laggard conscience, a prod to character creativity, and a ceaseless challenge to the manifold injustices of society. Clearly, then, the southern version of Christianity, which has been inimical to the interests of blacks, is highly idiosyncratic, if not *sui generis*. It endures, despite all the winds of change, because it pins a "badge of righteousness" on its adherents and wraps them in a Sabbath cloak which covers up—from most mortal eyes at least—their everyday misbehavior.

Some years ago Elie Halévy theorized that English evangelicalism, especially Methodism, may have prevented an eighteenth-century revolution in Britain by channeling the psychic energies of the English lower classes into revivalism and away from revolutionary preoccupations.[29] Reasoning analogically, one might also argue that over the past century and a half southern Protestantism, in similar fashion, has emasculated the South's working class (in an ideological sense) by focusing everybody's energies on soul-saving through never-ending evangelism. The specific functions performed by evangelicalism in this regard were the provision of outlets for emotional expression and the implanting of an ethic and theology that reconciled lower-class whites and blacks to the Jim Crow system, made that condition seem predestined, and made patient submission to it a sacred obligation. Stealing a metaphor from the Communists, may we not therefore say that evangelical Christianity has been an "opiate" for southerners of both races?

The basic hypothesis of this interpretive analysis has been that the chief proximate causes of Massive Resistance racism were political oligarchicalism, economic underdevelopment, the Calvin-Bacchus Syndrome, and evangelical Protestantism—with the first and last being causally the most efficacious. If this hypothesis has merit, it is obvious that a reduction of southern racism will require a greater degree of political democracy, modernization (and humanization) of the South's economy, increased educational opportunities for all, and a massive transformation of the ethics and theology of southern religion. Nothing is certain in explaining race conflicts—except that southern racism will continue to thrive as long as the institutional structures and religio-cultural patterns that created and reinforce it are left intact or but slightly altered.

EPILOGUE: CHALLENGE AND OPPORTUNITY

SINCE THE COMPLETION of this study, there has been no end to the dreary succession of flash-points on the national scene which prove that millions of Americans (black and white) have ceased to believe in the justice of the American, let alone the southern way of life. For many of the country's disadvantaged minorities, particularly the blacks, the American dream remains a nightmare. What began in the 1950's as a legal-constitutional revolution, affecting only the South's public schools, has now snowballed into a multifaceted, *permanent* revolution, reaching into every state and plunging the nation into its greatest crisis of faith and values in more than a century.

Massive Resistance, the southern response to that revolution, was dead as a viable political movement by the mid-1960's. Indeed, many would say it was dead by the late 1950's. Yet it is now apparent that the movement's operative myths—white supremacy and states'-rights federalism—still hold the southern mind in their trap-like grip. The myth lag remains a ubiquitous and tragic fact of southern existence.

In 1968 the President's National Advisory Commission on Civil Disorders (the so-called Kerner Commission) released a 250,000-word document, the findings of which parallel much of the critical analysis of this study.[1] The Commission minced no words in concluding that bigotry and racial segregation, as practiced in both the South and North, "threaten the future of every American."[2] Moreover, while stressing the complexity of the causation issue, the Commission found that there was one overriding reason for the racial conflicts of recent years—"white racism," which "has shaped our history decisively . . . [and] now threatens to affect our future."[3] As for future policy, the Kerner Report recommended that the nation's first priority be made "the creation of a true union—a single society and a single American identity."[4]

For the past four years the Nixon Administration has had the responsibility of trying to realize that "true union" of Americans described in the Kerner Report and, secondarily, of keeping the banked fires of Massive Resistance from flaring up again. The Administration's discharge of that responsibility remains a matter of great controversy. Nixon supporters maintain that the Administration's record represents a great leap forward toward equality of opportunity without the sacrifice of any group's vital interests. Critics, on the other hand, derogate the record as a "Southern Strategy" of retreat, the main purpose of which is to win the votes of unreconstructed Massive Resisters. As usual, the truth probably lies somewhere in between these extremes, for the last four years clearly have brought both progress and regression in desegregation.

Both in the 1968 campaign and later as President, Mr. Nixon made it plain that he favored a lowered federal profile in most areas of public policy. It was Mr. Nixon's view, and that of his closest advisers, that desegregation could be advanced more effectively if the President and federal bureaucrats spent less time berating the South and more time working behind the scenes to ease the transition to unitary schools. With that in mind, the Justice Department intervened in a Mississippi case and urged the courts to postpone the pending integration of that state's schools. The intervention understandably pleased the South, but the U. S. Supreme Court rejected the Justice Department's plea for delay.

One of the most controversial aspects of the Nixon record concerned the Administration's attitude toward the implementation of Title VI of the Civil Rights Act of 1964. By the end of the 1960's, it was generally felt that the federal government had finally established its credibility in the South respecting the maximum implementation of Brown. HEW had drawn up and widely publicized guidelines that called for complete desegregation of schools by September 1969, or, in a few cases, by September

1970. Furthermore it seemed that a majority of the South's counterrevolutionaries had reluctantly accepted the fact that the end of segregation was in sight and that further organized resistance would be futile. It was about this time that Governor McNair of South Carolina voiced the new mood surfacing in the South by remarking, "We have run out of time. We have run out of courts."

Mr. Nixon had said in his Inaugural Address that "No man can be fully free while his neighbor is not," and proponents of the egalitarian revolution praised him for the statement. A few months later, however, a series of events transpired which turned many of the egalitarians into the President's sharpest critics. For reasons that are still not clear, the desegregation deadlines were withdrawn, the cut-off of funds to recalcitrant school districts was curtailed, the administrative enforcement of Title VI was played down, and in 1970 the Nixon Administration announced it would henceforth rely on persuasion and court action to get dual school systems abolished. Between 1964 and 1970 HEW started proceedings to cut off funds to 600 school districts. In 1968–69, funds were actually cut off from forty-four districts. In 1972 a federal court found that no funds at all had been cut off since the summer of 1970, when the Administration's no-withholding policy took effect.

One can make a plausible case for applying the adjective "erratic" to Mr. Nixon's record on school desegregation, but the same adjective can be applied to the record of all recent Presidents. Neither Eisenhower, Kennedy, nor Johnson fought the Massive Resisters and supported the egalitarians with single-minded consistency. All of them wavered now and then on this or that issue, and each time they wavered they revived the flickering hopes of the segregationists. So it has been with Mr. Nixon.

Since Mr. Nixon is a self-confessed pragmatist, one would logically expect him to "waver" or change his mind on public policy as circumstances and the mood of the country change. But for whatever reasons, he does appear to have changed his mind somewhat on desegregation policy, and for that he has been both praised and criticized. The criticism has come not only for the changes noted above but also as a result of certain controversial personnel changes. These included the dropping of Leon Panetta as the director of HEW's Office of Civil Rights and the appointment of the conservative Robert C. Mardian as HEW's general counsel.

On March 24, 1970, President Nixon released his long-awaited "lawyer's brief" on school desegregation. Critics promptly attacked the statement as an unacknowledged abandonment of principle, but the majority of Americans appear to have found the statement timely and useful. The stated purpose of the brief was "to set forth in detail this Administration's policies on the subject of desegregation of America's elementary and secondary schools."[5] An additional purpose seems to have been to answer in a forceful way those critics among blacks and liberals who were saying that the Administration had made a "deal" with southern politicians and had, in effect, reenacted the Compromise of 1877. Presidential pronouncements rarely, if ever, change the minds of presidential critics, and this one was no exception. Supporters of Mr. Nixon claimed that the statement reaffirmed the President's commitment to desegregation, while opponents argued that it did no such thing.

In commenting on the law enunciated in Brown, Mr. Nixon made a sharp distinction between de jure segregation, which he said was unconstitutional, and de facto segregation, which he said is "undesirable but not generally held to violate the Constitution." To emphasize the distinction, he made reference to the Brown decision, which, he said, held that "separation *by law* establishes schools that are inherently unequal." Critics were quick to point out that the relevant holding in Brown was somewhat different— viz., that "Separate educational facilities are inherently unequal." And they tried, without visible success, to convince the people that President Nixon had deliberately misled them.

The President then proceeded to discourse at some length on the nature of schools and the educational process. He observed that two goals had recently been assigned the nation's schools— improving the quality of education and "lowering . . . artificial racial barriers." While he felt that both goals were commendable, he maintained that the pursuit of the first goal should be the primary task of the public schools. He did not agree that segregated schools in all cases cause psychic injury to black children, and he rejected the liberal belief "that blacks or others of minority races would be improved by association with whites" in all situations. He likewise suggested that it is a form of inverted racism to urge the integration of whites and blacks in the hope that blacks will benefit therefrom. He also, of course, reaffirmed his strong belief that no child should be "deprived" of his "own neighborhood school."

As for future desegregation policy, Mr. Nixon indicated that he would abide by five basic principles. He would continue to support the concept of the neighborhood school. He would not ask officials of his Administration to "go beyond the requirements of law" in dealing with local school boards. He would not initiate a federal campaign to destroy de facto segregation. He would set up a cabinet group under Mr. Agnew's direction to gather informational data about the entire educational process. He would divert additional federal funds from "other domestic problems" to aid disadvantaged schools.

The policy principles Mr. Nixon enunciated were neither novel nor shocking, but it appeared that they pleased conservatives more than liberals. Clearly the key commitments of the Nixon desegregation philosophy were to local control of schools, states' rights, minimal federal coercion of school boards, state-local voluntarism, and gradualism in the field of social reform. The principles were steeped in traditional Jeffersonianism, and if they were unlikely to accelerate school integration, there was a chance that they might defuse some of the bitter controversy swirling around the public schools.

Doubtless Mr. Nixon hoped that they would do just that. But black militants and white liberals continued to attack President Nixon's desegregation "brief" as a calculated retreat from Brown, and they linked it with Mr. Nixon's stated intention to appoint only "strict constructionist" conservatives to the federal courts. It was their view, in fact, that the President's judicial appointments would very likely have a greater long-term effect on the course of desegregation than any administrative decisions his bureaucratic agencies might make.

Mr. Nixon's liberal critics were not very happy when he nominated Warren Burger to succeed Earl Warren as Chief Justice of the

Supreme Court. But their unhappiness and anger knew no bounds when he nominated two conservative southerners, Clement Haynsworth and G. Harrold Carswell, to fill an additional vacancy on the Court. Haynsworth had a mixed record in civil rights cases, while Carswell had a pronounced segregationist record, but neither was able to gain Senate confirmation. Mr. Nixon's other first-term Supreme Court appointments—Blackmun, Rehnquist, and Powell—were from the conservative side of the political spectrum, but they were not segregationists. Despite the fears of egalitarians, there was little if any evidence by the end of 1972 that the Supreme Court had retreated from, or seriously modified the Warren Court's Brown holding.

Some of the achievements of the Nixon Administration in the field of desegregation, which liberals tend to ignore, should be noted. Whether they outweigh the signs of "regression" discussed above is a question each individual must settle for himself.

In 1969 the Administration brought forty-three lawsuits against recalcitrant school districts and joined in more than a dozen others initiated by private parties. It also initiated the first enforcement proceedings against a non-southern school system (Ferndale, Michigan), and filed the first statewide desegregation suit when it charged that Georgia officials were trying to perpetuate rather than eliminate that state's dual school systems.

When the Whitten Amendment was reviving the hopes of the Massive Resisters, the Administration at first seemed to favor it. But in the end, it helped to defeat the amendment, which would have forbidden HEW to cut off funds to any district with a freedom of choice plan.

In his message of March 1970, Mr. Nixon promised that he would ask Congress to provide $1.5 billion over the next two years to aid school districts in both the South and North to desegregate.

In the summer of that year, the Justice Department brought statewide school desegregation suits against Mississippi and Texas, similar to the one filed against Georgia in the preceding year.

Finally, also in 1970, the Internal Revenue Service let it be known that it would be stricter in the future in granting tax-exempt status to new private schools in the South. And on August 19, it shocked segregationists by revoking the tax exemptions of eleven all-white private schools in Mississippi.

Whether or not the actions of the Nixon Administration were responsible, it now is clear that there has recently been a mini-revival of Massive Resistance in the states of the Old Confederacy. Just as the original Massive Resistance movement was a response to the Brown decision, the current tentative revival is largely a response to the school busing controversy. But it differs from the counterrevolution of the fifties in being more national in scope.

No other public issue—save perhaps Vietnam—has posed a greater challenge to American democracy in the past decade than the issue of busing to achieve racial balance in schools. No issue has offered so few opportunities for conflict resolution and creative statesmanship. Richard Nixon certainly did not invent the busing issue—George Wallace seems to have done that—but as President he is stuck with it, and he is likely to get the bulk of the credit and blame for its ultimate outcome.

This Epilogue is obviously not the place for a full-scale analysis of the busing issue, yet a few general comments are germane to the discussion of the current resurgence of Massive Resistance. The first thing to be said is that both sides have misrepresented the facts in the busing controversy, though the segregationists seem to have been more culpable. The slogan "No Busing!" is being used today by unreconstructed Massive Resisters in the same way that they used the slogans "states' rights" and "freedom of choice" in the fifties and sixties—namely, to rationalize their white supremacy racism and make it more palatable to the courts and the nation at large. The issue of busing is so emotional, complex, and politicized that it will almost certainly be around to trouble the waters of American politics long after Richard Nixon has retired from public office.[6]

The busing issue, to a great extent, is a pseudo-issue, since there is more inflated rhetoric than solid substance in most debates about it. This is most clearly revealed in the propaganda of the southern opponents of busing and their northern sympathizers. Their manipulation of symbols and their manner of argumentation are closely reminiscent of the anti-Brown propaganda which the Massive Resistance movement spawned in the 1950's, except that there is less explicit discussion of race in the anti-busing polemics. The "Neo-Massive Resisters," for example, never admit that in the rural South consolidated schools and large-scale busing have made unitary education a viable reality, beneficial to both races. They deliberately ignore the fact that the Supreme Court has never decreed a fixed mathematical racial balance in public schools. They fail to point out that only about three per cent of all children bused to school are transported to achieve desegregation. They seem not to be aware of the fact that in the early seventies more pupils were being bused to racially segregated schools than to integrated ones. They seek to hide the fact that nearly half of the nation's public school children are regularly bused to school for reasons having little or nothing to do with integration. They ignore the statistical fact that the number of children bused nationally changed very little between 1967 and the early 1970's. They are unwilling to admit that before George Wallace "discovered" the busing issue, the majority of southerners were calmly and sensibly adjusting to court-ordered busing. They adamantly refuse to recognize the fact that when courts issue busing orders to school districts, they do so in order to vindicate a fourteenth-amendment right announced in Brown and other school cases. They are very clever in disguising the fact that court-ordered busing has usually involved far more black than white children. And despite their insinuations, they have never proved that white children are being bused in large numbers from superior suburban schools to inferior central-city schools.

When one carefully analyzes the anti-busing propaganda popularized in the South during the past four years, one cannot avoid the conclusion that it is largely a delayed attempt by southern segregationists to "get" Brown and to achieve by indirection what the Massive Resistance counterrevolution was unable to achieve by direct action. It is quite clearly an attempt by white southerners to keep blacks in their central-city ghetto schools and forever away from the lily-white, suburban "neighborhood schools." Doubtless there are many good reasons for wanting to minimize the busing of small children, but in light of the white southerners' universal acceptance of the busing of black children in pre-Brown days, it is hard to believe that the current anti-busing campaign is not, at least in part, racially motivated.

It needs also to be said that liberals and egalitarians are not without blame for the extraordinary escalation of the busing issue. True, they have not indulged in as much polemical distortion as have the anti-busing zealots, yet they have failed to do their duty in a number of ways. They have not adequately informed themselves about the intricacies of the busing issue. They have not always been willing to support greater taxes for central-city schools. They have been something less than creative in proposing alternatives to busing. They have underestimated the hold that the neighborhood school concept has on the American mind. And far too many of them have turned their backs on the public schools and enrolled their children in elitist private schools, where there is minimal desegregation and maximal freedom from busing controversy.

In the election year of 1972 very few national or state politicians were willing to commit themselves unequivocally to a position of supporting busing to advance school desegregation. The politicians were convinced that the people were opposed to busing (the polls confirmed that belief), and they tended to go along with the *vox populi* without trying to change it. Southerners were particularly pleased when President Nixon, along with most Democratic candidates, put himself solidly in the anti-busing camp, and this presidential decision was undoubtedly one of the major reasons why southerners voted for Mr. Nixon in record numbers in the 1972 election.

His position on the busing issue was made clear in a number of public statements and recommendations to Congress during his first term. He praised the neighborhood school at every opportunity. He criticized the courts for going too far in demanding an artificial racial balance in public schools. He rejected the liberal idea that schools should be a major instrument of social reform. And in March of 1972, shortly after George Wallace won the Florida presidential primary, he addressed the nation by television and radio on the subject of busing.

Mr. Nixon said that he was sending to Congress two bills that would codify and clarify his policy on busing. One of these proposed that Congress legislate a moratorium on all new busing orders for a period of up to fifteen months. The other proposed that Congress, after freezing the status quo by the first bill, establish "a clear, rational, and uniform standard for determining the extent to which a local educational agency is required to reassign and transport its students in discharging its obligation under the Fourteenth Amendment . . . to desegregate its schools." The President also indicated that he was willing to consider, on its merits, an anti-busing constitutional amendment which southerners in Congress were busily preparing.

Mr. Nixon's busing speech and the bills he subsequently sent to Congress created even more controversy between desegregationists and defenders of the status quo than his speech of March 1970 had done. The diehards of the Massive Resistance movement seemed especially pleased, though they criticized the President for taking an equivocal position on an anti-busing amendment. Critics of the Nixon bills, including most but not all black leaders, urged Congress to reject the bills on the ground that they would be bad policy and raise grave constitutional questions. The critics, supported by many constitutional law experts, also alleged that the bills violated the spirit, if not the letter of the Supreme Court's Swann decision, and of a related decision outlawing North Carolina's anti-busing law.[7]

Eventually the Nixon proposals passed the House as the Equal Opportunities Act of 1972. The Act initially provided funds for compensatory education for slum children and all but barred courts from requiring busing to desegregate public schools. However, by the time the bill cleared the House, the compensatory funds had been dropped, and it amounted to little more than an anti-busing measure. The House-passed bill also permitted school desegregation cases already decided by the courts to be reopened —something the South's segregationists had long been advocating.

The anti-busing bill reached the Senate floor in the closing days of the 92nd Congress, and the ensuing debate was one of the most dramatic chapters in the desegregation struggle since the debate on the 1964 Civil Rights Act. The South's tutelary geniuses in the Senate made daily headlines in October 1972, as they had done in 1964, but in the end the Senate killed the anti-busing bill. Ironically, the liberals who opposed the bill were able to defeat it only by resorting to the southerners' favorite weapon—the fili-buster. After three attempts to invoke cloture failed, the southern-ers admitted defeat—for the time being at least—and the Senate moved on to other business.

While busing is certainly no panacea for the ills that plague public education, liberals were right to view the anti-busing bill as a symbol of the resurgence of Massive Resistance. Had the bill passed, a full-scale revival of the South's counterrevolution might well have ensued. Even so, it is probable that the 1972 busing controversy has damaged the cause of peaceful desegregation by rekindling the fires of racial bitterness and by making anti-busing sentiments more "respectable" than they previously had been.

The fight over school busing, while the most dramatic, was by no means the only sign of a resurgence of Massive Resistance. From 1969 on there were numerous signs and portents of this phenomenon. There was, for instance, the picture of Lester Mad-dox in the restaurant of the U. S. House of Representatives pass-ing out replicas of the ax handles he had used to bar blacks from his Pickrick Chicken House in Atlanta. There was also the deci-sion of several southern school boards to reopen the litigation that had forced desegregation on them. Revelatory, too, was the revival of editorial intransigence in the more conservative papers. More significant than that were the renewed attacks on the federal courts which had seemed to abate when Chief Justice Warren retired, and the impressive showing George Wallace made in the 1972 presidential primaries before he was wounded by an assas-sin's bullets. Both revelatory and tragic was the resurgence of interracial violence—confined largely but not entirely to the public schools—such as had disfigured the counterrevolutionary fifties. And perhaps most ominous of all was the demagogic J. B. Ston-er's 1972 reentry into Georgia politics on an unabashed white supremacist platform. He must have thrilled the unreconstructed Massive Resisters when he bragged to Georgia voters that he was "the only candidate for U. S. senator who is for the white people and the only candidate who is against integration."

Despite the obstructionist backlash of the segregationists, which this book has detailed, it now seems certain that the expanding egalitarian revolution is destined to change in the coming years not only our creaky political system but also our social, religious, educational, and economic institutions. Tocqueville was profoundly on target when he wrote (more than a century ago) that the forward march of democracy, of which our contemporary civil rights struggle is but one campaign, is an "irresistible revolution which has advanced for centuries in spite of every obstacle and which is still advancing in the midst of the ruins it has caused."[8] To be sure, neither the South nor the nation is likely to forge a truly integrated society in the near future. Yet progress continues on many fronts—North and South—and Tocqueville's revolution, while not quite irresistible, shows no sign of stopping.

The persistence of racism in the South and the mini-revival of Massive Resistance discussed above underscore the gap separating democratic ideals from democratic practice in both South and North. While it is not a purpose of this study to predict the ultimate fate of American blacks, the competing perspectives on this issue have been duly noted. Some pose serious challenges to American democracy.

The South's militant counterrevolutionaries still believe that segregation is God-ordained and ought therefore to remain a feature of the southern way of life. Most liberal and progressive democrats, anchored to the Melting Pot perspective, hope (and predict) that the nation's black minority will one day be fully assimilated into the American mainstream. Marxists insist that segregation and racism will end only when capitalism ends. Black separationists, who were the avant-garde of the egalitarian revolution in the 1960's, now advocate a kind of autonomous parallel development of black people. Some of these, such as Brother Imari's Republic of New Africa, are demanding $400 billion dollars in "damages" from five southern states with which to initiate the black man's autonomous development. It is their view— apparently not shared by the majority of black people—that the granting of sovereignty (and reparations) to a black nation in Mississippi or somewhere else in the South would be the simplest, cheapest, and most logical way to end racism.

Most Americans would probably agree that of these four perspectives on the race issue, those of the extreme segregationists and the Marxists have the least merit and are least likely to be the "wave of the future." As between the liberal and the black militant perspectives, the conscientious democrat will probably opt for the one that seems most feasible and closest to his view of equality.

The assimilationist perspective of the liberals, though psychologically and ideologically appealing, seems flawed with an excess of optimism and, more important, is on the verge of being totally discredited. Yet it remains the "traditional" American perspective on the race problem, and it was brilliantly argued by Robert E. Park back in 1926:

> In the relations of races there is a cycle which tends everywhere to repeat itself. . . . The race relations cycle, which takes the form . . . of contacts, competition, accommodation and eventual assimilation, is apparently progressive and irreversible. . . . Racial barriers may slacken the tempo of the movement, but cannot change its direction. . . . The forces which have brought about the existing interpenetration of peoples are so vast and irresistible that the resulting changes assume the character of a cosmic process.[9]

This dream of the eventual assimilation of the races—an offshoot of the Melting Pot thesis—is surely not an ignoble one. Nor should it be lightly dismissed because it is not immediately feasible. On the other hand, the realities of today's world will not permit a rational man to believe, uncritically, in the inevitability of assimilation as a "cosmic process."

From the beginning, equality has been one of the most protean themes of the American Dream. Jefferson proclaimed it in the Declaration of Independence by asserting that "all men are created equal." Lincoln reaffirmed it at Gettysburg with the words, "our fathers brought forth on this continent a new nation conceived in liberty, and dedicated to the proposition that all men are created equal." The framers of the fourteenth amendment constitutionalized it in the equal protection clause. And in 1954 the Warren Court gave it a vast new dimension by outlawing segregation in the public schools.

In the end, both the egalitarian revolution and the Massive Resistance counterrevolution came down to a conflict over equality—its meaning, scope, and policy imperatives. As history has shown, this is the most ancient of issues dividing Right and Left. There is therefore every reason to assume that Americans will be fighting (and sometimes dying) over equality as long as the Republic stands. That in itself is not bad. The important thing is for future Americans to view egalitarian (and racial) conflicts not as life-and-death challenges to be surmounted, but as opportunities to make the democratic ideals of freedom and equality everyday practices.

How different things might have been after 1954 if the South's Massive Resisters had not acted as though freedom were a "zero-sum" game in which the black man's gain must be the white man's loss. Freedom for whites and freedom for blacks are not, and never have been, polar opposites. Rather they are complementary parts of that seamless, polychromatic web which forms the core of all just societies.

APPENDIX AND TABLES

"THE SOUTHERN MANIFESTO"
(MARCH 12, 1956)

Declaration of Constitutional Principles

THE UNWARRANTED DECISION of the Supreme Court in the public school cases is now bearing the fruit always produced when men substitute naked power for established law.

The Founding Fathers gave us a Constitution of checks and balances because they realized the inescapable lesson of history that no man or group of men can be safely entrusted with unlimited power. They framed this Constitution with its provisions for change by amendment in order to secure the fundamentals of government against the dangers of temporary popular passion or the personal predilections of public officeholders.

We regard the decision of the Supreme Court in the school cases as a clear abuse of judicial power. It climaxes a trend in the Federal judiciary undertaking to legislate in derogation of the authority of Congress, and to encroach upon the reserved rights of the States and the people.

The original Constitution does not mention education. Neither does the 14th amendment nor any other amendment. The debates preceding the submission of the 14th amendment clearly show that there was no intent that it should affect the systems of education maintained by the States.

The very Congress which proposed the amendment subsequently provided for segregated schools in the District of Columbia.

When the amendment was adopted, in 1868, there were 37 States of the Union. Every one of the 26 States that had any substantial

---

* *Congressional Record*, 84th Cong., 2nd Sess. (March 12, 1956), 4459–64.

racial differences among its people either approved the operation of segregated schools already in existence or subsequently established such schools by action of the same lawmaking body which considered the 14th amendment.

As admitted by the Supreme Court in the public school case (*Brown* v. *Board of Education*), the doctrine of separate but equal schools "apparently originated in *Roberts* v. *City of Boston* . . . (1849), upholding school segregation against attack as being violative of a State constitutional guarantee of equality." This constitutional doctrine began in the North, not in the South, and it was followed not only in Massachusetts, but in Connecticut, New York, Illinois, Indiana, Michigan, Minnesota, New Jersey, Ohio, Pennsylvania, and other northern States until they, exercising their rights as States through the constitutional processes of local self-government, changed their school systems.

In the case of *Plessy* v. *Ferguson* in 1896 the Supreme Court expressly declared that under the 14th amendment no person was denied any of his rights if the States provided separate but equal public facilities. This decision has been followed in many other cases. It is notable that the Supreme Court, speaking through Chief Justice Taft, a former President of the United States, unanimously declared in 1927 in *Lum* v. *Rice* that the "separate but equal" principle is "within the discretion of the State in regulating its public schools and does not conflict with the 14th amendment."

This interpretation, restated time and again, became a part of the life of the people of many of the States and confirmed their habits, customs, traditions, and way of life. It is founded on elemental humanity and commonsense, for parents should not be deprived by Government of the right to direct the lives and education of their own children.

Though there has been no constitutional amendment or act of Congress changing this established legal principle almost a century old, the Supreme Court of the United States, with no legal basis for such action, undertook to exercise their naked judicial power and substituted their personal political and social ideas for the established law of the land.

This unwarranted exercise of power by the Court, contrary to the Constitution, is creating chaos and confusion in the States principally affected. It is destroying the amicable relations between the white and Negro races that have been created through 90 years of patient effort by the good people of both races. It has planted hatred and suspicion where there has been heretofore friendship and understanding.

Without regard to the consent of the governed, outside agitators are threatening immediate and revolutionary changes in our public-school systems. If done, this is certain to destroy the system of public education in some of the States.

With the gravest concern for the explosive and dangerous condition created by this decision and inflamed by outside meddlers:

We reaffirm our reliance on the Constitution as the fundamental law of the land.

We decry the Supreme Court's encroachments on rights reserved to the States and to the people, contrary to established law and to the Constitution.

We commend the motives of those States which have declared the intention to resist forced integration by any lawful means.

We appeal to the States and people who are not directly affected by these decisions to consider the constitutional principles involved against the time when they, too, on issues vital to them, may be the victims of judicial encroachment.

Even though we constitute a minority in the present Congress, we have full faith that a majority of the American people believe in the dual system of Government which has enabled us to achieve our greatness and will in time demand that the reserved rights of the States and of the people be made secure against judicial usurpation.

We pledge ourselves to use all lawful means to bring about a reversal of this decision which is contrary to the Constitution and to prevent the use of force in its implementation.

In this trying period, as we all seek to right this wrong, we appeal to our people not to be provoked by the agitators and troublemakers invading our States and to scrupulously refrain from disorders and lawless acts.

(The names of the signers were affixed to the text—19 from the Senate and 77 from the House of Representatives, making a total of 96 signatures.)

TABLE A

Major Legislation on School Desegregation

17 Southern and Border States, Plus District of Columbia (1954–1964)

Legislation	ALA.	ARK.	DEL.	D.C.*	FLA.	GA.	KY.	LA.	MD.	MISS.	MO.	N.C.	OKLA.	S.C.	TENN.	TEX.	VA.	W. VA.
Anti-NAACP/Barratry	X	X			X	X		X		X				X	X	X	X	
Closure of Schools Permitted	X	X			X	X		X		X		X		X		X	X	
Compulsory Attendance Amended or Repealed	X	X			X	X		X		X		X			X	X	X	
Emergency Powers to Officials	X				X	X		X		X		X			X		X	
Freedom of Choice—Seg./Deseg.	X	X	X	X	X	X		X		X		X	X		X**		X	
Human Rights Commissions				X			X		X		X		X		X**			X
Interposition/Protest	X	X			X	X		X		X				X	X	X	X	
Legal Defense Authorized	X	X			X	X		X		X				X	X	X	X	
Limitations of Federal Powers Proposed	X	X			X	X		X						X	X	X	X	
Private Schools: Authorized/Encouraged	X				X	X		X					X				X	
Property Sold/Leased to	X				X	X		X		X							X	
Pupil Assignment	X	X			X	X		X		X		X		X		X	X	
Racial Designations: Removed	X	X									X	X						X
Required												X			X		X	X
Scholarships Out-of-State	X	X	X		X	X	X	X	X	X	X	X	X	X	X	X	X	X
Segregation by Sex	X		X					X		X				X	X		X	
Segregation Committees	X**	X**				X		X		X		X			X	X**	X	X
Sovereignty Commissions	X	X			X	X		X		X		X		X	X		X	
State Constitutional Provision for Public Schools Removed	X									X								
Teachers: Tenure/Removal	X	X				X		X				X		X			X	
Protected in Private Schools	X	X			X	X		X						X			X	
Tuition Grants to Schools/Students	X	X				X		X		X		X		X	X	X	X	X
Withheld Aid to Deseg. Schools	X	X			X	X		X				X		X	X	X	X	X

note: The table indicates types of legislation passed, not the number. One bill often included several features; several bills might duplicate each other. Several laws included have been held unconstitutional or been repealed.

* D.C. Board of Commissioners
** Appointed without legislation
source: *Southern School News*, X (May, 1964), 5–B.

TABLE B

SEGREGATION-DESEGREGATION STATUS

(Figures are for 1964–1965 School Year unless otherwise noted)

	DISTRICTS			ENROLLMENT		IN DESEGREGATED DISTRICTS		NEGROES IN SCHOOLS WITH WHITES	
	Total	With Negroes and Whites	Deseg.	White	Negro	White	Negro	No.	%
Alabama	118	118	9	549,593**	293,426**	131,241**	87,457**	101	.034
Arkansas	411	220	24	333,630†	114,651†	93,072	28,943	930	.811
Florida	67	67	22	1,014,920	247,475	817,842	175,969	6,612	2.67
Georgia	196	180	12	686,761	334,126	200,127	133,454	1,337	.400
Louisiana	67	67	3	472,923*	313,314*	63,591	88,677	3,581	1.14
Mississippi	163	163	4	299,748	279,106	34,620	21,929	57	.020
North Carolina	170	170	86	828,638	349,282	555,997	207,551	4,963	1.42
South Carolina	108	108	18	371,921	260,667	173,833	96,196	265	.102
Tennessee	152	141	65	724,327	173,673	475,877	136,936	9,289	5.35
Texas	1,379	862	450*	2,086,752*	344,312*	1,600,000*	245,000*	27,000*	7.84
Virginia	130	127	81	736,017	233,070	600,000*	200,000*	12,000*	5.15
TOTAL	2,961	2,223	774	8,105,230	2,943,102	4,746,200	1,422,112	66,135	2.25
Delaware	79	45	45	83,164	19,367	78,942	14,064	12,051	62.2
District of Columbia	1	1	1	17,487	123,906	17,487	123,906	106,578	86.0
Kentucky	204	165	165	607,522	55,215	540,000*	55,215	37,585	68.1
Maryland	24	23	23	566,375	169,207	561,300	169,207	86,205	50.9
Missouri	1,056	212*	203*	818,000*	104,000*	NA	95,000*	44,000*	42.3
Oklahoma	1,090	321	211	555,000*	45,000*	334,000*	38,000*	14,000*	31.1
West Virginia	55	54	54	426,500*	21,300*	426,500*	21,300*	13,500*	63.4
BORDER	2,509	821	702	3,074,048	537,995	1,958,229††	516,692	313,919	58.3
REGION	5,470	3,044	1,476	11,179,278	3,481,097	6,704,429††	1,938,804	380,054	10.9

* Estimated   ** 1963–64   † 1962–63   †† Missouri not included
SOURCE: *Southern School News,* XI (June, 1965), 11.

TABLE C

COLLEGE DESEGREGATION
(1964–1965 School Year)

	Predominantly White No.-Deseg.	Predominantly Negro No.-Deseg.	Total No.-Deseg.	ENROLLMENT		NEGROES IN SCHOOLS WITH WHITES	
				Predominantly White Schls.	Predominantly Negro Schls.	Predominantly White Schls.	Predominantly Negro Schls.
Alabama	9—4	2—1	11—5	32,839	3,384	68	0
Arkansas	7—7	1—1	8—8	21,985	2,200	51	0
Florida	24—15	11—11	35—26	115,633	13,691	1,715	0
Georgia	17—9	3—0	20—9	34,225	3,714	71	0
Louisiana	11—11	3—3	14—14	46,749	10,282	1,178	10,275
Mississippi	19—1	6—0	25—1	31,020	6,302	2	0
North Carolina	12—12	5—5	17—17	42,965	9,136	489	9,122
South Carolina	5—3	1—0	6—3	19,356	1,724	24	0
Tennessee	6—6	1—1	7—7	48,208	5,704	1,035	4,669
Texas	50—50	4—4	54—54	184,411	8,482	2,553	8,306
Virginia	21—15	2—2	23—17	42,420	4,173	132	4,170
SOUTH	181—133	39—28	220—161	619,811	68,792	7,318	36,542
Delaware	1—1	1—1	2—2	4,500*	769*	17	750
District of Col.	0—0	1—1	1—1	0	1,293		1,110
Kentucky	7—7	1—1	8—8	39,000*	1,150*	1,700*	980*
Maryland	16—16	4—4	20—20	39,581	4,714	965	4,352
Missouri	17—17	1—1	18—18	58,000*	1,100*	2,500*	1,100*
Oklahoma	22—22	1—1	23—23	60,502	925	851*	923*
West Virginia	10—10	1—1	11—11	24,487*	1,189*	1,200*	325
BORDER	73—73	10—10	83—83	226,070	11,140	7,233	9,540
REGION	254—206	49—38	303—244	845,881	79,932	14,551	46,082

* Estimated

SOURCE: *Southern School News*, XI (June, 1965), 11.

TABLE D

VOTER REGISTRATION IN THE SOUTHERN STATES

Spring–Summer, 1970

STATE	White Voting Age Population*	Black Voting Age Population	Whites Registered	Percent White VAP* Registered	Blacks Registered (1968 figure in parentheses)		Percent Black VAP* Registered
Alabama	1,353,058	481,320	1,300,000	96.1	308,000	(273,000)	64.0
Arkansas	850,643	192,626	683,000	80.3	138,000	(130,000)	71.6
Florida	2,617,438	470,261	2,465,000	94.2	315,000	(292,000)	67.0
Georgia	1,797,062	612,910	1,610,000	89.6	390,000	(344,000)	63.6
Louisiana	1,289,216	514,589	1,137,000	88.2	318,000	(305,000)	61.8
Mississippi	748,266	422,256	650,000	86.9	285,000	(251,000)	67.5
North Carolina	2,005,955	550,929	1,598,000	79.6	302,000	(305,000)	54.8
South Carolina	895,147	371,873	656,000	73.3	213,000	(189,000)	57.3
Tennessee	1,779,018	313,873	1,570,000	88.3	240,000	(228,000)	76.5
Texas	4,884,765	649,512	3,599,000	73.7	550,000	(540,000)	84.7
Virginia	1,876,167	436,720	1,472,000	78.4	265,000	(255,000)	60.7
TOTALS	20,096,735	5,016,100	16,740,000	83.3	3,324,000	(3,112,000)	66.3

* VAP—Voting Age Population, 1960 Census
SOURCE: Voter Education Project Inc.

NOTES AND REFERENCES

INTRODUCTION

1. Until quite recently, very few Americans—black or white—knew even the rudiments of the black man's history in the United States. To the extent that this ignorance resulted from a scarcity of books on black history, one must assume that the ignorance is receding in light of the recent flood of books detailing the facts of black experience in America from colonial days to the present. Among the best books on the subject are these: B. A. Botkin, *Lay My Burden Down* (Chicago, 1965); Kenneth Clark, *Dark Ghetto* (Scranton, Pa., 1965); Melvin Drimmer, ed., *Black History: A Reappraisal* (Garden City, N. Y., 1968); W. E. B. Du Bois, *The Souls of Black Folk* (Greenwich, Conn., 1961); John Hope Franklin, *From Slavery to Freedom* (New York, 1967); Harold Isaacs, *The New World of Negro Americans* (New York, 1964); Rayford W. Logan, *The Betrayal of the Negro* (New York, 1965); Ulrich B. Phillips, *American Negro Slavery* (Baton Rouge, La., 1966); Benjamin Quarles, *The Negro in the American Revolution* (Chapel Hill, 1961); Kenneth Stampp, *The Peculiar Institution* (New York, 1956); and C. Vann Woodward, *The Strange Career of Jim Crow* (Fair Lawn, N.J., 1966).

Until the 1950's, most American historians and social scientists wrote about the black experience from a false perspective. They tended either to write patronizingly about blacks or simply to ignore them. In either case they appeared to view black people as a mere appendage to American history rather than an organic part of it. Among other things, this book aims to take a fresh look at black history as it impinged in the 1950's and 1960's on the presumed interests of the South's white majority.

2. The section deleted from the Declaration, which John Adams called the "vehement philippic against negro slavery," was this:

He [George III] has waged cruel war against human nature itself, violating its most sacred rights of life and liberty in the persons of a distant people who never offended him, captivating and carrying them into slavery in another hemisphere, or to incur miserable death in their transportation thither. This piratical warfare, the opprobrium of infidel *powers, is the warfare of the* Christian *king of Great Britain. Determined to keep open a market where MEN should be bought and sold, he has prostituted his negative for suppressing every legislative attempt to prohibit or to restrain this execrable commerce; and that this assemblage of horrors might want no fact of distinguished die, he is now exciting these very people to rise in arms among us, and to purchase that liberty of which* he *deprived them, by murdering the people upon whom* he *also obtruded them; thus paying off former crimes committed against the* liberties *of one people, with crimes which he urges them to commit against the* lives *of another.*

3. Four state actions were consolidated under one citation: *Brown* v. *Board of Education of Topeka; Briggs* v. *Elliott; Davis* v. *County School Board of Prince Edward County*; and *Gebhart* v. *Belton*, 347 U.S. 483 (1954). This litigation will henceforth be referred to as the desegregation decision, the Brown case, the Brown opinion, the Brown decision, Brown I, or simply Brown.

In terms of constitutional law, the central importance of Brown was that it rejected the conclusions of the Supreme Court in *Plessy* v. *Ferguson*, 163 U.S. 537 (1896), a landmark case around which southern segregationists had woven a vast congeries of obfuscating myths. Plessy dealt with public transportation rather than with education, and thus the seeming legitimation of school segregation in the decision was a dictum. Moreover, the phrase "separate but equal" did not actually appear in the Plessy decision. Justice Harlan used the phrase once in dissent, and the Louisiana statute which was at issue in Plessy included the phrase but in reverse order—"equal but separate." See *Louisiana Laws*, 1890, No. 111, pp. 152–54. Though it is not generally known, it is a fact that the "equal but separate" phrase originated in the mid-1880's in the writings of Henry Grady and his New South prophets. See, for example, Atlanta *Constitution*, October 21, 1883, and January 1, 1885. See also Leonard W. Levy and Harlan B. Phillips, "The *Roberts* Case: Source of the 'Separate but Equal' Doctrine," *American Historical Review*, 56 (1951), 510–18.

4. *Bolling* v. *Sharpe*, 347 U.S. 497 (1954).

5. 349 U.S. 294 (1955). For the origins of the "all deliberate speed" formula, see Alwin Thaler, "With All Deliberate Speed," *Tennessee Law Review*, 27 (1960), 510–17.

6. *Alexander* v. *Holmes County Board of Education*, 396 U.S. 19 (1969).

CHAPTER 1

1. Samuel Lubell, "Racial War in the South," *Commentary*, 24 (August 1957), 113.

2. *Congressional Record*, 83rd Cong., 2nd Sess. (May 27, 1954), 7254.

3. *Dred Scott* v. *Sandford*, 19 Howard 303 (1857). In this case, the Supreme Court held that a slave could not become a citizen of the United States or enjoy the constitutional rights and privileges of citizenship.

4. James Bryce, *The American Commonwealth* (New York, 1899), Vol. 1, p. 509.

5. Presbyterian Church in the United States, General Assembly, *Minutes*, 1954 (n.p., n.d.), 193, 197.

6. Southern Baptist Convention, *Annual*, 1954 (Nashville, Tenn., 1954), 87.

7. Baptist General Association of Virginia, *Journal*, 1954 (Richmond, n.d.), 88.

CHAPTER 2

1. Dwight D. Eisenhower, *The White House Years: Mandate for Change*, 1953–1956 (Garden City, New York, 1963), p. 230. Cf. Emmet John Hughes, *The Ordeal of Power: A Political Memoir of the Eisenhower Years* (New York, 1963), pp. 242, 244.

2. From the *Charleston News and Courier*, as quoted in the *Southern School News*, II (January, 1956), 5.

3. See Lucy v. Adams, in *Race Relations Law Reporter*, I (February, 1956), 85–89, II (April 1957), 350–58.

4. Quoted in the *New York Times*, September 6, 1956. For an account of the Mansfield crisis, see John Howard Griffin and Theodore Freedman, *Mansfield, Texas: A Report on the Crisis Situation Resulting from Efforts to Desegregate the School System* (New York, 1957).

5. The appendix contains the full text of the Manifesto.

6. A good summary of the details of the Manifesto's composition can be found in Numan V. Bartley, *The Rise of Massive Resistance: Race and Politics in the South during the 1950's* (Baton Rouge, La., 1969), pp. 116–117.

7. Quoted in Richmond *News Leader*, March 12, 1956.

CHAPTER 3

1. As a distinctive term, ideology goes back to the 1790's when it was used in revolutionary France to describe the views of certain *savants* or *Idéologues*, the most prominent of whom was Antoine Destutt de Tracy. The *Idéologues*, who were members of the newly founded *Institut de France*, formulated a theory of ideas derived from sensationist philosophical principles similar to those of Locke. According to their theory, ideology was a "science of ideas." Napoleon, who became an honorary member of the *Institut* in 1797, at first sided with the *Idéologues*. Later, however, he broke with them and set out to discredit their *"ténébreuse métaphysique,"* which he felt undermined his authority and tended to subvert the body politic. Due largely to Napoleon's opposition, "ideology" and "ideologue" were soon transformed into pejorative labels.

On the general subject of ideology, see Richard H. Cox, ed., "The Original Concept of Ideology," *Ideology, Politics, and Political Theory* (Belmont, Calif., 1969); A. Destutt de Tracy, *Éléments d'Idéologie*, 5 vols. (Paris, 1817); Ben Halpern, " 'Myth' and 'Ideology' in Modern Usage," *History and Theory*, I, 2 (1961), 129–49; George Lichtheim, "The Concept of Ideology," History and Theory, IV, 2 (1965), 164–77, 193–96; Willard A. Mullins, "On the Concept of Ideology in Political Science," *The American Political Science Review*, 66 (June, 1972), 498–510; Fr. Picavet, *Les Idéologues* (Paris, 1891); Jay W.

Stein, "Beginnings of 'Ideology,' " *South Atlantic Quarterly*, 55 (April, 1956), 163–70; and Hans Barth, *Warheit und Ideologie*, 2nd ed. (Zurich, 1961).

Although some scholars say that Comte, Feuerbach, and the Young Hegelians were the legitimate heirs of the *Idéologues*, it was Karl Marx who made ideology a common term in modern scholarship. In his *Theses on Feuerbach* and in other works, Marx defined ideology as "false consciousness," or more specifically as distorted ideas in defense of the status quo. Marx believed that one of his most important tasks was "unmasking" the bourgeoisie's conservative (and therefore distorted) ideology.

In the twentieth century Karl Mannheim in his early writings also used the term ideology to denote distorted conservative ideas. However, in his later writings Mannheim, like Max Weber before him, accepted the conservative bent of ideologies but recognized that they are not necessarily distorted in the sense of being unscientific. He also distinguished ideologies from utopias, which he called the belief systems of aspiring radicals.

Professor Carl Friedrich of Harvard has defined ideologies as simply "ideas in action, political action." See Carl Joachim Friedrich, *Man and His Government: An Emprical Theory of Politics* (New York, 1963), p. 11.

A few modern scholars consider political theory and ideology to be mutually exclusive because of the bias, non-objectivity, and "messianic humanism" inherent in the latter. See, for example, Dante Germino, *Beyond Ideology: The Revival of Political Theory* (New York, 1967), pp. 45–46. This view has something in common with the theory of certain conservative social scientists that we are coming to "the end of ideology" in advanced industrial societies.

The definition of ideology used in this chapter and throughout this volume owes a good deal to the conception found in A. James Gregor, *Contemporary Radical Ideologies: Totalitarian Thought in the Twentieth Century* (New York, 1968), pp. 8–9.

2. R. M. MacIver, *The Web of Government* (New York, 1947), pp. 3–12.

3. G. Sorel, *Reflections on Violence*, trans. T. E. Hulme and J. Roth (Glencoe, Ill., 1950), pp. 20–21. There is also an insightful discussion of myth in Friedrich, *op. cit.*, pp. 94–105. In Chapter 5, which is called "The Political Myth, Its Symbols and Utopian Order," the author examines a wide variety of myths: theogonic, cosmogonic, cosmological, anthropological, soteriological, eschatological, heroic, and the founder myth.

4. Scholars sometimes make a distinction between the concepts "racialism" and "racism." Those who do so define the former as the *theory* of racial discrimination and the latter as its *practice*. This study makes no such distinction, chiefly because the theory and practice of discrimination were so intertwined in the Massive Resistance movement that it seemed pointless to try to separate them. Racism is used in this chapter instead of racialism because it is a shorter, more comprehensive, and more common term.

5. An earlier and quite different version of this myth by the author appeared in Meyer Weinberg and Oscar E. Shabat, *Society and Man*, 2nd ed. (Englewood Cliffs, N. J., 1965), p. 340. About half of Chapter 14 of the Weinberg-Shabat book, entitled "Racial Discrimination," was devoted to an appraisal of the Harvard doctoral dissertation on which this study is based. For more about the ideas discussed in this section, see Barry N. Schwartz and Robert Disch, *White Racism: Its History, Pathology and Practice* (New York, 1970); Philip Mason, *Common Sense About Race* (New York, 1961); and James W. Vander Zanden, "The Ideology of White Supremacy," *Journal of the History of Ideas*, XX (June–September, 1959), 385–402.

6. Thomas Dixon, *The Clansman* (New York, 1905), p. 291.

7. *Southern School News*, I (November, 1954), 3.

8. Thomas Dixon, *The Leopard's Spots* (New York, 1902), p. 244.

9. Attorneys for North Carolina, Prince Edward County, Virginia, and Texas. Leon Friedman, ed., *Argument* (New York, 1969).

10. William M. Brown, *The Crucial Race Question* (Little Rock, Ark., 1907), p. 125.

11. Henry W. Grady, "What of the Negro," *The Possibilities of the Negro in Symposium* (Atlanta, 1904), pp. 64–65.

12. H. E. Talmadge, *You and Segregation* (Birmingham, Ala., 1955), pp. 44–45.

13. Sutton E. Griggs, *Wisdom's Call* (Nashville, Tenn., 1911), p. 113.

14. One of the best recent works demonstrating that white racism is not supported by the findings of the biological and social sciences is Thomas F. Pettigrew, *A Profile of the Negro American* (New York, 1964). See also L. C. Dunn and T. Dobzhansky, *Heredity, Race and Society*, rev. ed. (New York, 1952), and Melville J. Herskovitz, *The American Negro: A Study in Racial Crossing* (New York, 1928).

15. Ashley Montague, *Man's Most Dangerous Myth: The Fallacy of Race*, 4th ed., revised and enlarged (New York, 1964), p. 316. [In the 1950's, one of the most extreme expressions of white supre-

macy was Tom P. Brady's *Black Monday*, 2nd ed. (Winona: Association of Citizens' Councils of Mississippi, 1955).]

16. *Congressional Record*, 83rd Cong., 2nd Sess. (August 5, 1954), 13375.

17. "South Carolina Brief" in the case of *Harry Briggs, Jr. v. R. W. Elliott, Chairman, J. D. Carson, Members of Board of Trustees of School District No. 22, Clarendon Co., S. C.* This was one of the original actions eventually brought together in the Brown case.

18. *Barron* v. *Mayor and City Council of Baltimore*, 32 U.S. (7 Pet.) 243 (1833).

19. A typical scholarly definition of interposition is that found in Jack C. Plano and Milton Greenberg, *The American Political Dictionary* (New York, 1962), p. 34. For southern views of the doctrine, see Committee for Courts of Justice, Senate of Virginia, *The Doctrine of Interposition: Its History and Application* (Richmond, Division of Purchase and Printing, 1957), and Judge L. H. Perez, *Interposition: What is It?* (Pamphlet of speech, New Orleans, 1956). For contrasting views, see R. Brisbane, "Interposition: Theory and Fact," *Phylon*, XVII (March, 1956), 12–16; Mitchell Franklin, "The Unconstitutionality of Interposition," *Lawyers Guild Review*, XVI (Spring, 1956), 50–60; and Herbert O. Reid, "The Supreme Court Decision and Interposition," *The Journal of Negro Education*, XXV (Spring, 1956), 109–17.

CHAPTER 4

1. One of the best recent books about leadership is A. W. Gouldner, *Studies in Leadership* (New York, 1950). Also valuable are C. I. Barnard, *Organization and Management* (Cambridge, Mass., 1948), and Andrew S. McFarland, *Power and Leadership in Pluralist Systems* (Stanford, 1969).

2. Calhoun's letters, speeches, and reports are collected in *The Papers of John C. Calhoun*, ed. Robert Meriwether (Columbia, S. C., 1959). One of the most perceptive biographies of Calhoun is Charles M. Wiltse, *John C. Calhoun, Nationalist* (Indianapolis, Ind., 1944).

3. *Richmond Times-Dispatch*, May 18, 1954.

4. *Congressional Record*, 81st Cong., 1st Sess. (January 27, 1949), 569.

5. As quoted in Charles J. Bloch, *We Need Not Integrate to Educate* (Atlanta, Ga., n. d.), p. 11.

6. *Congressional Record*, 84th Cong., 1st Sess. (May 26, 1955), 7124.

7. Excerpted from an Eastland speech delivered in 1954 and printed in the Memphis *Commercial Appeal*, December 29, 1955.

8. A stimulating study of southern political leaders, which includes analyses of what this book calls "tutelary geniuses" and "charismatic demagogues," is Robert Sherrill, *Gothic Politics in the Deep South* (New York, 1969). In parts of the book, Sherrill weakens the force of his argument by an excess of rhetoric and passion.

9. Ross R. Barnett, "Address to Statewide Citizens' Council Banquet, Columbia, South Carolina, January 29, 1960" (press release copy, Southern Regional Council files), 4.

10. The definitive study of these men is I. A. Newby, *Challenge to the Court, Social Scientists and the Defense of Segregation, 1954–1966*, rev. ed. (Baton Rouge, La., 1969).

11. On the general subject of the attitudes of scientists toward race, see Thomas F. Gossett, *Race, The History of an Idea in America* (Dallas, 1963), and John S. Haller, Jr., *Outcasts From Evolution: Scientific Attitudes of Racial Inferiority, 1859–1900* (Urbana, Ill., 1971). The Haller book, which won the Anisfield-Wolf Award in Race Relations for 1971, shows how science "verified" the inferiority of the Negro and helped to rationalize the politics of disfranchisement and segregation.

12. Quoted in Benjamin Muse, *Ten Years of Prelude: The Story of Integration Since the Supreme Court's 1954 Decision* (New York, 1964), p. 29.

13. *Des Moines Tribune*, February 12, 1972.

CHAPTER 5

1. The history of the Klan has been the subject of several scholarly and journalistic works as well as the object of at least two congressional investigations. Particularly useful are these works: Charles C. Alexander, *The Ku Klux Klan in the Southwest* (Lexington, Ky., 1965); David M. Chalmers, *Hooded Americanism: The First Century of the Ku Klux*

Klan, 1865–1965 (Garden City, N. Y., 1965); David M. Chalmers, "The Ku Klux Klan and the Radical Right," *The Radical Right: Proceedings of the Sixth Annual Intergroup Relations Conference at the University of Houston, Houston, Texas, March 27, 1965* (n.p., n.d.); Stanley F. Horn, *Invisible Empire: The Story of the Ku Klux Klan, 1866–1871* (Boston, 1939); and Arnold S. Rice, *The Ku Klux Klan in American Politics* (Washington, 1962). See also "The Present-Day Ku Klux Klan Movement," *Report by the Committee on Un-American Activities, House of Representatives,* 90th Cong., 1st Sess. (Washington, D.C., 1967).

2. The best history of the Reconstruction Klan is Allen W. Trelease, *White Terror: The Ku Klux Klan Conspiracy and Southern Reconstruction* (New York, 1971).

3. Sherrill, *op. cit.*, pp. 315–16, 352.

4. See Jerome H. Skolnick, *The Politics of Protest* (New York, 1969), pp. 218–23.

5. See James W. Vander Zanden, "The Klan Revival," *American Journal of Sociology,* LXV (March, 1960), 456–62. Vander Zanden doubts that the Klan membership ever exceeded 10,000.

6. The best published study of the Councils is Neil R. McMillen, *The Citizens' Council: Organized Resistance to the Second Reconstruction 1954–64* (Urbana, Ill., 1971). Other published sources are the files of *The Citizen,* the newsletters of local Council organizations, the issues of the *Southern School News,* pro-Council Southern newspapers (notably the Birmingham *Dixie-American,* the Augusta *Courier,* the Charleston *News and Courier,* and the Jackson *Daily News*), the clipping files of the Anti-Defamation League and the Southern Regional Council, the NAACP's *Annual Reports,* and Hodding Carter, III, *The South Strikes Back* (Garden City, N. Y., 1959). In university archives one can also find a good many unpublished M.A. and Ph.D. theses that deal with various aspects of the Council movement. Among the many journal articles dealing with the subject, these are especially useful: Samuel DuBois Cook, "Political Movements and Organizations," *Journal of Politics,* XXVI (February, 1964), 130–53; David Halberstam, "The White Citizens' Councils: Respectable Means for Unrespectable Ends," *Commentary,* XXII (October, 1956), 293–302; Frederick B. Routh and Paul Anthony, "Southern Resistance Forces," *Phylon Quarterly,* XVIII (First Quarter, 1957), 50–58; and James W. Vander Zanden, "The Citizens' Council," *Alpha Kappa Deltan,* XXVIII (Spring, 1959), 3–9; and "A Note on the Theory of Social Movements," *Sociology and Social Research,* XLIV (September–October, 1959), 3–7.

The Councils were embarrassed when it turned out that the accused slayer of the NAACP leader Medgar Evers was Byron de la Beckwith, a fertilizer salesman and prominent member of the Greenwood, Mississippi, Citizens' Council. During his trial Beckwith was strongly supported by the statewide Council organization, however, and key Council leaders formed a White Citizens' Legal Fund to underwrite the expenses of their comrade's trial. The case finally ended in two mistrials. The Beckwith case was not typical of normal Council resistance.

7. Bartley, *op. cit.*, p. 86.

8. Newby, *op. cit.*, pp. 228–30. It was perhaps no mere coincidence that several of the top leaders of the Councils were John Birchers, including Simmons, Louis W. Hollis (national director), and Medford Evans (managing editor of their official journal). Council organizers outside the South included a large number of Birchers, most notably Kent H. Steffgen, who was first field director for California and a Birch Society member since its inception in 1958. See McMillen, *op. cit.*, pp. 200–01.

9. Bartley, *op. cit.*, p. 96.

CHAPTER 6

1. See Murray Edelman, *The Symbolic Uses of Politics* (Urbana, Ill., 1967).

2. Paul M. Gaston, *The New South Creed: A Study in Southern Mythmaking* (New York, 1970), p. 9.

3. A brief but excellent analysis of the South's attack upon the NAACP is *Assault Upon Freedom of Association, A Study of the Southern Attack on the National Association for the Advancement of Colored People*, American Jewish Congress (New York, 1957).

4. Educational Fund of the Citizens' Councils, *The Ugly Truth About the NAACP: An Address by Attorney General Eugene Cook of Georgia Before the 55th Annual Convention of the Peace Officers Association of Georgia* (Greenwood, n. d.), 10.

5. *Ibid.*, p. 2.

6. *Ibid.*, p. 10.

7. An excellent analysis of the psychological process of scape-

goating is G. W. Allport, *The Nature of Prejudice* (Cambridge, Mass., 1954).

8. Richard Hofstadter, *The Paranoid Style in American Politics and Other Essays*, Vintage ed. (New York, 1967).

CHAPTER 7

1. The use of such phrases as "dual sovereignty" and "sovereign states" in the Fabisinski Committee's report was a clear sign that the state's legal establishment was fully committed to the myth of states'-rights federalism. Governor Collins later changed his mind about segregation and broke with his state's Massive Resisters in a dramatic statewide television broadcast. After his change of heart, Collins said he wanted "solutions, not scapegoats."

2. The "Pearsall Plan" was named after Thomas J. Pearsall of Rocky Mount, who was chairman of the Governor's Advisory Committee on Education and a former Speaker of the North Carolina House of Representatives.

3. It appears that the concept of interposition was rediscovered (or disinterred) by William Olds, a Virginia country lawyer, who published a pamphlet on the subject soon after the announcement of Brown. After the pamphlet was given wide publicity by James Jackson Kilpatrick, Jr., of the *Richmond News Leader*, the word entered the vocabulary (and mythology) of Massive Resisters throughout the South.

4. U.S. House of Representatives, 84th Cong., 2nd Sess., *Investigation of Public School Conditions: Report of the Subcommittee to Investigate Public School Standards and Conditions and Juvenile Delinquency in the District of Columbia of the Committee on the District of Columbia* (Washington, 1957), 46.

5. An excellent account of Almond's address and of the general assembly's 1959 special session can be found in Benjamin Muse, *Virginia's Massive Resistance* (Bloomington, Ind., 1961), pp. 131–39.

6. Maryland had refused to ratify the fourteenth amendment in 1867, the year before it became part of the Constitution.

7. The authoritative work on this aspect of Massive Resistance is Leon Friedman, ed., *Southern Justice* (New York, 1966).

CHAPTER 8

1. The definitive work on the role of the federal courts in combating the South's counterrevolution is J. W. Peltason, *Fifty-Eight Lonely Men, Southern Federal Judges and School Desegregation* (New York, 1961). A new edition of this work was issued by the University of Illinois Press in 1971, with epilogue by Kenneth N. Vines and bibliographic essay by Numan V. Bartley. See also Note, "Judicial Performance in the Fifth Circuit," *Yale Law Journal*, 73 (1963), 90.

2. *Briggs* v. *Elliott*, 132 F. Supp. 776 (E.D.S.C. 1955). This was one of the original cases in the Brown litigation.

3. A man in his seventies in 1956 and a native of Rockingham County, Virginia, Judge Paul was appointed to the federal bench by President Hoover. Since 1932 he had presided, with distinction, over the Western District Federal Court in Virginia. His father, a Confederate Army veteran, had been a federal judge in the same district. It is ironic that one of those originally urging Paul's appointment to the bench was Harry Flood Byrd, who doubtless disagreed with most of the Judge's opinions in the field of race relations.

4. *Hoxie School District* v. *Brewer*, 1 *Race Relations Law Reporter*, 229 and 1027 (1956).

5. *Cooper* v. *Aaron*, 358 U.S. 1 (1958).

6. *NAACP* v. *Alabama ex rel Patterson*, 357 U.S. 449 (1958).

7. *Griffin* v. *Prince Edward School Board*, 377 U.S. 218 (1964).

8. Peltason, *op. cit.*, p. 245.

9. *Garner* v. *Louisiana*, 368 U.S. 157 (1961).

10. *Peterson* v. *Greenville*, 373 U.S. 244 (1963).

11. *Simkins* v. *Moses H. Cone Memorial Hospital*, 323 F.2d 959 (4th Cir., 1963), *cert. denied*, 376 U.S. 938, 84 S. Ct. 793 (1964).

12. *Jones* v. *Mayer Co.*, 392 U.S. 409 (1969). Justices Harlan and White filed a lengthy dissent in this case. They have recently been supported in their views by a legal historian who contends that "in *Jones* v. *Mayer* the Court appears to have had no feeling for the truth

of history, but only to have read it through the gloss of the Court's own purpose." Charles Fairman, *Reconstruction and Reunion 1864–88: Part One* (New York, 1971), p. 1258.

13. *Green* v. *County Board of New Kent County*, 391 U.S. 430 (1968). The Court also evidenced its impatience with the slow pace of school desegregation in these *per curiam* opinions: *Carter* v. *West Feliciana Parish School Bd.*, 296 U.S. 226 (1969); *Dowell* v. *Board of Education*, 396 U.S. 269 (1969); *Carter* v. *West Feliciana Parish School Bd.*, 396 U.S. 290 (1970); and *Northcross* v. *Board of Education*, 397 U.S. 232 (1970).

14. *Alexander* v. *Holmes*, 396 U.S. 19 (1969).

15. Archibald Cox, *The Warren Court: Constitutional Decisions as an Instrument of Reform* (Cambridge, Mass., 1967), p. 26.

16. The Little Rock crisis has been analyzed in Virgil T. Blossom, *It Has Happened Here* (New York, 1959); Daisy Bates, *The Long Shadow of Little Rock: A Memoir* (New York, 1962); Ernest Q. Campbell and Thomas F. Pettigrew, *Christians in Racial Crisis: A Study of Little Rock's Ministry* (Washington, 1959); B. Hays, *A Southern Moderate Speaks* (Chapel Hill, N. C., 1958); W. Record and J. C. Record, *Little Rock, U.S.A.* (San Francisco, 1960); and Peltason, *op. cit.*, pp. 155–65.

17. President Eisenhower's legal authority for dispatching federal troops to Little Rock was a Civil War statute of July 29, 1861, and the second clause of the Ku Klux Klan Act of 1871, codified as Sections 332 and 333 respectively, Title 10, of the United States Code (1964). The 1861 law authorized the President to call out the militia or use the army to suppress riots or violence whenever because of "unlawful obstructions . . . or rebellion against the authority of the Government of the United States, it shall become impracticable . . . to enforce, by the ordinary course of judicial proceedings, the laws of the United States within any State." The second clause of the Ku Klux Klan Act provided for the use of the army or militia whenever "domestic violence . . . opposes or obstructs the exclusion of the laws of the United States or impedes the course of justice under those laws."

18. The basic facts of the New Orleans showdown are well described in the files of *Southern School News* and the *New Orleans Times-Picayune* as well as in Peltason, *op. cit.*, pp. 221–43. See also Robert L. Crain, *The Politics of School Desegregation* (Garden City, N. Y., 1969), pp. 250–322; and E. L. Pinney and R. S. Friedman, *Political Leadership and the School Desegregation Crisis in Louisiana* (Eagleton Institute of Politics, "Cases in Practical Politics," Case No. 31, New York, 1963).

19. *Orleans Parish* v. *Bush; United States* v. *Louisiana, 5 Race Relations Law Reporter* 10008 (1960).

20. *Bush* v. *New Orleans,* 364 U.S. 500 (1960).

21. On December 15, 1961, President Kennedy announced that he was appointing Judge Wright to the United States Court of Appeals for the District of Columbia. He had originally planned to appoint Wright to the Court of Appeals for the Fifth Circuit, which includes Louisiana and several other southern states. Senator Russell Long, however, objected, and under the custom of "senatorial courtesy," President Kennedy deferred to the Louisiana Senator and appointed Wright to the District of Columbia court.

22. The text of Governor Barnett's interposition proclamation can be found in the *Southern School News,* IX (October, 1962), 10.

23. The two fatalities were a French correspondent of the *Agence France Presse,* Paul Guihard, and Ray Gunter, an Oxford onlooker.

24. After Meredith had been admitted to Ole Miss, Harry S. Murphy, Jr., a New York City black, revealed that he had attended the university as a Navy V–12 student in 1945–46. University records confirmed his statement, which meant that Meredith was the second black to attend Ole Miss. Another black, Cleve McDowell, was admitted to the university, under a federal court order, on June 5, 1963. He, however, was expelled the following September after he was found carrying a concealed weapon on campus. In the early seventies, there were approximately 300 black students at Ole Miss representing about 3.5 per cent of the student body. By 1972 there were blacks on the freshman football squad and a black student newspaper, *The Spectator.* There was also a Black Student Union. The Stars and Bars of the Confederacy still wave over the campus, and the band still plays "Dixie," but the days of crude, overt racism appear to have passed.

25. Miss Lucy had earlier graduated from Miles College and had hoped to receive a graduate degree in library science from the University of Alabama. She subsequently married a black Baptist minister, left Alabama, and in the late 1960's was a substitute English teacher at a black elementary school in Shreveport, Louisiana. Her later counterpart at the University of Georgia, Charlayne Hunter, took a rather different road. In 1963 she secretly married a white classmate, Walter Stovall, and after graduation they moved to New York's Greenwich Village, where Charlayne became an editorial assistant with *The New Yorker.* Her husband meanwhile became an Associated Press reporter. Later Miss Hunter wrote a book about her experiences and took a position as a Russell Sage fellow at St. Louis's Washington University.

CHAPTER 9

1. A good summary of congressional legislation in the field of civil rights is that contained in the Congressional Quarterly Service's *Congress and the Nation, 1945–1964, A Review of Government and Politics in the Postwar Years* (Washington, D.C., 1965), pp. 1620–42.

2. *Heart of Atalanta Motel, Inc.* v. *United States*, 379 U.S. 241 (1964). See also *Katzenbach* v. *McClung*, 379 U.S. 294 (1964). In the Atlanta case Justice Clark, writing for the Court, concluded that "the action of the Congress in the adoption of the Act as applied here to a motel which concededly serves interstate travelers is within the power granted it by the Commerce Clause of the Constitution as interpreted by this Court for 140 years."

3. *South Carolina* v. *Katzenbach*, 383 U.S. 301 (1966).

4. *Katzenbach* v. *Morgan*, 384 U.S. 641 (1966).

5. *Harper* v. *Virginia Board of Education*, 383 U.S. 667 (1966).

CHAPTER 10

1. The best recent study of the Klan is Dwayne Walls' *The Klan: Collapsed and Dormant*, Special Report (Race Relations Information Center, 1970). In this pamphlet Mr. Walls, a reporter for *The Charlotte Observer*, devotes most of his analysis to Klan groups in North Carolina.

2. The chief factors contributing to Atlanta's racial liberalism are these: a series of progressive mayors, an enlightened economic oligarchy, two liberal white newspapers, a crusading black daily newspaper (the *Atlanta Daily World*, founded in 1928 as a weekly), a tradition of biracial community action led by the Southern Regional Council, activist black churches and pastors, an aggressive NAACP chapter, a large and cohesive black middle class, an outstanding black

university establishment, a progressive police department, and the reform work of the Southern Christian Leadership Conference, which is headquartered in the city. For the best recent study of Atlanta, see Doris Lockerman and Patricia LaHatte, *Discover Atlanta* (New York, 1969).

3. The most authoritative and scholarly work on the subject of the politicization of southern blacks is Donald R. Matthews and James W. Prothro, *Negroes and the New Southern Politics* (New York, 1966). The following are other useful sources: Charles Aikin, *The Negro Votes* (San Francisco, 1962); Harry A. Bailey, Jr., *Negro Politics in America* (Columbus, Ohio, 1967); Margaret Price, *The Negro and the Ballot in the South* (Southern Regional Council, 1959); Olive H. Shadgett, *Voter Registration in Georgia: A Study of its Adminstration* (Bureau of Public Administration, University of Georgia, 1955); Donald S. Strong, *Registration of Voters in Alabama* (Bureau of Public Administration, University of Alabama, 1956); Bernard Taper, *Gomillion versus Lightfoot: The Tuskegee Gerrymander Case* (New York, 1962); Pat Watters and Reese Cleghorn, *Climbing Jacob's Ladder: The Arrival of Negroes in Southern Politics* (New York, 1967); James Q. Wilson, *Negro Politics, The Search for Leadership* (New York, 1960); "The Negro Voter in the South," *The Journal of Negro Education*, XXVI (Yearbook issue, 1957), 213–431; and U. S. Senate Committee on the Judiciary, Subcommittee on Constitutional Rights, *Literacy Tests and Voter Requirements in Federal and State Elections*, Hearings, March 27–April 12, 1962 (87th Congress, 2nd session). Not enough credit for increasing the number of black registrants in the South has been given to the Voter Education Project of the Southern Regional Council. The VEP has been operating since 1962, and has scrupulously sought to avoid partisanship in its work. See in this regard the pamphlet, *Voter Registration in the South, Summer, 1968* (Atlanta, Ga., 1968). This is one of a series of valuable statistical compilations prepared by the Southern Regional Council's Voter Education Project.

4. The changing aspects of southern politics are well described in Chandler Davidson, *Biracial Politics: Conflict and Coalition in the Metropolitan South* (Baton Rouge, La., 1972); Albert Gore, *Let the Glory Out: My South and Its Politics* (New York, 1972); and William C. Havard, ed., *The Changing Politics of the South* (Baton Rouge, La., 1972). Each of these books, in its own way, underscores the fact that the fluid and chaotic politics of the present South contain many unpredictable possibilities.

Chapter 11

1. Louis Hartz, *The Liberal Tradition in America* (New York, 1955), pp. 145–77.

2. George Fitzhugh, *Cannibals All: Or Slaves Without Masters* (1857), ed. C. Vann Woodward (Cambridge, Mass., 1960), p. 72.

3. Hartz, *op. cit.*, p. 177.

4. Hinton Rowan Helper, *The Impending Crisis of the South: How to Meet It* (New York, 1857), p. 357. Ironically, in later life Helper became famous for writing books that attacked blacks.

5. See Daniel R. Goodloe, *Inquiry into the Causes which Have Retarded the Accumulation of Wealth and Increase of Population in the Southern States* (Washington, D.C., 1846). This was a bitter denunciation of the slavery system that preceded the publication of Helper's more famous book. To a certain extent, the antebellum views of Helper and Goodloe were precursors of that naive, postbellum "industrial determinism" that disfigured so much of the New South literature. See Henry Woodfin Grady, *The New South*, ed. Oliver Dyer (New York, 1890) and Paul M. Gaston, *The New South Creed: A Study in Southern Mythmaking* (New York, 1970).

6. See William A. Dunning, *Reconstruction, Political and Economic, 1865–1867* (New York, 1907); Claude G. Bowers, *The Tragic Era* (Boston, 1929); and E. Merton Coulter, *The Story of Reconstruction, 1865–1877* (Baton Rouge, La., 1947).

7. See Twelve Southerners, *I'll Take My Stand: The South and the Agrarian Tradition* (New York and London, 1930), p. 12.

8. A thoroughgoing Marxist analysis of southern history and character is James S. Allen's *Reconstruction: The Battle for Democracy, 1865–1876* (New York, 1937). See also W. E. B. DuBois, *Black Reconstruction* (New York, 1935), which was written before DuBois became a full-fledged Marxist, and Herbert Aptheker, *A Documentary History of the Negro People in the United States* (New York, 1966), especially Vol. 2.

9. W. J. Cash, *The Mind of the South* (New York, 1941; Doubleday Anchor Edition, 1954), p. 426.

10. Two books by C. Vann Woodward are particularly recommended: *The Burden of Southern History* (Baton Rouge, La., 1960)

and *American Counterpoint: Slavery and Racism in the North-South Dialogue* (New York, 1972).

11. Hodding Carter, *Southern Legacy* (Baton Rouge, La., 1950) and *The Angry Scar* (New York, 1959). See also Hodding Carter III, *The South Strikes Back* (Garden City, N. Y., 1959).

12. Other useful interpretations of southern behavior are these: David Bertelson, *The Lazy South* (New York, 1967); Dewey W. Grantham, Jr., *The Democratic South* (Athens, Ga., 1963); Samuel Lubell, *White and Black: Test of a Nation* (New York, 1964); Keith F. McKean, *Cross Currents in the South* (Denver, Colo., 1960); William H. Nicholls, *Southern Tradition and Regional Progress* (Chapel Hill, N. C., 1960); James W. Silver, *Mississippi: The Closed Society* (New York, 1964); Francis Butler Simkins, *The Everlasting South* (Baton Rouge, La., 1963); Pat Watters, *The South and the Nation* (New York, 1970); and T. Harry Williams, *Romance and Realism in Southern Politics* (Athens, Ga., 1961).

13. The late Professor Key made much of the southern phenomenon of "bi-factionalism." See V. O. Key, Jr., *Southern Politics in State and Nation* (New York, 1949). Key does not appear to have fully grasped the fact that when the Democratic party of the South has faced grave crises, be it white-black fusion in the Populist years or court-ordered school integration in the 1950's, its various factions have invariably coalesced to present a common front to the challenging foe. One is, therefore, tempted to call Key's theory of factionalism in the Democratic party a case of "pseudomorphic-factionalism."

14. *Ibid.*, p. 119.

15. The views on Populism expressed in this section are derived from an article which the author wrote and published in a black journal some years ago. See Francis M. Wilhoit, "An Interpretation of Populism's Impact on the Georgia Negro," *The Journal of Negro History*, LII (April, 1967), 116–27. The pioneering work on this subject was A. M. Arnett, *The Populist Movement in Georgia* (New York, 1922). See also John D. Hicks, *The Populist Revolt* (New York, 1931), and C. Vann Woodward, *Tom Watson, Agrarian Rebel* (New York, 1938).

16. Quoted in Mrs. William H. Felton, *My Memoirs of Georgia Politics* (Atlanta, Ga., 1911), p. 6.

17. In addition to Dollard's classic work on caste, see Allison Davis, Burleigh B. Gardner, and Mary R. Gardner, *Deep South* (Chicago, 1941); and W. Lloyd Warner, "American Caste and Class," *American Journal of Sociology*, XXXII (September, 1936), 234–37.

18. For an inventory of national-character studies, see H. C. J.

Duijker and N. H. Frijda, *National Character and National Stereo-types* (Amsterdam, 1960). Two much-discussed recent studies of white racism appear to have gone overboard in emphasizing the importance of psychological factors. See Joel Kovel, *White Racism: A Psychohistory* (New York, 1971), and Lawrence J. Friedman, *The White Savage: Racial Fantasies in the Postbellum South* (Englewood Cliffs, N. J., 1970).

19. The best analysis of the Protestant "Southern accent in religion" in Samuel S. Hill, Jr., *Southern Churches in Crisis* (Boston, 1968). See also Kenneth K. Bailey, *Southern White Protestantism in the Twentieth Century* (New York, 1964); Dwight W. Culver, *Negro Separation in the Methodist Church* (New Haven, Conn., 1955); Jeffrey K. Hadden, *The Gathering Storm in the Churches* (New York, 1969); Frank S. Loescher, *The Protestant Church and the Negro* (New York, 1948); Philip Mason, *Christianity and Race* (New York, 1956); Liston Pope, *The Kingdom Beyond Caste* (New York, 1957); Edwin McNeill Poteat, Jr., "Religion in the South," *Culture in the South*, ed. W. T. Couch (Chapel Hill, N. C., 1934); Robert Root, *Progress Against Prejudice* (New York, 1957); James Sellers, *The South and Christian Ethics* (New York, 1962); Wesley Shrader, "Segregation in the Churches," *Esquire*, XLIX (May, 1958), 119–21; E. Tilson, *Segregation and the Bible* (Nashville, Tenn., 1963); W. D. Weatherford, *American Churches and the Negro: A Historical Study from Early Slavery Days to the Present* (Boston, 1956); and R. F. West, *Preaching on Race* (St. Louis, Mo., 1963).

While southern black Protestantism is also basically evangelical, it appears, to an outsider, to be rather more emotional and less puritanical. Surprisingly, there is as yet no outstanding scholarly work on the southern black church. The latest study of evangelicalism without regard to race is John B. Boles, *The Origins of the Southern Evangelical Mind* (Lexington, Ky., 1972).

20. Francis B. Simkins, *The Everlasting South* (Baton Rouge, La., 1963), p. 79.

21. Hill, *op. cit.*, pp. 12–16.

22. It may well be that the eighteenth-century conversion of the South from deism and episcopacy to evangelicalism was both a regional and a national tragedy, since it meant that the South of the future would value emotion over reason, religion over education. It is also interesting to note that at the time the South was changing its religion, it was changing its regional drinking habits—from mild wines, beer, and rum to corn liquor, produced in copious quantities by the distilling ingenuity of the region's Scotch-Irish Calvinist immi-

grants. It is more than likely that these changes had something to do with the violence that escalated in the South throughout the nineteenth century. And it should not be forgotten that the ancestors of most of today's southern whites came from the rugged Highlands of Scotland, where physical violence and Calvinistic fundamentalism have for centuries driven the natives to recurring cycles of ascetic deprivation and promiscuous hedonistic indulgence.

23. The proper relationship between secular law and the enforcement of religious (and other) morality has been a central concern of western jurisprudence. Theories about the relationship range from the view of medieval canonists and extreme Calvinists that "sins" and "crimes" should in effect be merged to the view of modern libertarians that only those "sins" should be proscribed by the state's criminal law that directly injure another person. The recent tendency of Western democracy has been in the direction of libertarianism, though not everywhere consistently so.

Jefferson well expressed the libertarian view of law when he wrote: "They [English judges] have taken the whole leap, and declared at once that the whole Bible and Testament, in a lump, make a part of the English code, laws made for the Jews alone, and the precepts of the gospel, intended by their benevolent author as obligatory only in *foro conscientiae*; and they arm the whole with the coercions of municipal law." *The Works of Thomas Jefferson*, ed. Paul L. Ford (New York, 1904–05), I, 463–64. In the nineteenth century, Bentham and John Stuart Mill were the leading spokesmen for the view that law and morals should be separated. The best short study of this general subject is David H. Flaherty, "Law and the Enforcement of Morals in Early America," *Perspectives in American History*, V, eds. Donald Fleming and Bernard Bailyn (Cambridge, Mass., 1971), pp. 201–53.

Concerning the southern evangelicals' crusade for the criminalization of alcohol, it is now widely believed that a major reason for the southern church's support of prohibition, which was not an original Calvinist position, was the desire to keep the black man sober and industrious, and thus more securely under the control of whites. It was assumed by the segregationist evangelicals—wrongly as it turned out —that the black man could not find the money to buy bootleg whiskey.

24. Quoted in Robert Moats Miller, "The Protestant Churches and Lynching, 1919–1939," *The Journal of Negro History*, XLIII (April, 1957), 118.

25. See C. W. de Kiewiet, *The Anatomy of South African Misery* (New York, 1956).

26. Robert Bingham, *The New South: An Address in the Interest of National Aid to Education* (n.p., 1884), p. 13.

27. Liston Pope, *op. cit.*, p. 25.

28. Shrader, *loc. cit.*, p. 119.

29. Elie Halévy, *A History of the English People*, 6 vols. (London, 1960), vol. 1.

EPILOGUE

1. *Report of the National Commission on Civil Disorders* (New York, 1968).

2. *Ibid.*, p. 1.

3. *Ibid.*, p. 10.

4. *Ibid.*, p. 23.

5. The text in its entirety can be found in the *New York Times*, March 25, 1970, pp. 26–27.

6. For an excellent brief analysis of the busing issue, see United States Commission on Civil Rights, *Your Child and Busing* (Washington, D.C., 1972). This publication discusses the history and background of busing and analyzes the arguments that are commonly used against it. See also Lillian B. Rubin, *Busing and Backlash* (Berkeley, Calif., 1972), and Christopher Jencks, "Busing—The Supreme Court Goes North," *New York Times Magazine*, November 19, 1972, pp. 40–41, 118–21, 125–27.

7. In *Swann* v. *Charlotte-Mecklenburg Board of Education*, 402 U.S. 1. (1971), the Supreme Court unanimously reaffirmed its policy of requiring school boards (and in their failure, federal district courts) to "come forward with a plan that promises realistically to work now . . . until it is clear that state-imposed segregation has been completely removed." Speaking for the Court, Chief Justice Burger rejected the argument of segregationists that the proviso of Title IV of the Civil Rights Act of 1964 forbidding courts to order busing "to achieve a racial balance" was meant to restrict the federal courts' equitable remedial powers. Instead, he said, it was designed to foreclose any interpretation of the Act as expanding the courts' present powers to enforce equal protection.

In *North Carolina State Board of Education* v. *Swann*, 402 U.S. 43 (1971), a proceeding ancillary to *Charlotte-Mecklenburg*, the Supreme Court invalidated North Carolina's anti-busing law on the ground it prevented implementation of desegregation plans required by the fourteenth amendment. Said the Court: "The legislation before us flatly forbids assignment of any student on account of race or for the purpose of creating a racial balance or ratio in the schools. . . . [The] statute exploits an apparently neutral form to control school assignment plans by directing that they be 'color blind'; that requirement, against the background of segregation, would render illusory the promise of Brown v. Board of Education. . . . Just as the race of students must be considered in determining whether a constitutional violation has occurred, so also must race be considered in formulating a remedy. . . . Similarly the flat prohibition against assignment of students for the purpose of creating a racial balance must inevitably conflict with the duty of school authorities to disestablish dual school systems. . . . We likewise conclude that an absolute prohibition against transportation of students assigned on the basis of race, 'or for the purpose of creating a balance or ratio,' will similarly hamper the ability of local authorities to effectively remedy constitutional violations."

8. Alexis de Tocqueville, *Democracy in America*, Henry Reeve Text, rev. by Francis Bowen, I (New York, 1957), p. 7.

9. Robert E. Park, *Race and Culture* (Glencoe, Ill., 1950), pp. 149–50. An excellent survey and critique of the scholarly literature on this subject can be found in L. Paul Metzger's "American Sociology and Black Assimilation: Conflicting Perspectives," *American Journal of Sociology*, LXXVI (January, 1971), 627–47. A list of references is included at the end of this article, which includes the Park quotation (pp. 631–32).

Index